THE SILENCE OF OUR FRIENDS

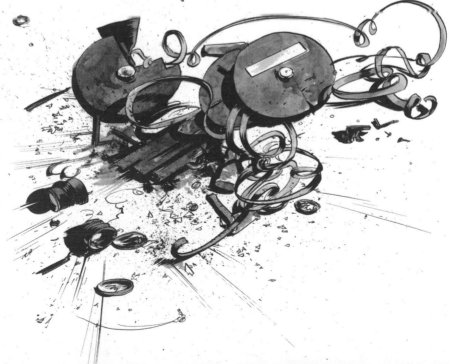

THE SILENCE OF OUR FRIENDS

WRITTEN BY
MARK LONG &
JIM DEMONAKOS

ART BY
NATE POWELL

First Second
NEW YORK & LONDON

First Second
New York & London

Text copyright © 2012 Mark Long and Jim Demonakos
Illustration copyright © 2012 Nate Powell
Compilation copyright © 2012 Mark Long, Jim Demonakos, and Nate Powell

Published by First Second
First Second is an imprint of Roaring Brook Press, a division of Holtzbrinck
Publishing Holdings Limited Partnership
175 Fifth Avenue, New York, New York 10010
All rights reserved

Distributed in the United Kingdom by Macmillan Children's Books, a division of
Pan Macmillan.

Cataloging-in-Publication Data is on file at the Library of Congress

First Second books are available for special promotions and premiums.
For details, contact: Director of Special Markets, Holtzbrinck Publishers.

First edition 2012
Book design by Colleen AF Venable
Art production assistance by Erin Tobey
Printed in the United States of America

10 9 8 7 6 5

TO
JOHN V. LONG

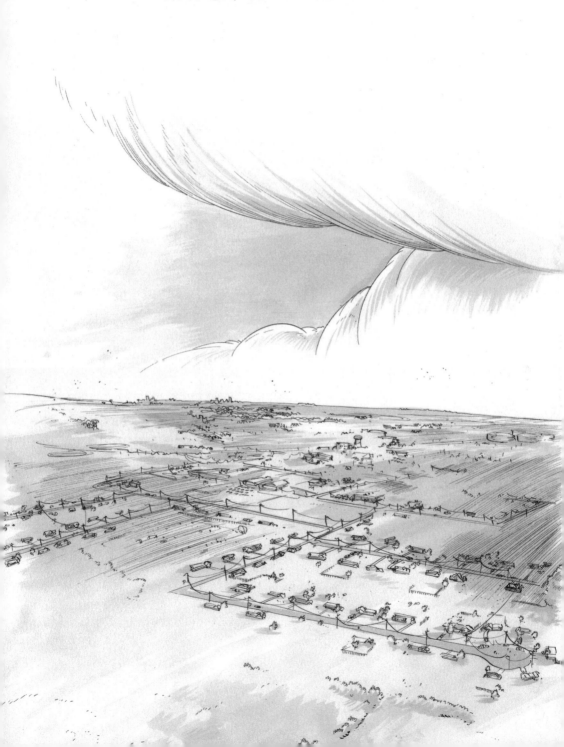

HOUSTON, TEXAS 1968

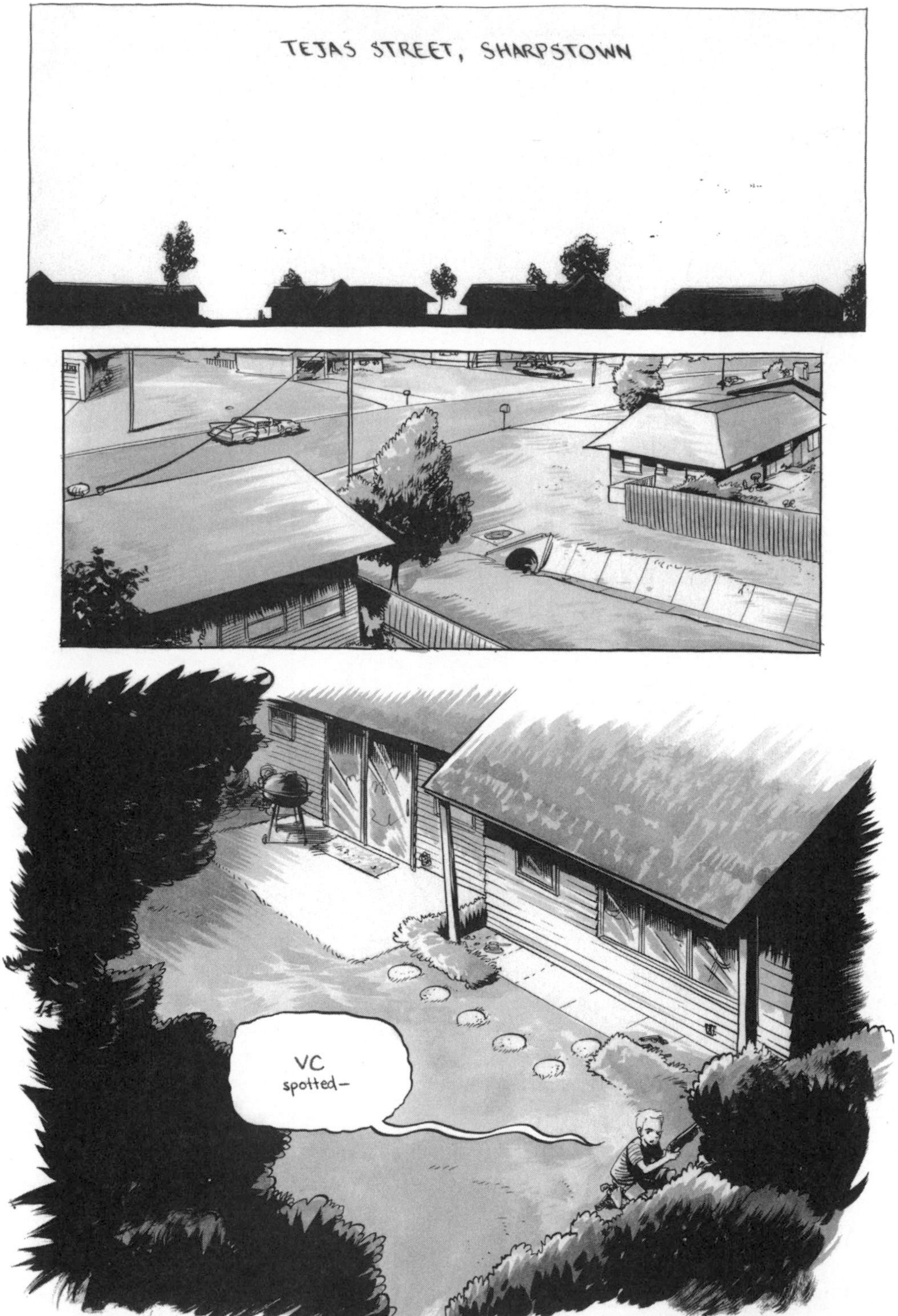
TEJAS STREET, SHARPSTOWN
VC spotted—

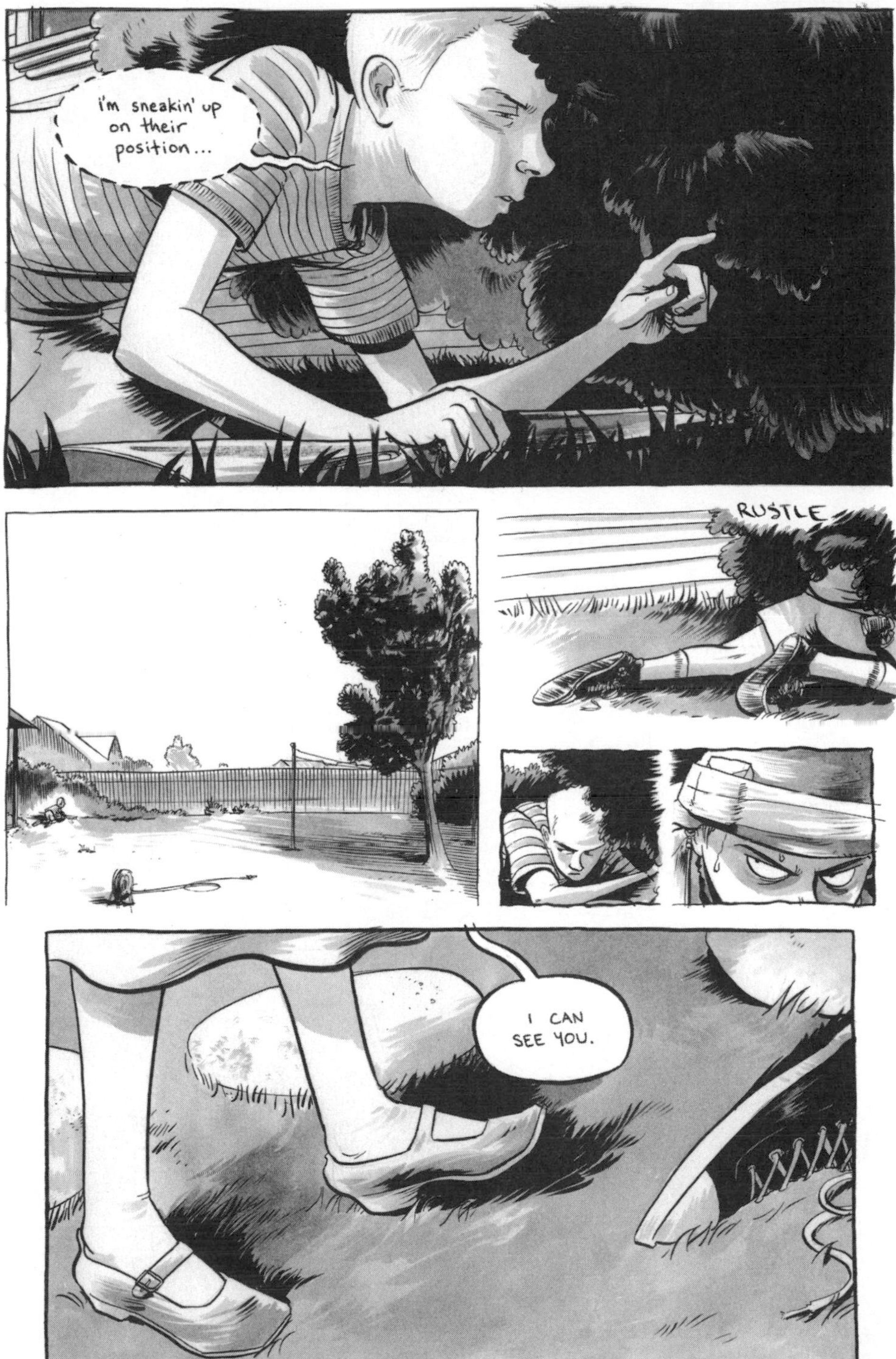
i'm sneakin' up on their position...
RUSTLE
I CAN SEE YOU.

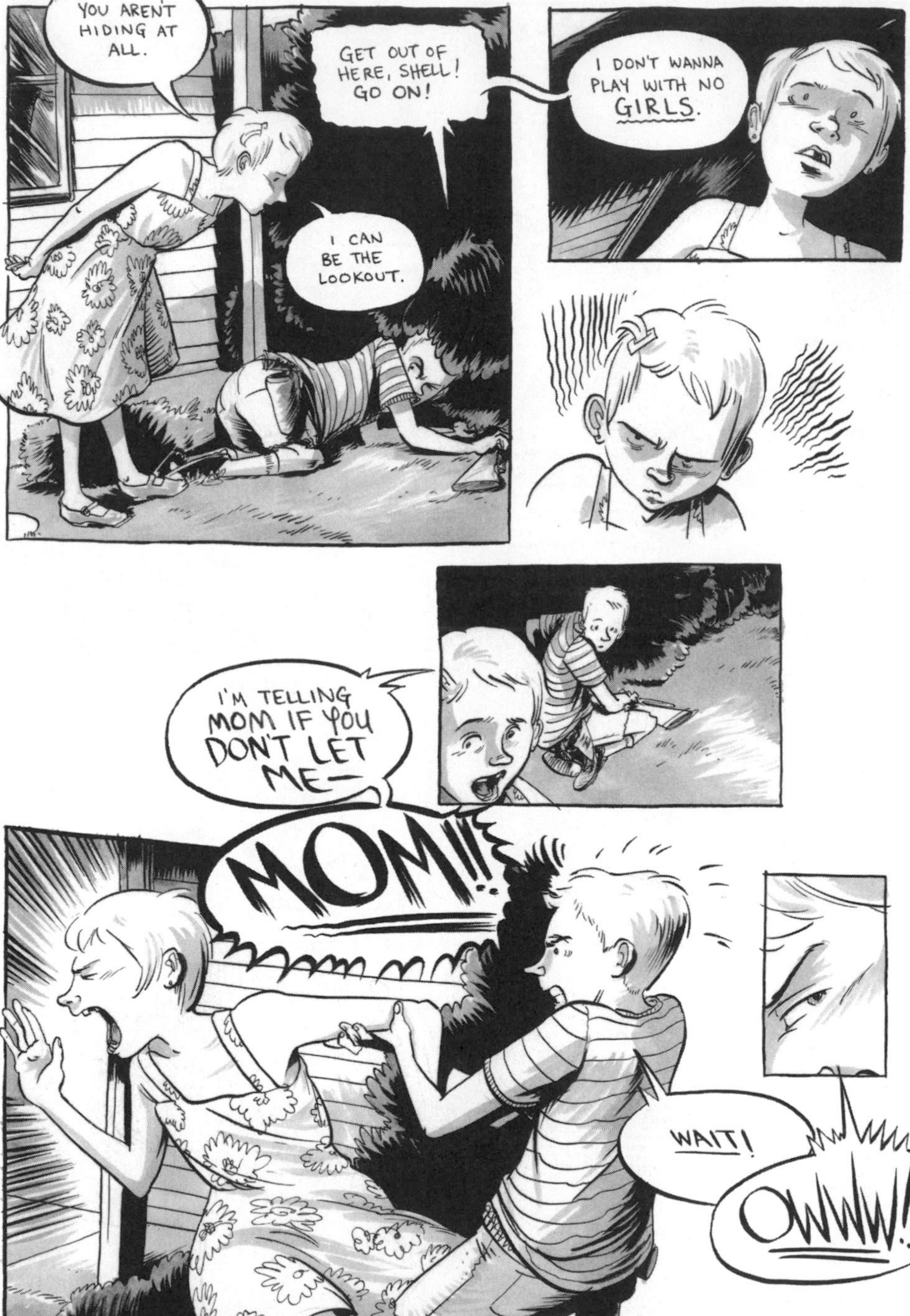
YOU AREN'T HIDING AT ALL.
GET OUT OF HERE, SHELL! GO ON!
I CAN BE THE LOOKOUT.
I DON'T WANNA PLAY WITH NO GIRLS.
I'M TELLING MOM IF YOU DON'T LET ME—
MOM!!
WAIT!
OWWW!!

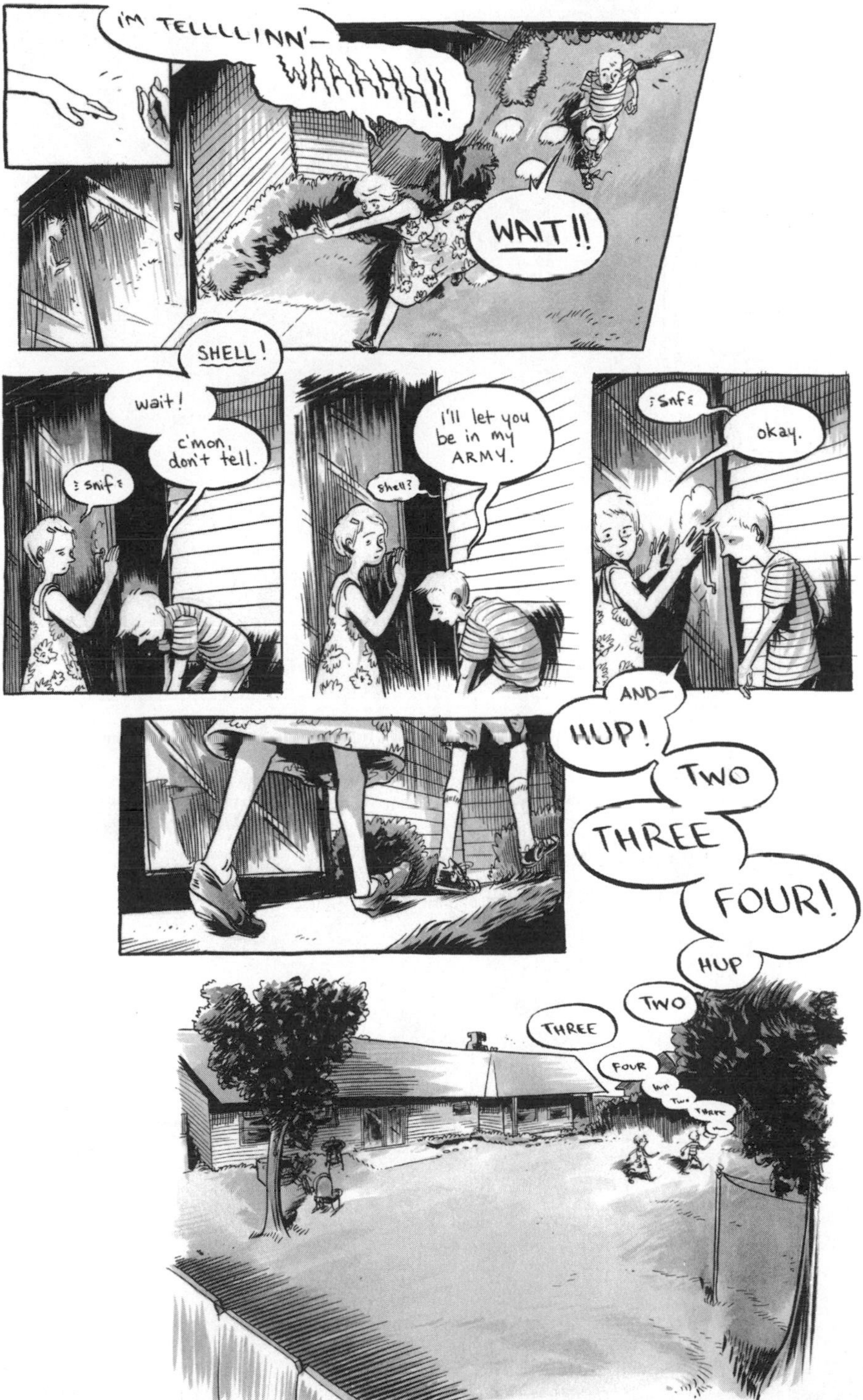
I'M TELLLLLINN'—
WAAAHHH!!
WAIT!!
SHELL!
wait!
c'mon, don't tell.
snif
shell?
i'll let you be in my ARMY.
Snf
okay.
AND—
HUP!
TWO
THREE
FOUR!
HUP
TWO
THREE
FOUR

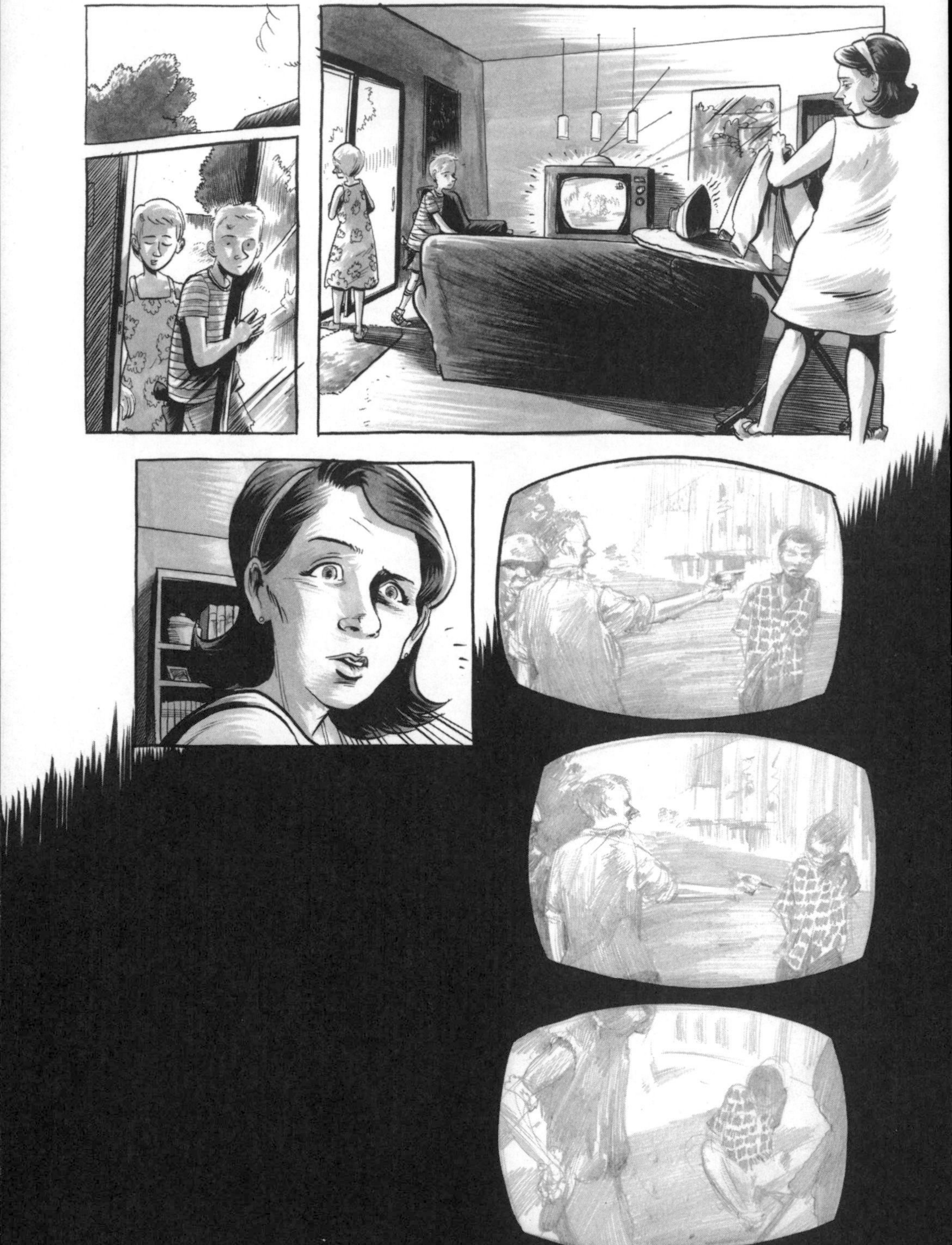

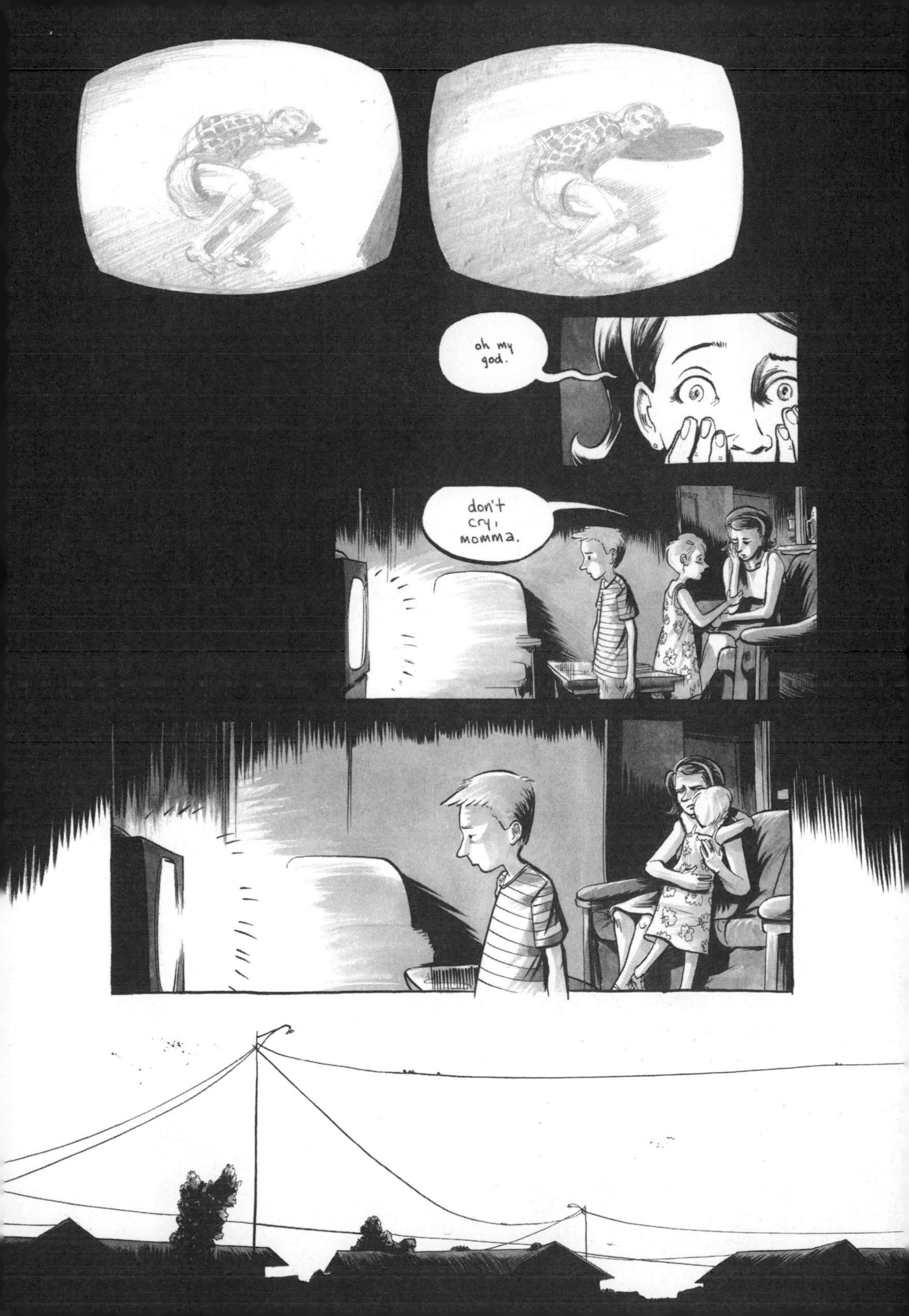
oh my god.
don't cry, momma.

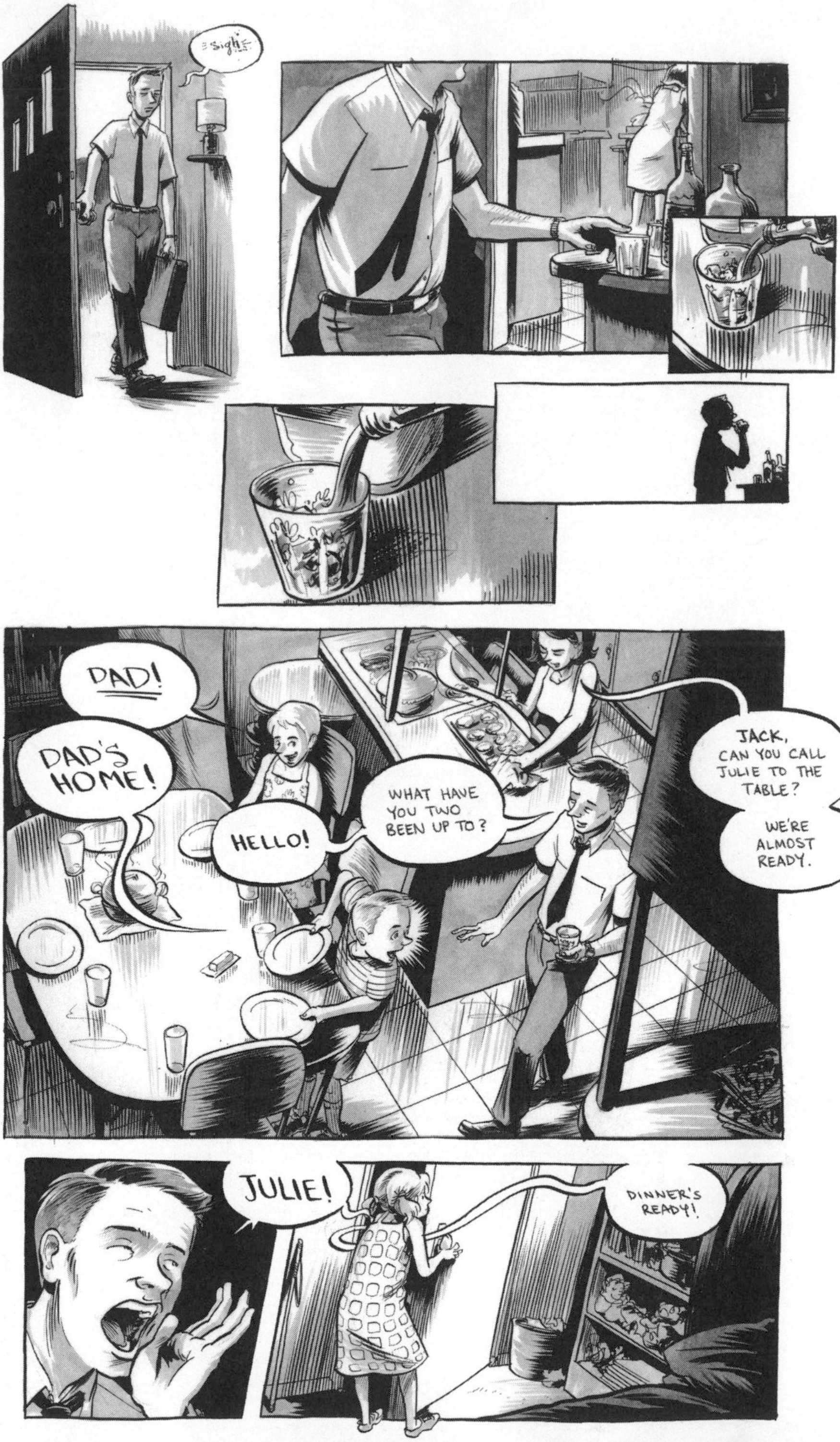
Sigh
DAD!
DAD'S HOME!
HELLO!
WHAT HAVE YOU TWO BEEN UP TO?
JACK, CAN YOU CALL JULIE TO THE TABLE?
WE'RE ALMOST READY.
JULIE!
DINNER'S READY!

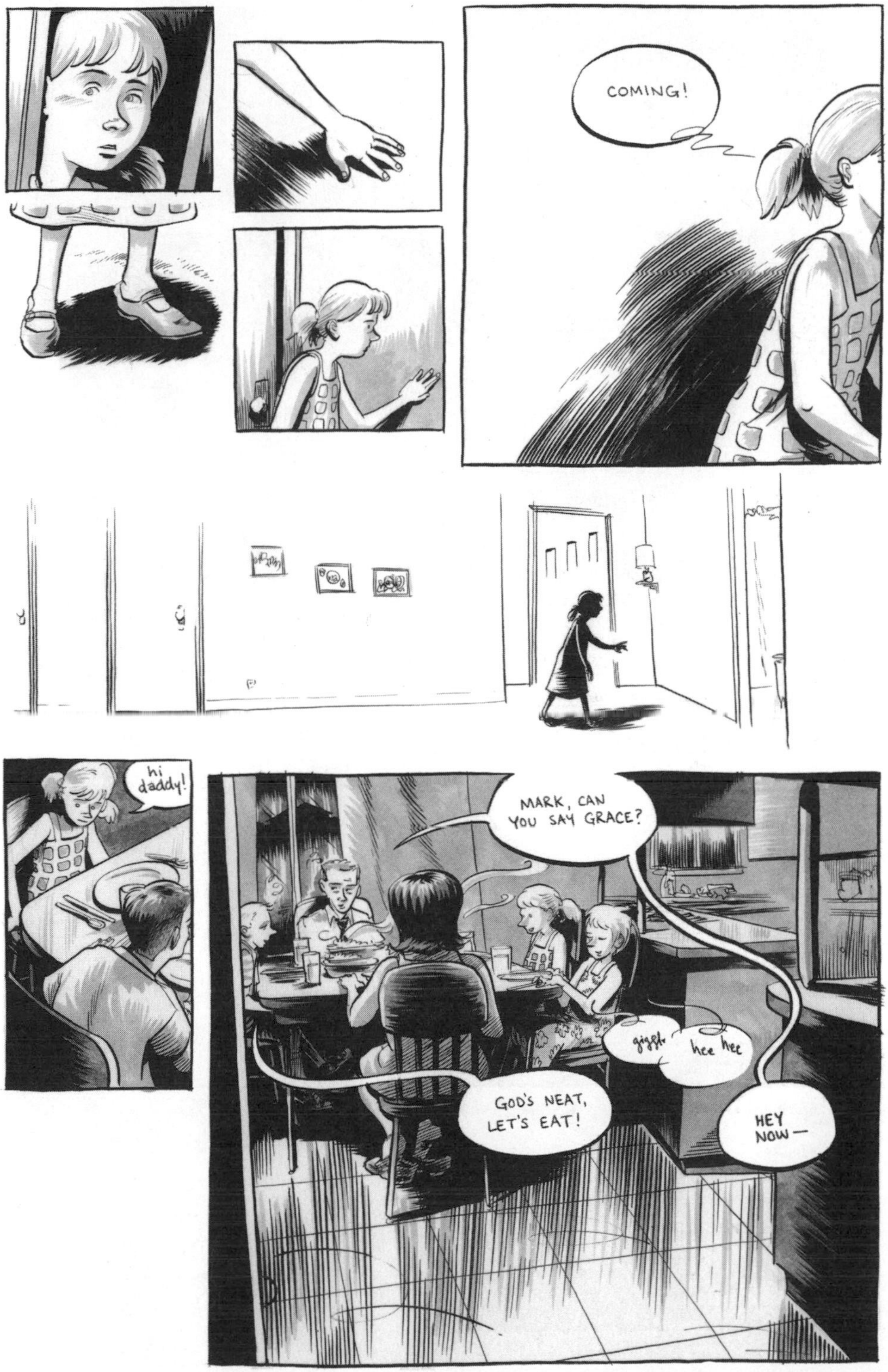
COMING!
hi daddy!
MARK, CAN YOU SAY GRACE?
GOD'S NEAT, LET'S EAT!
giggle
hee hee
HEY NOW—

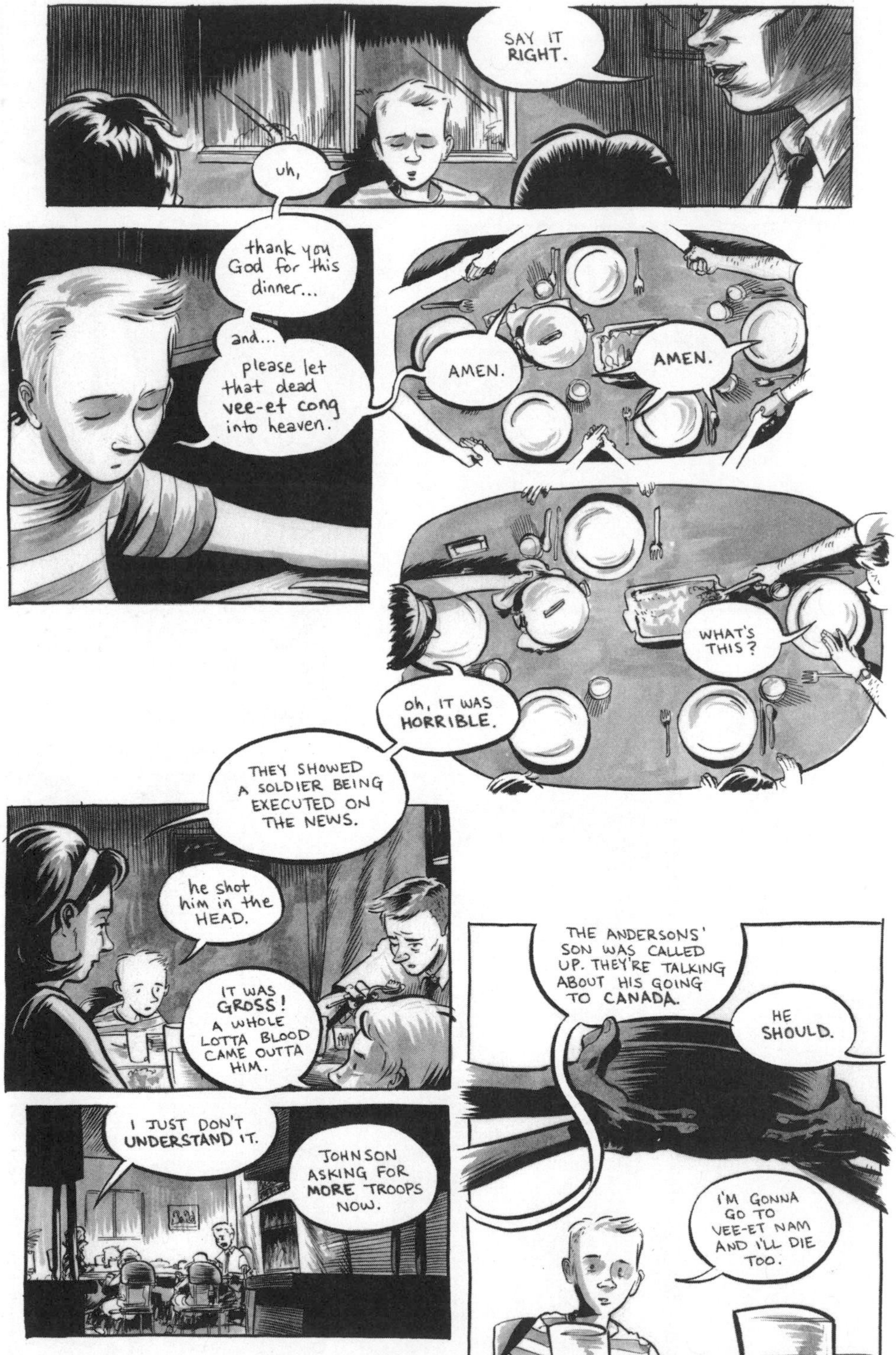
SAY IT RIGHT.
uh,
thank you God for this dinner...
and...
please let that dead vee-et cong into heaven.
AMEN.
AMEN.
WHAT'S THIS?
oh, IT WAS HORRIBLE.
THEY SHOWED A SOLDIER BEING EXECUTED ON THE NEWS.
he shot him in the HEAD.
IT WAS GROSS! A WHOLE LOTTA BLOOD CAME OUTTA HIM.
I JUST DON'T UNDERSTAND IT.
JOHNSON ASKING FOR MORE TROOPS NOW.
THE ANDERSONS' SON WAS CALLED UP. THEY'RE TALKING ABOUT HIS GOING TO CANADA.
HE SHOULD.
I'M GONNA GO TO VEE-ET NAM AND I'LL DIE TOO.

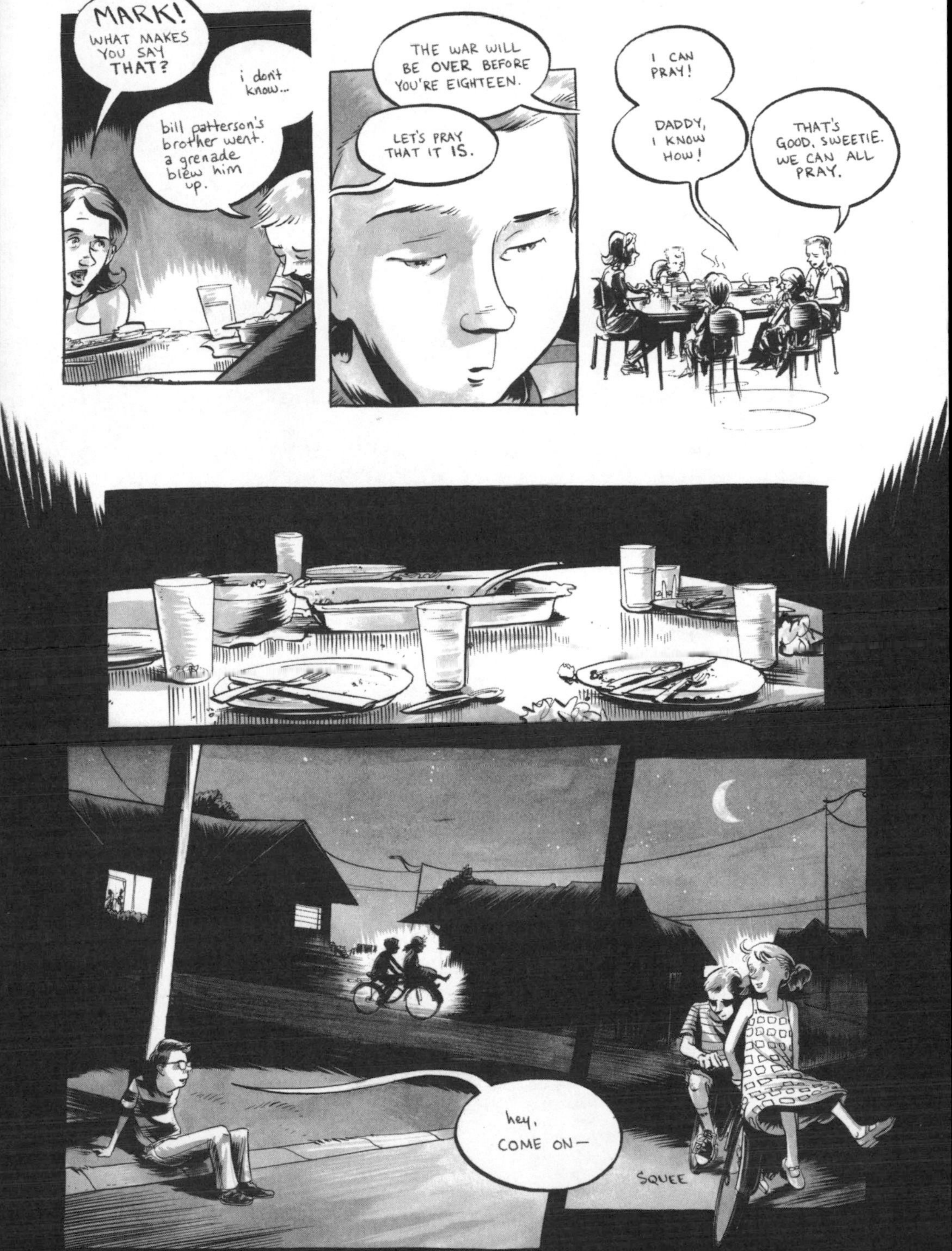
MARK! WHAT MAKES YOU SAY THAT?
i don't know...
bill patterson's brother went. a grenade blew him up.
THE WAR WILL BE OVER BEFORE YOU'RE EIGHTEEN.
LET'S PRAY THAT IT IS.
I CAN PRAY!
DADDY, I KNOW HOW!
THAT'S GOOD, SWEETIE. WE CAN ALL PRAY.
hey, COME ON—
SQUEE

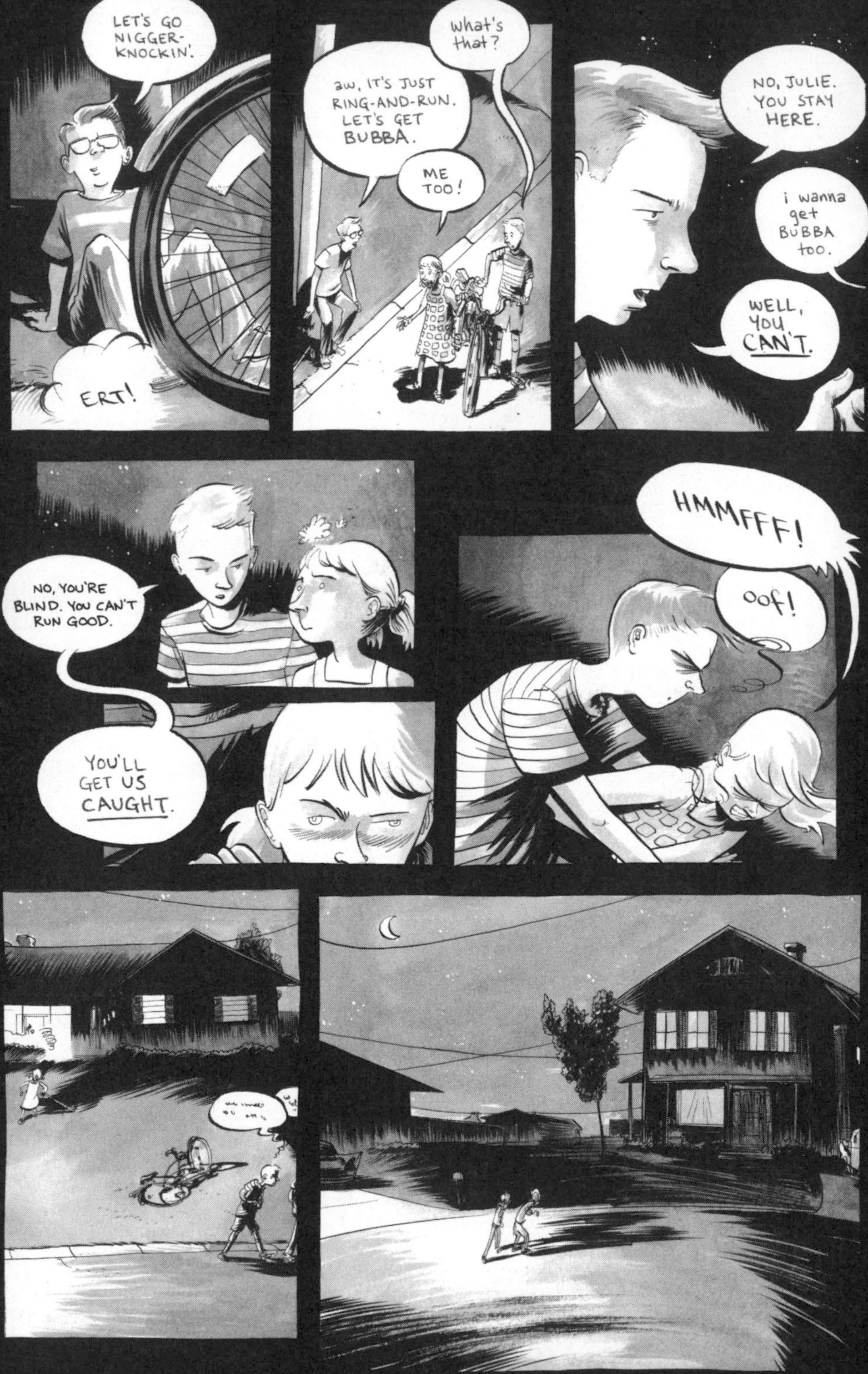
LET'S GO NIGGER-KNOCKIN'.
ERT!
what's that?
aw, IT'S JUST RING-AND-RUN. LET'S GET BUBBA.
ME TOO!
NO, JULIE. YOU STAY HERE.
i wanna get BUBBA too.
WELL, YOU CAN'T.
NO, YOU'RE BLIND. YOU CAN'T RUN GOOD.
YOU'LL GET US CAUGHT.
HMMFFF!
oof!

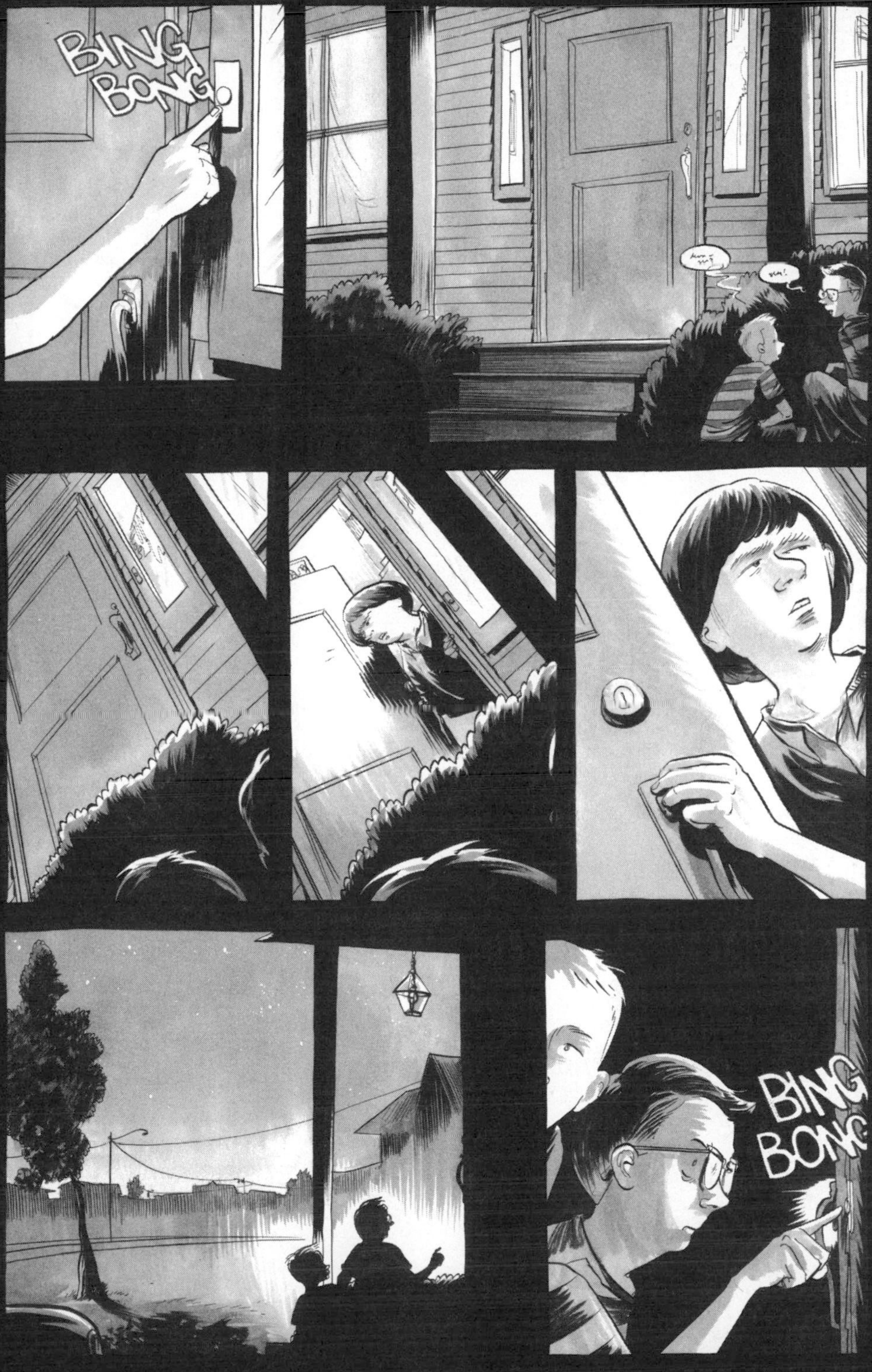
BING BONG
BING BONG

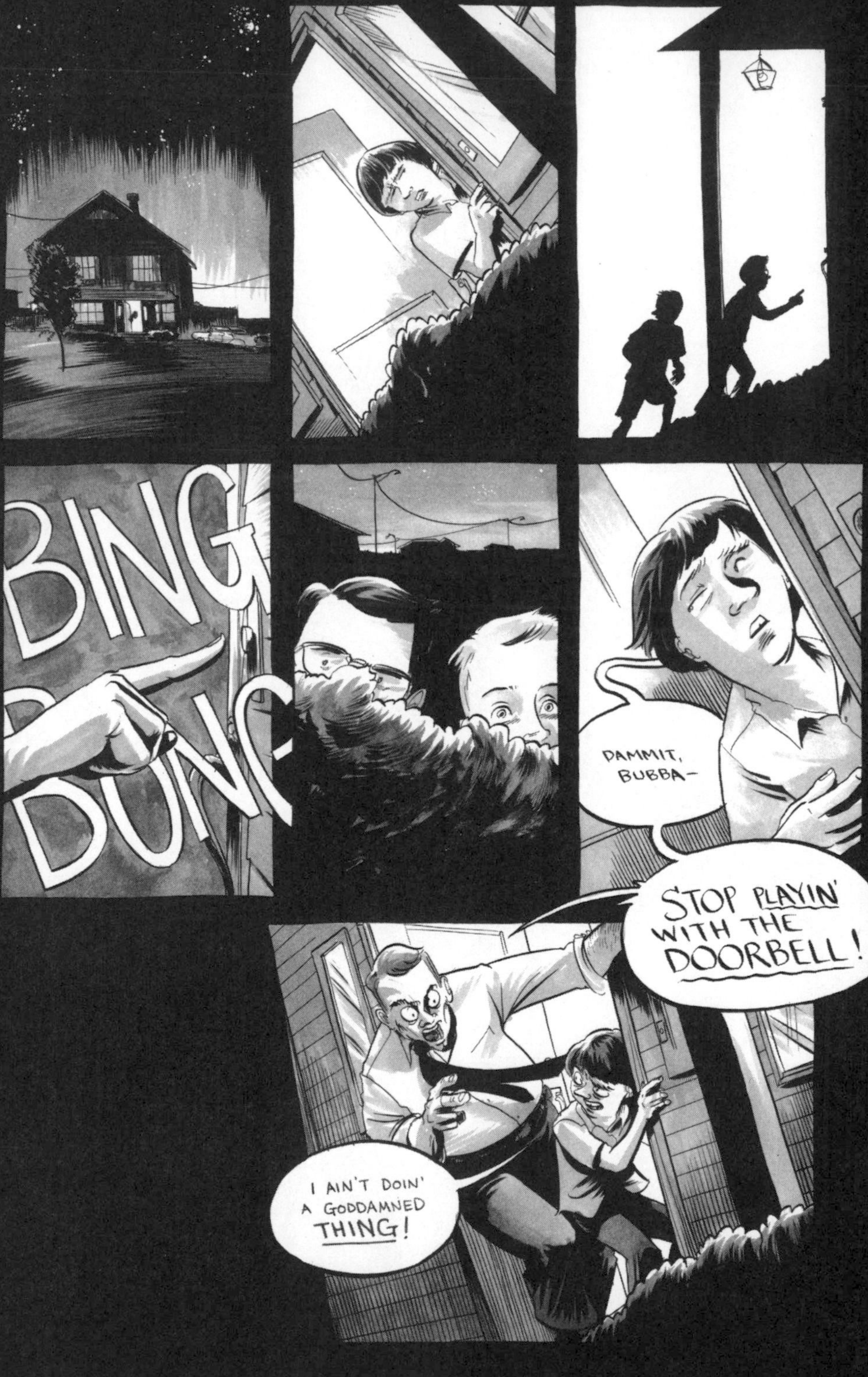
BING
BONG
DAMMIT, BUBBA-
STOP PLAYIN' WITH THE DOORBELL!
I AIN'T DOIN' A GODDAMNED THING!

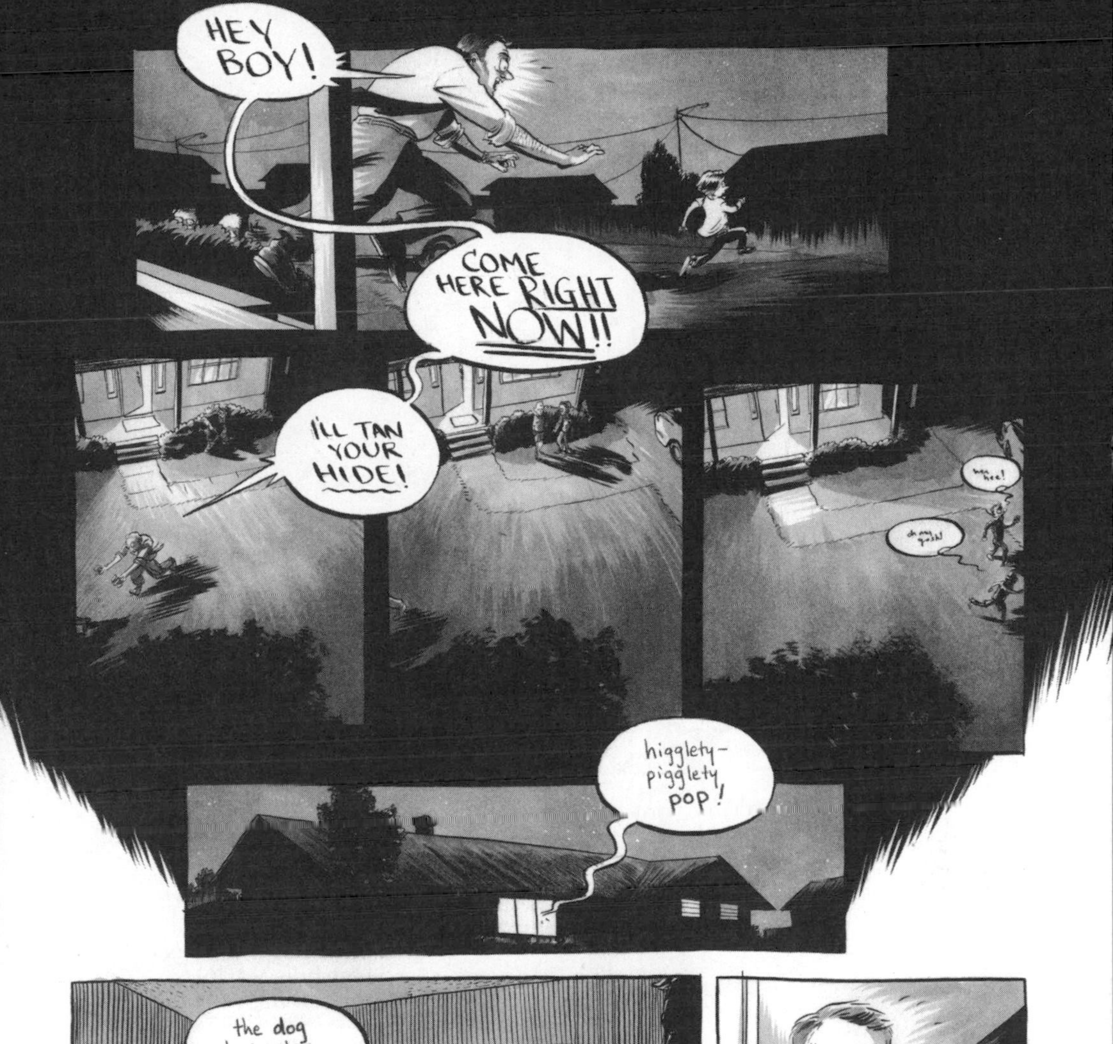
HEY BOY!
COME HERE RIGHT NOW!!
I'LL TAN YOUR HIDE!
higglety-pigglety pop!
the dog has eaten the mop!
the pig's in a hurry the cat's in a flurry
higglety-pigglety pop!

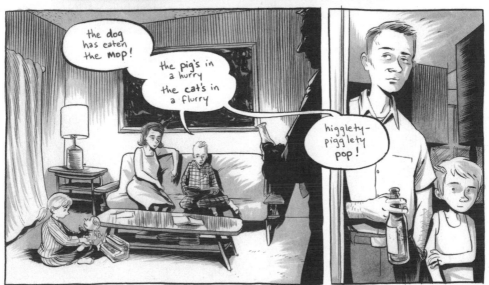

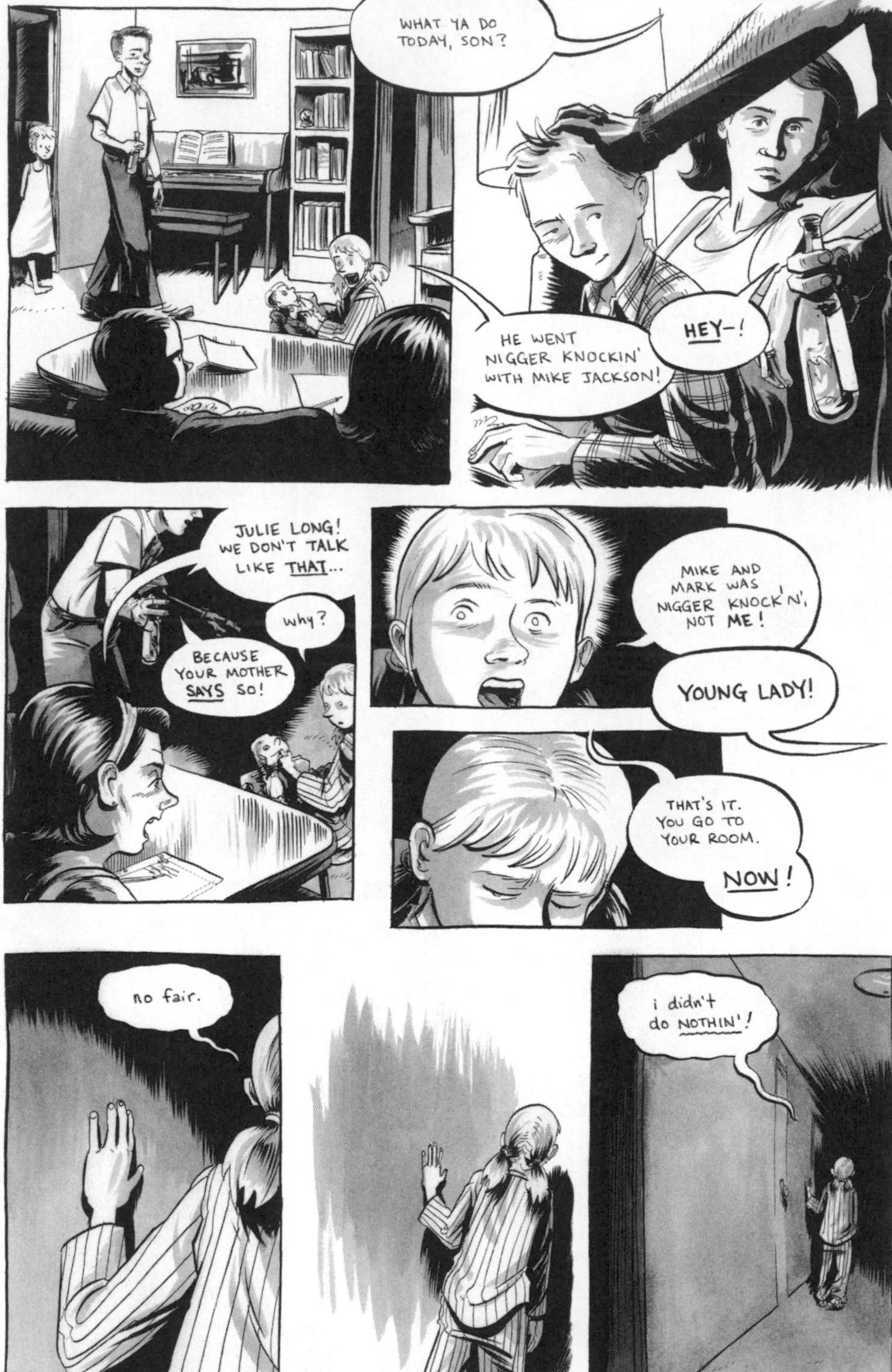
WHAT YA DO TODAY, SON?
HE WENT NIGGER KNOCKIN' WITH MIKE JACKSON!
HEY-!
JULIE LONG! WE DON'T TALK LIKE THAT...
why?
BECAUSE YOUR MOTHER SAYS SO!
MIKE AND MARK WAS NIGGER KNOCK'N', NOT ME!
YOUNG LADY!
THAT'S IT. YOU GO TO YOUR ROOM.
NOW!
no fair.
i didn't do NOTHIN'!

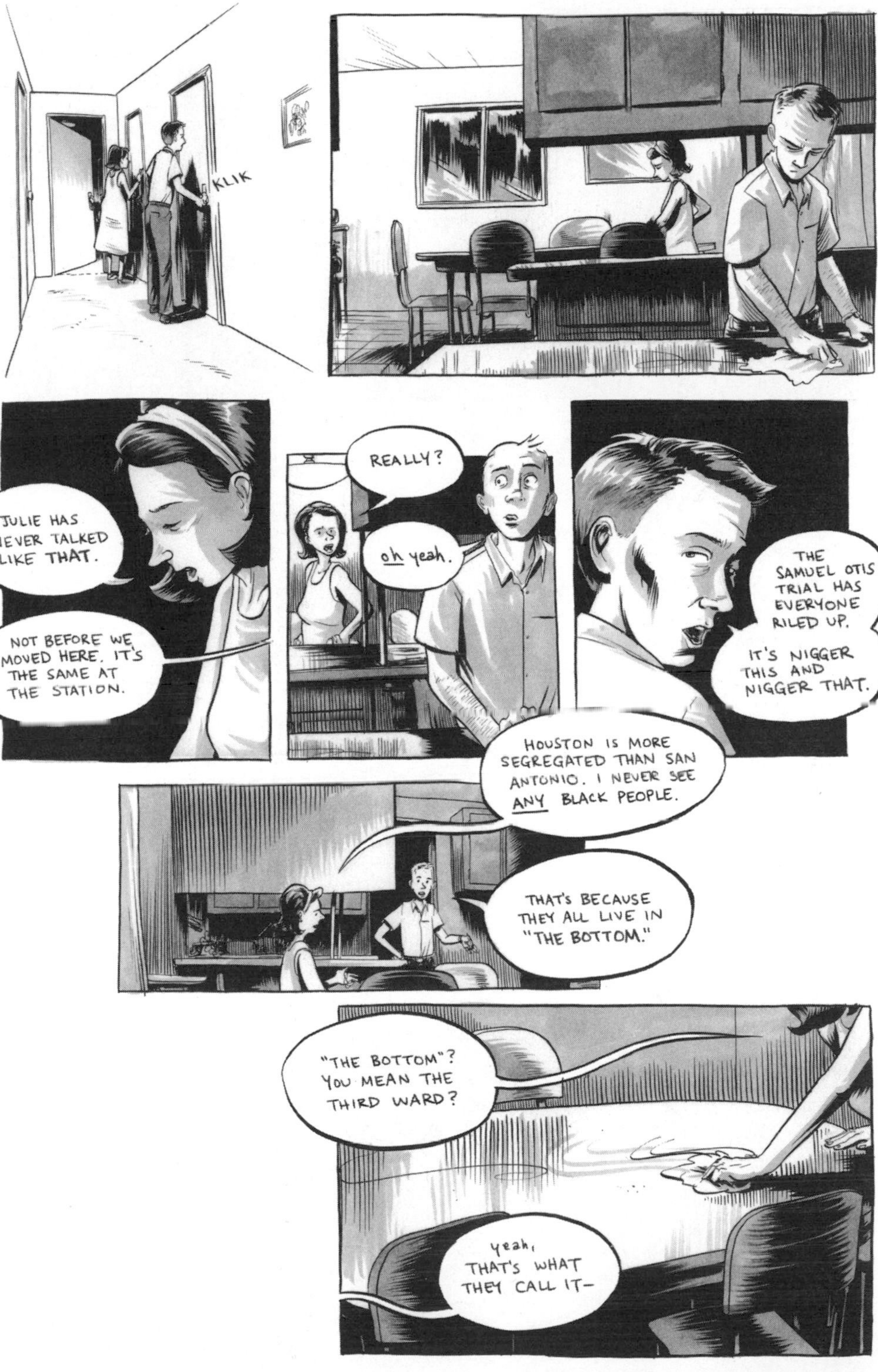
KLIK
JULIE HAS NEVER TALKED LIKE THAT.
NOT BEFORE WE MOVED HERE. IT'S THE SAME AT THE STATION.
REALLY?
oh yeah.
THE SAMUEL OTIS TRIAL HAS EVERYONE RILED UP.
IT'S NIGGER THIS AND NIGGER THAT.
HOUSTON IS MORE SEGREGATED THAN SAN ANTONIO. I NEVER SEE ANY BLACK PEOPLE.
THAT'S BECAUSE THEY ALL LIVE IN "THE BOTTOM."
"THE BOTTOM"? YOU MEAN THE THIRD WARD?
yeah, THAT'S WHAT THEY CALL IT—

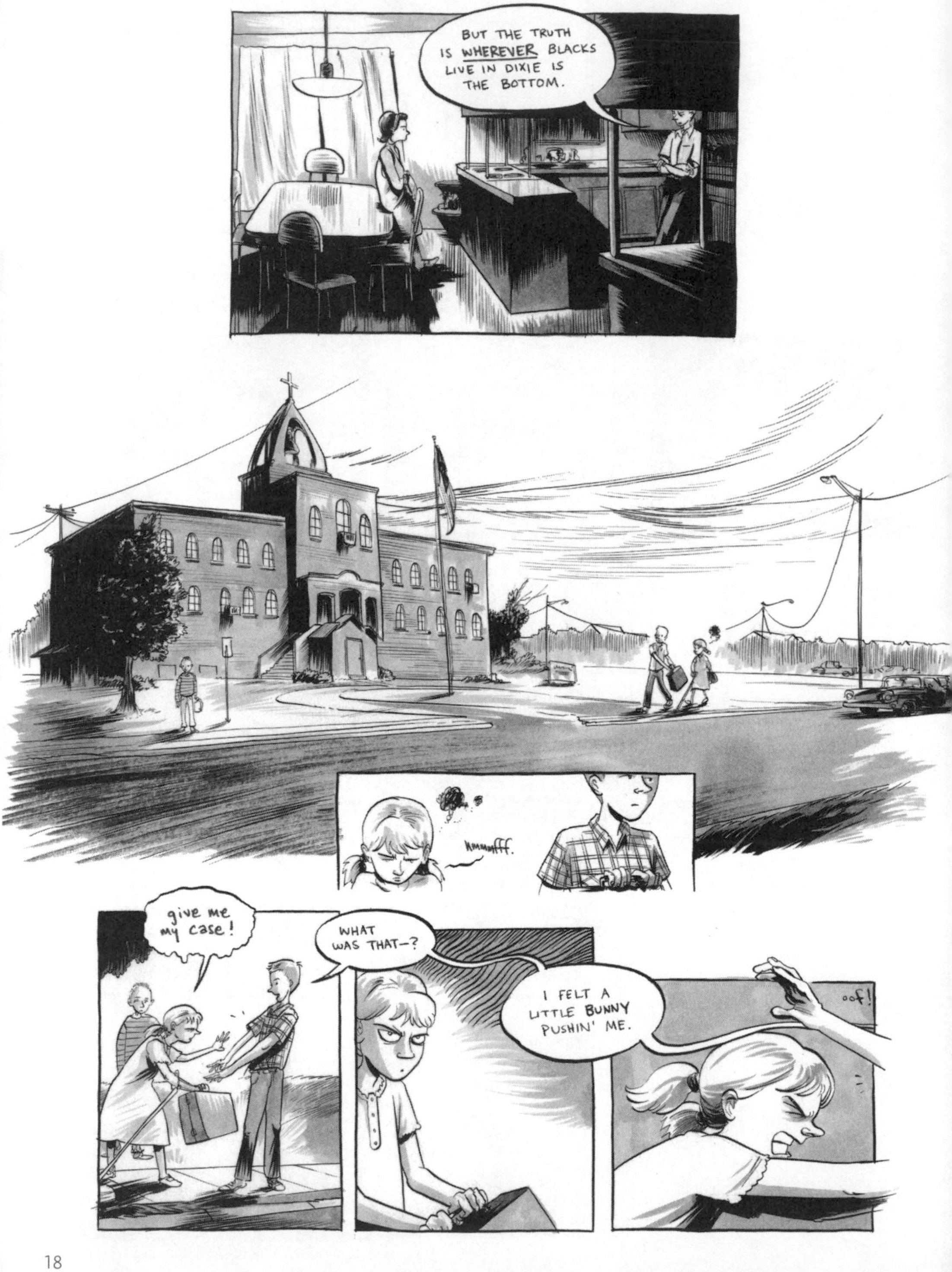

BUT THE TRUTH IS WHEREVER BLACKS LIVE IN DIXIE IS THE BOTTOM.
Hmmmfff.
give me my case!
WHAT WAS THAT—?
I FELT A LITTLE BUNNY PUSHIN' ME.
oof!

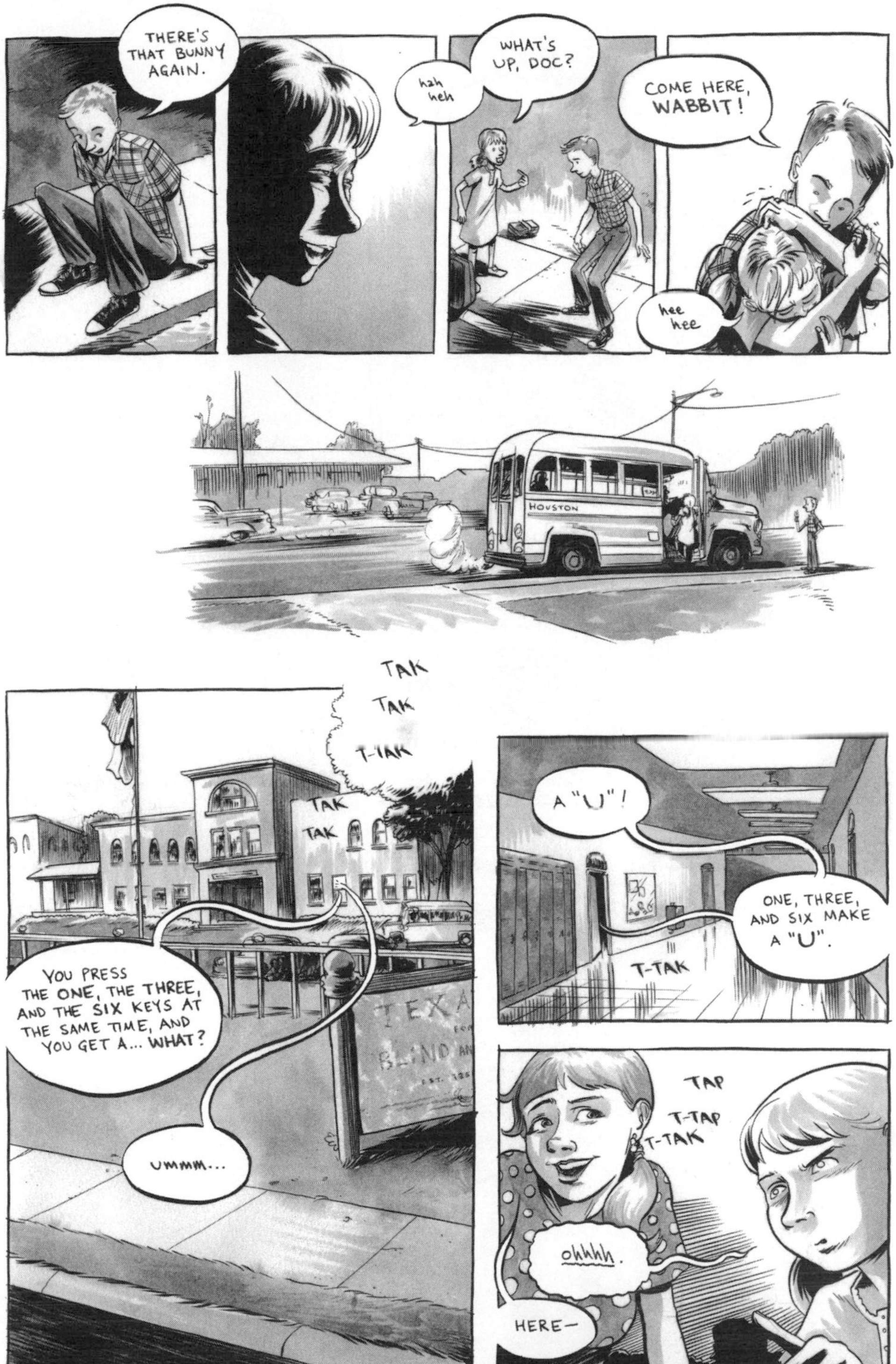
THERE'S THAT BUNNY AGAIN.
hah heh
WHAT'S UP, DOC?
COME HERE, WABBIT!
hee hee
HOUSTON
TAK
TAK
T-TAK
TAK
TAK
YOU PRESS THE ONE, THE THREE, AND THE SIX KEYS AT THE SAME TIME, AND YOU GET A... WHAT?
UMMM...
A "U"!
ONE, THREE, AND SIX MAKE A "U".
T-TAK
TAP
T-TAP
T-TAK
ohhhh.
HERE—

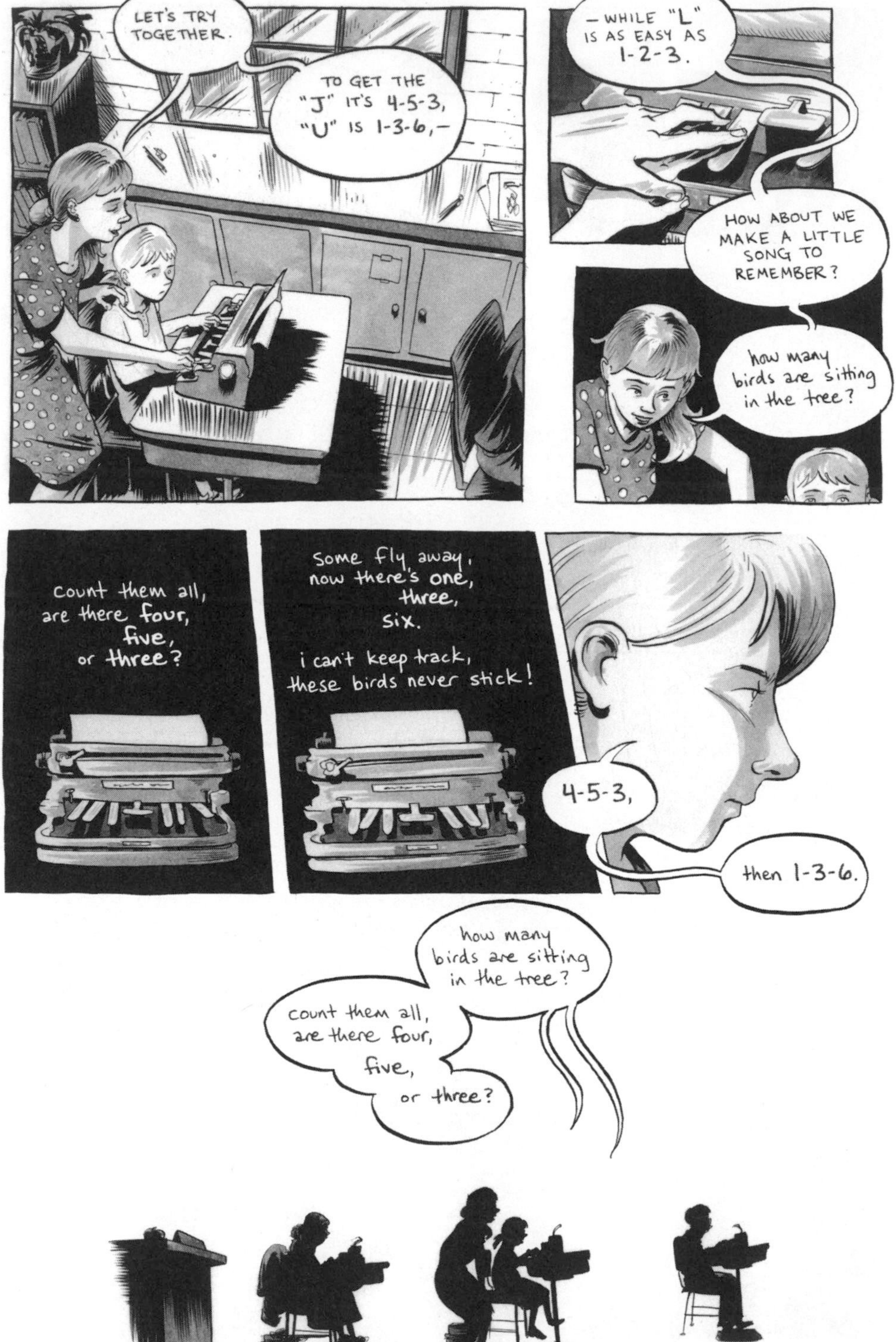
LET'S TRY TOGETHER.
TO GET THE "J" IT'S 4-5-3, "U" IS 1-3-6,—
—WHILE "L" IS AS EASY AS 1-2-3.
HOW ABOUT WE MAKE A LITTLE SONG TO REMEMBER?
how many birds are sitting in the tree?
count them all, are there four, five, or three?
Some fly away, now there's one, three, six.
i can't keep track, these birds never stick!
4-5-3,
then 1-3-6.
how many birds are sitting in the tree?
count them all, are there four, five, or three?

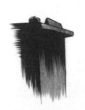

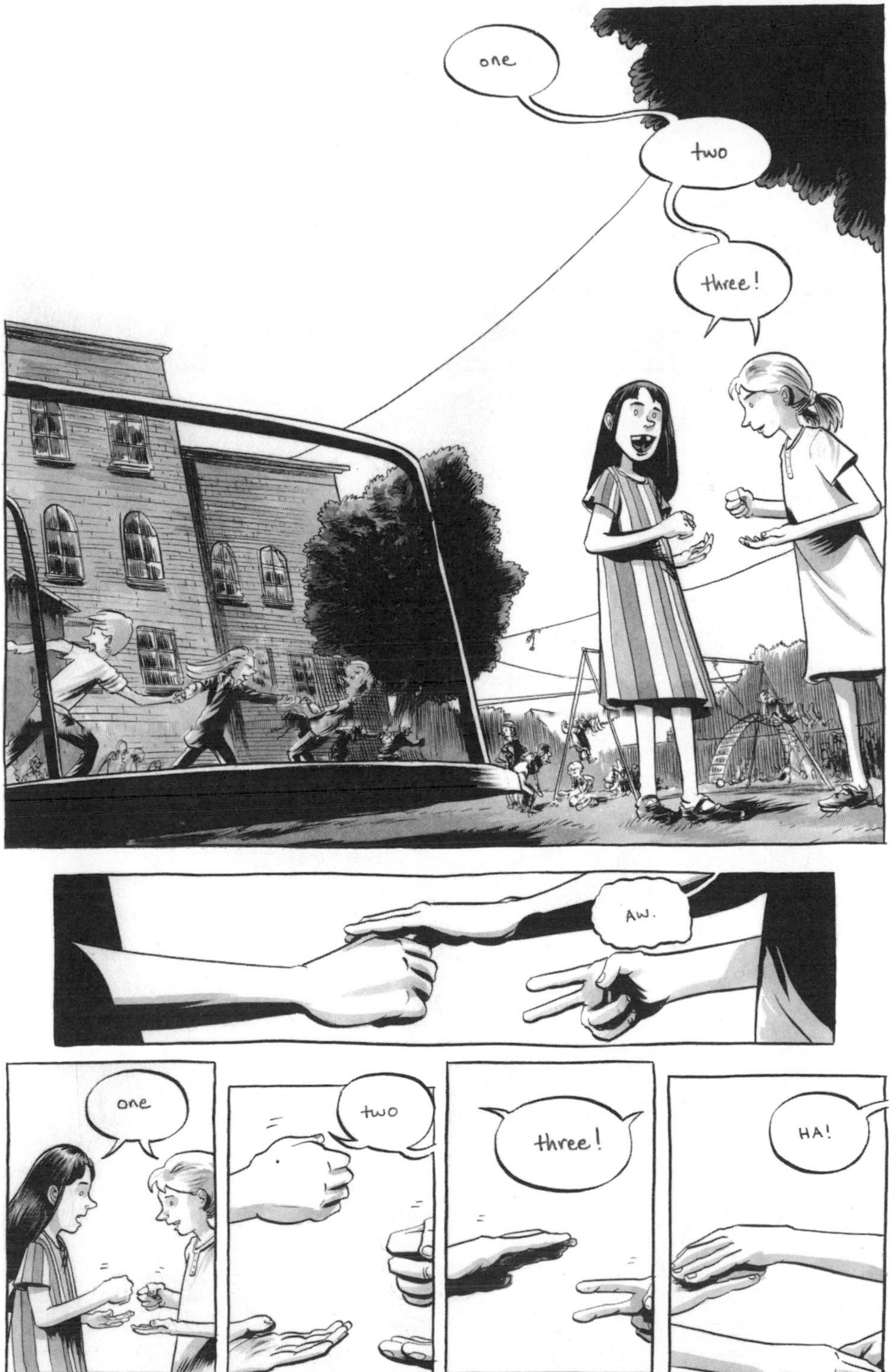
one
two
three!
AW.
one
two
three!
HA!

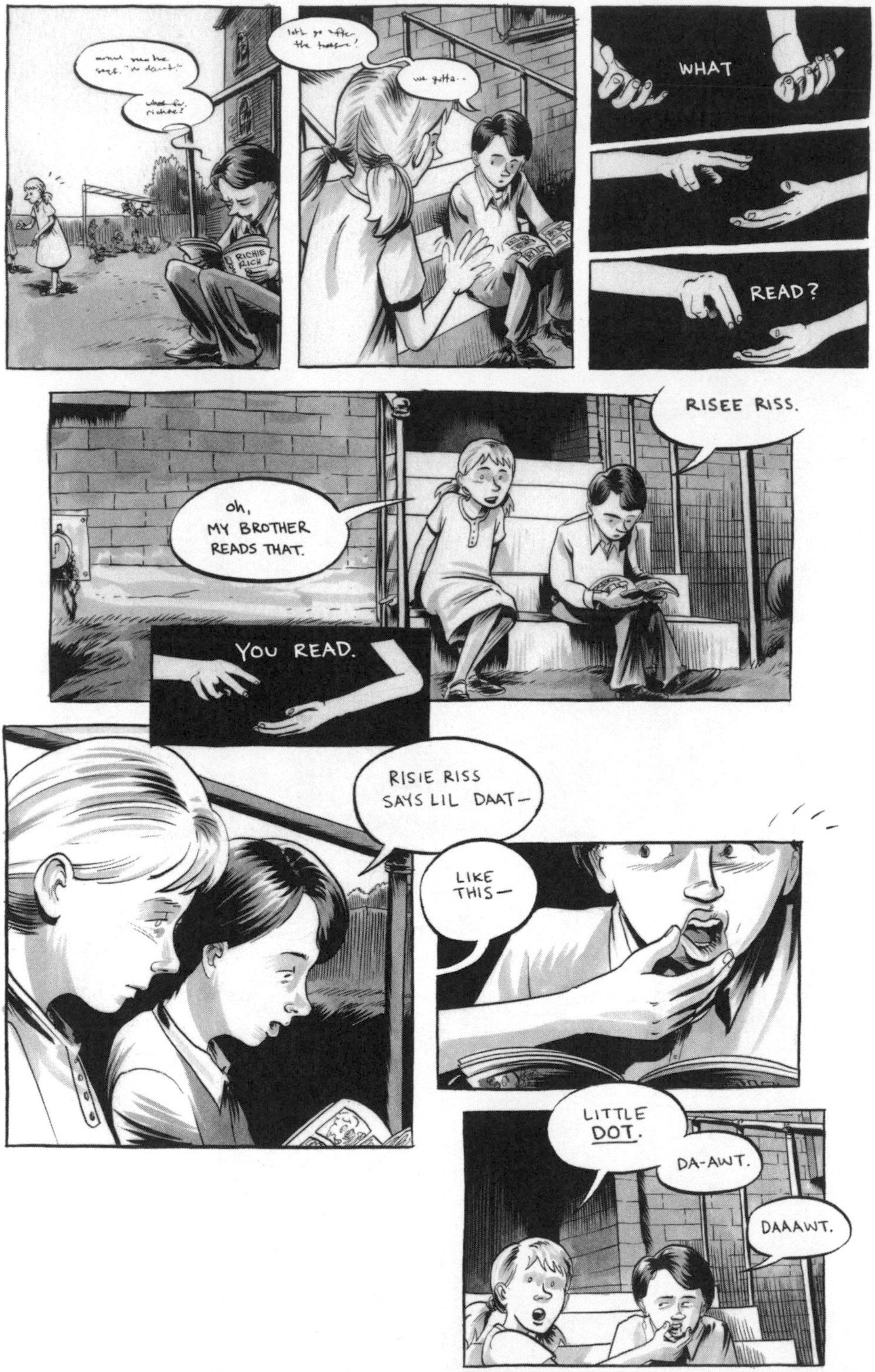

we gotta..
WHAT
READ?
RISEE RISS.
oh, MY BROTHER READS THAT.
YOU READ.
RISIE RISS SAYS LIL DAAT—
LIKE THIS—
LITTLE DOT.
DA-AWT.
DAAAWT.

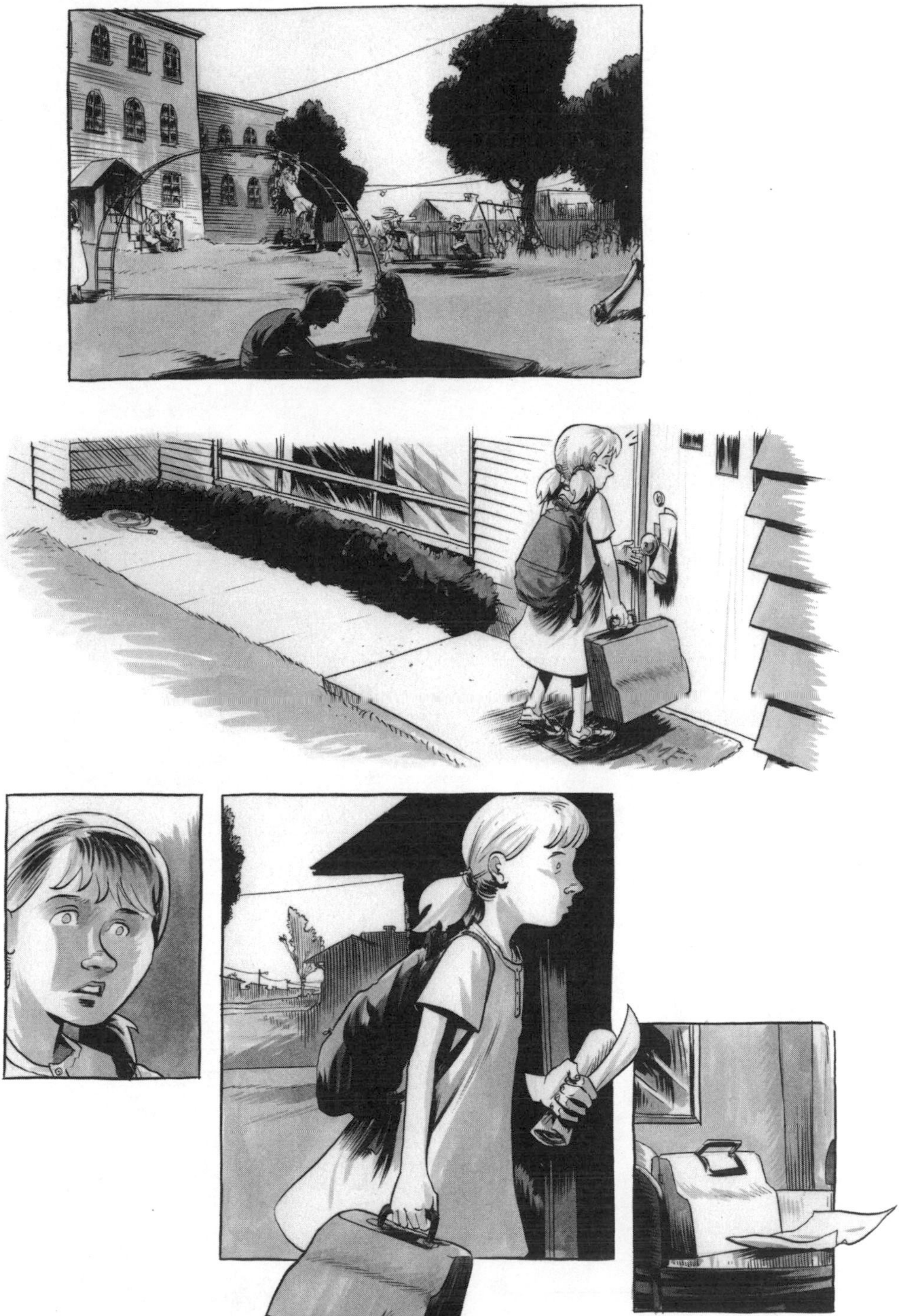

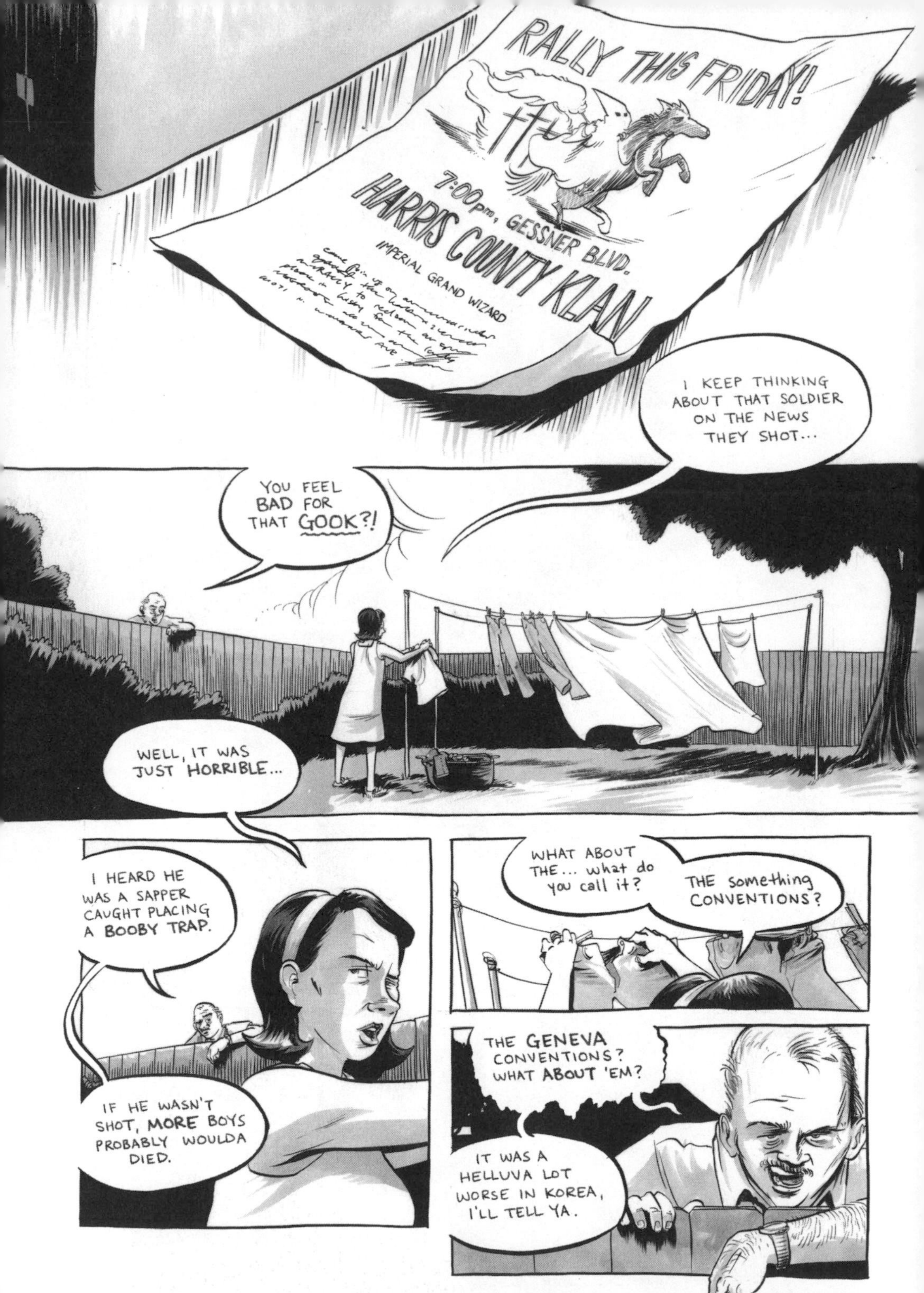

RALLY THIS FRIDAY!
7:00pm, GESSNER BLVD.
HARRIS COUNTY KLAN
IMPERIAL GRAND WIZARD
I KEEP THINKING ABOUT THAT SOLDIER ON THE NEWS THEY SHOT...
YOU FEEL BAD FOR THAT GOOK?!
WELL, IT WAS JUST HORRIBLE...
I HEARD HE WAS A SAPPER CAUGHT PLACING A BOOBY TRAP.
IF HE WASN'T SHOT, MORE BOYS PROBABLY WOULDA DIED.
WHAT ABOUT THE... what do you call it?
THE something CONVENTIONS?
THE GENEVA CONVENTIONS? WHAT ABOUT 'EM?
IT WAS A HELLUVA LOT WORSE IN KOREA, I'LL TELL YA.

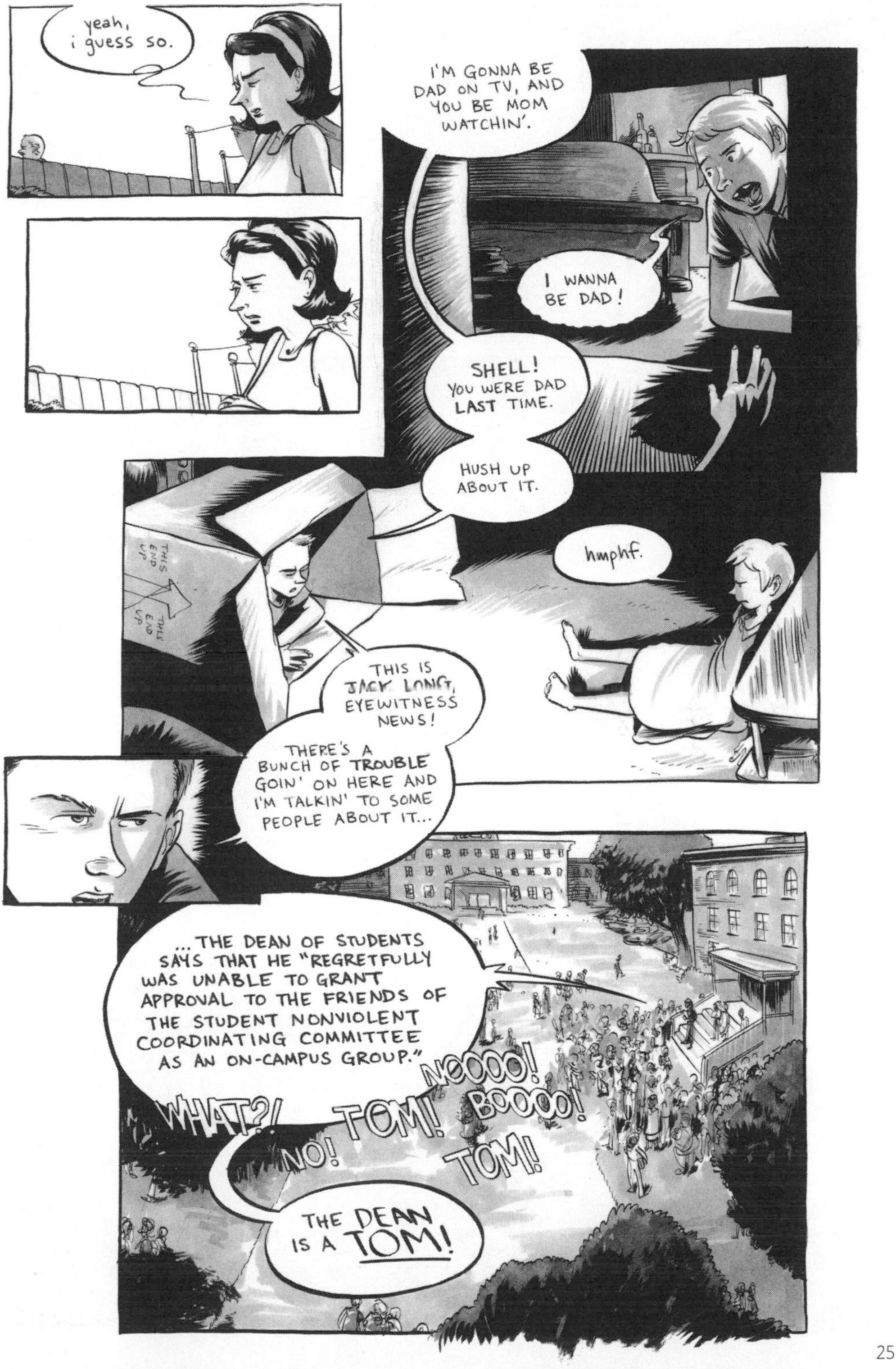
yeah, i guess so.
I'M GONNA BE DAD ON TV, AND YOU BE MOM WATCHIN'.
I WANNA BE DAD!
SHELL! YOU WERE DAD LAST TIME.
HUSH UP ABOUT IT.
hmphf.
THIS END UP
THIS END UP
THIS IS JACK LONG, EYEWITNESS NEWS!
THERE'S A BUNCH OF TROUBLE GOIN' ON HERE AND I'M TALKIN' TO SOME PEOPLE ABOUT IT...
...THE DEAN OF STUDENTS SAYS THAT HE "REGRETFULLY WAS UNABLE TO GRANT APPROVAL TO THE FRIENDS OF THE STUDENT NONVIOLENT COORDINATING COMMITTEE AS AN ON-CAMPUS GROUP."
WHAT?!
NO!
TOM!
NOOOO!
BOOOO!
TOM!
THE DEAN IS A TOM!

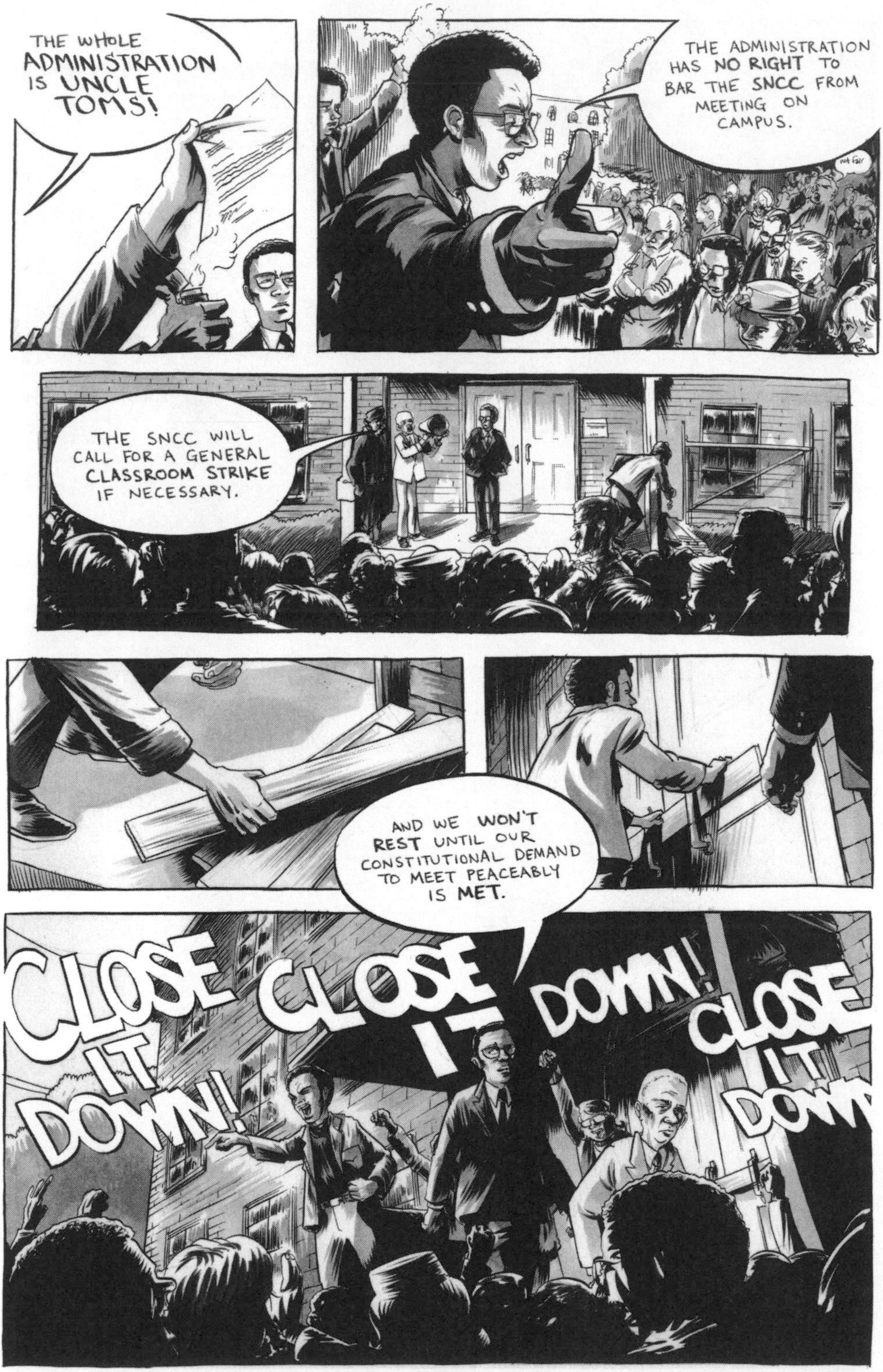
THE WHOLE ADMINISTRATION IS UNCLE TOMS!
THE ADMINISTRATION HAS NO RIGHT TO BAR THE SNCC FROM MEETING ON CAMPUS.
THE SNCC WILL CALL FOR A GENERAL CLASSROOM STRIKE IF NECESSARY.
AND WE WON'T REST UNTIL OUR CONSTITUTIONAL DEMAND TO MEET PEACEABLY IS MET.
CLOSE IT DOWN!
CLOSE IT DOWN!
CLOSE IT

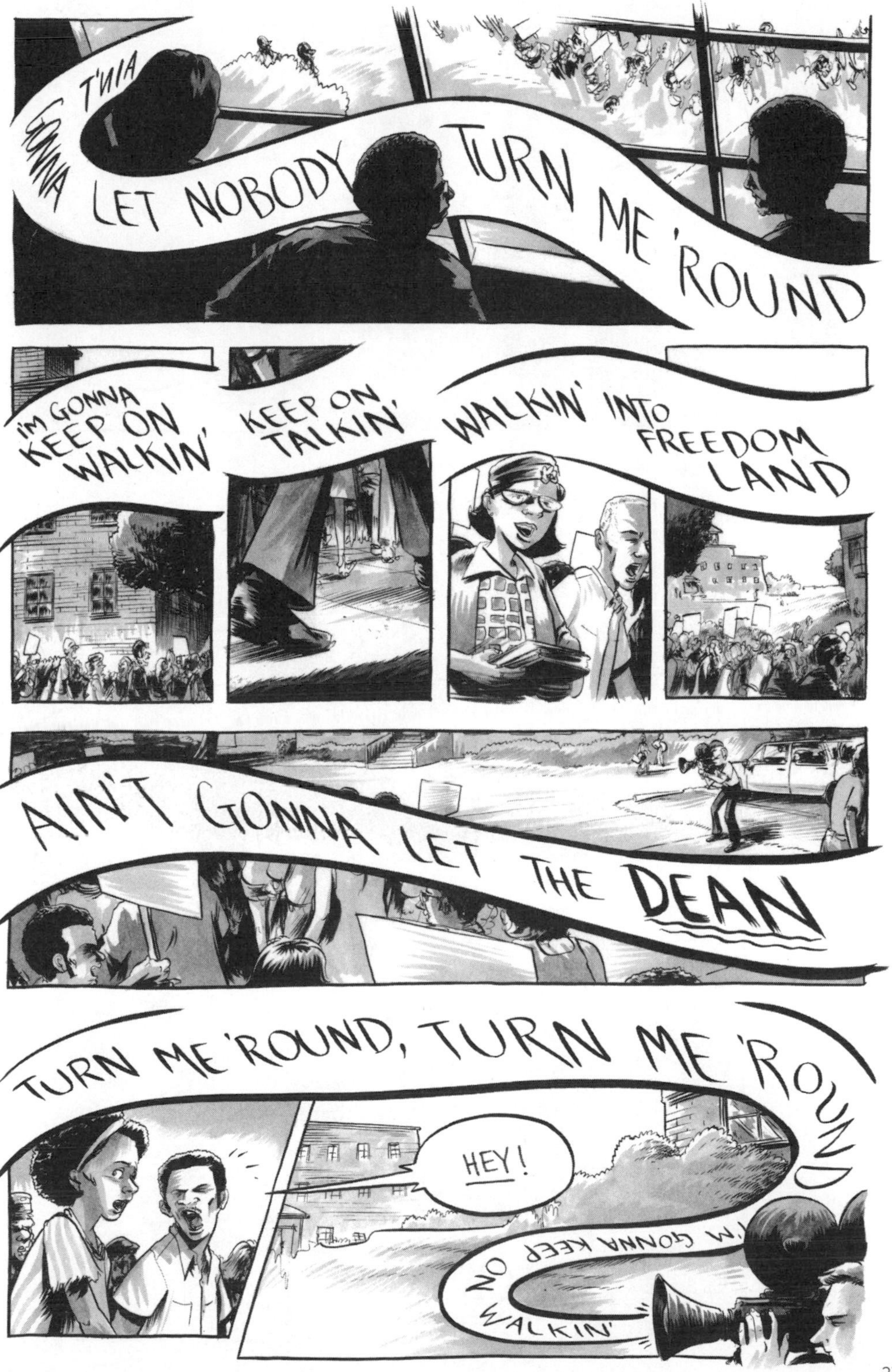

GONNA LET NOBODY TURN ME 'ROUND
I'M GONNA KEEP ON WALKIN' KEEP ON TALKIN' WALKIN' INTO FREEDOM LAND
AIN'T GONNA LET THE DEAN
TURN ME 'ROUND, TURN ME 'ROUND
HEY!
I'M GONNA KEEP ON WALKIN'

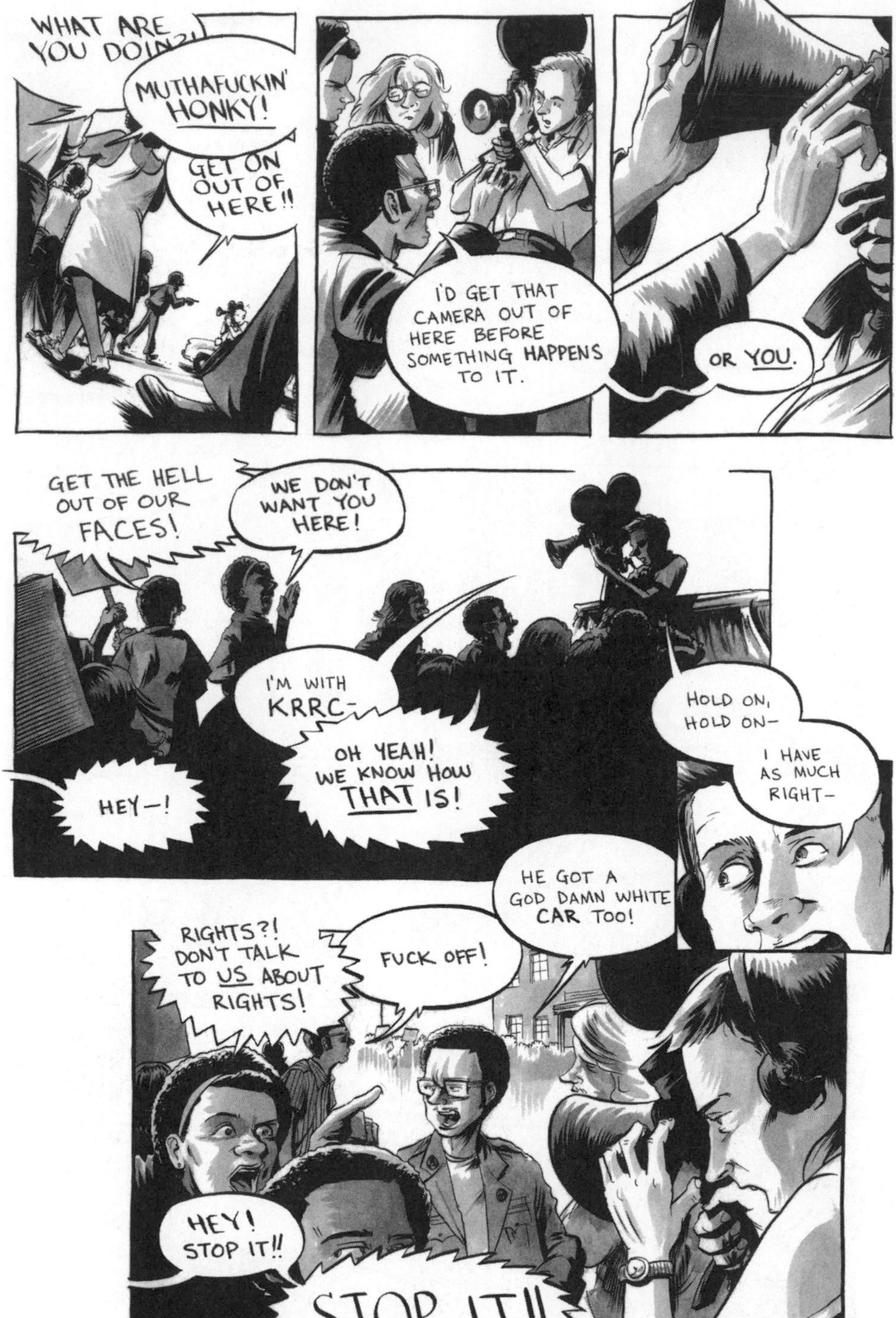
WHAT ARE YOU DOIN?!
MUTHAFUCKIN' HONKY!
GET ON OUT OF HERE!!
I'D GET THAT CAMERA OUT OF HERE BEFORE SOMETHING HAPPENS TO IT.
OR YOU.
GET THE HELL OUT OF OUR FACES!
WE DON'T WANT YOU HERE!
I'M WITH KRRC-
OH YEAH! WE KNOW HOW THAT IS!
HEY-!
HOLD ON, HOLD ON-
I HAVE AS MUCH RIGHT-
HE GOT A GOD DAMN WHITE CAR TOO!
RIGHTS?! DON'T TALK TO US ABOUT RIGHTS!
FUCK OFF!
HEY! STOP IT!!
STOP IT!!

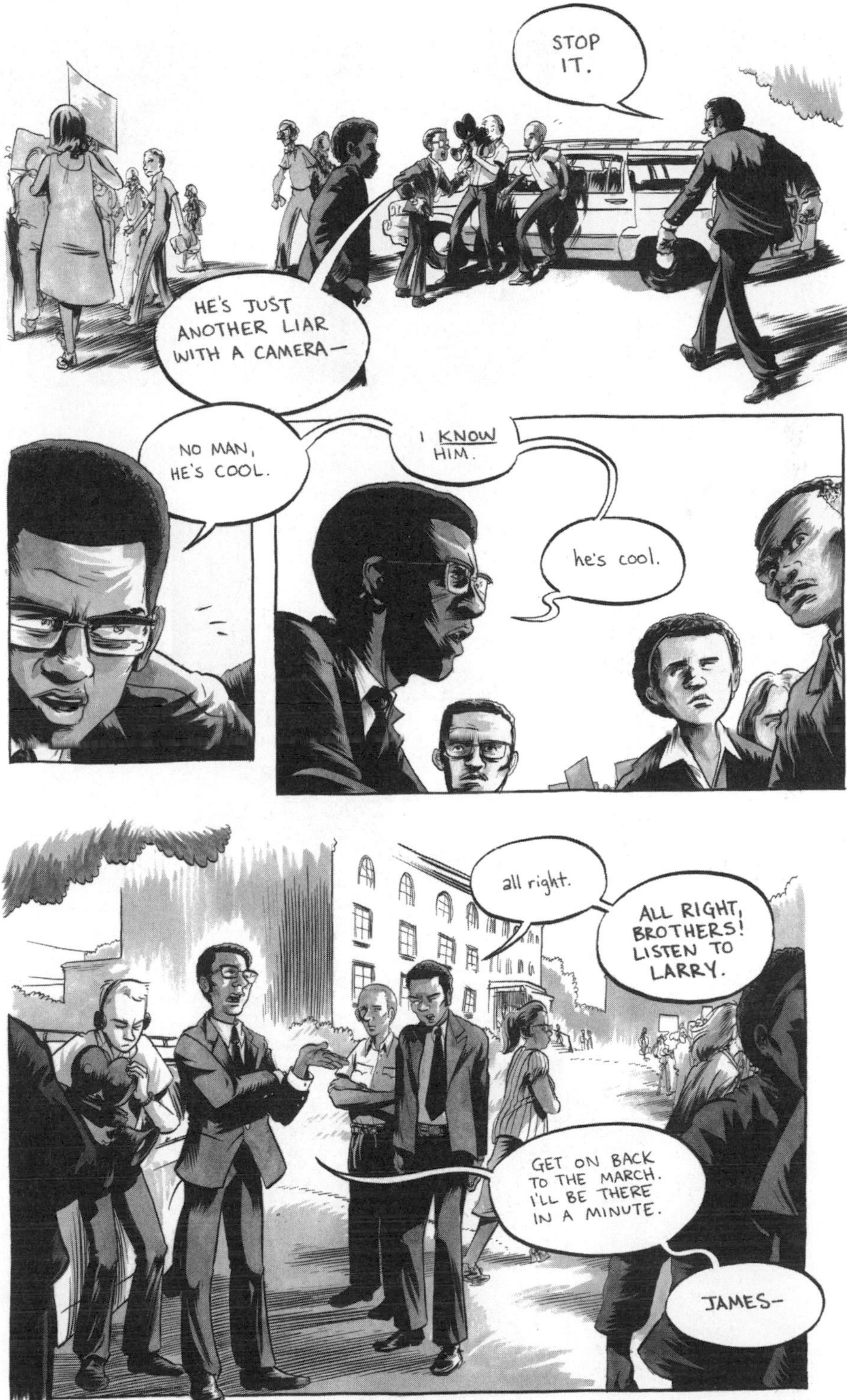
STOP IT.
HE'S JUST ANOTHER LIAR WITH A CAMERA—
NO MAN, HE'S COOL.
I KNOW HIM.
he's cool.
all right.
ALL RIGHT, BROTHERS! LISTEN TO LARRY.
GET ON BACK TO THE MARCH. I'LL BE THERE IN A MINUTE.
JAMES—

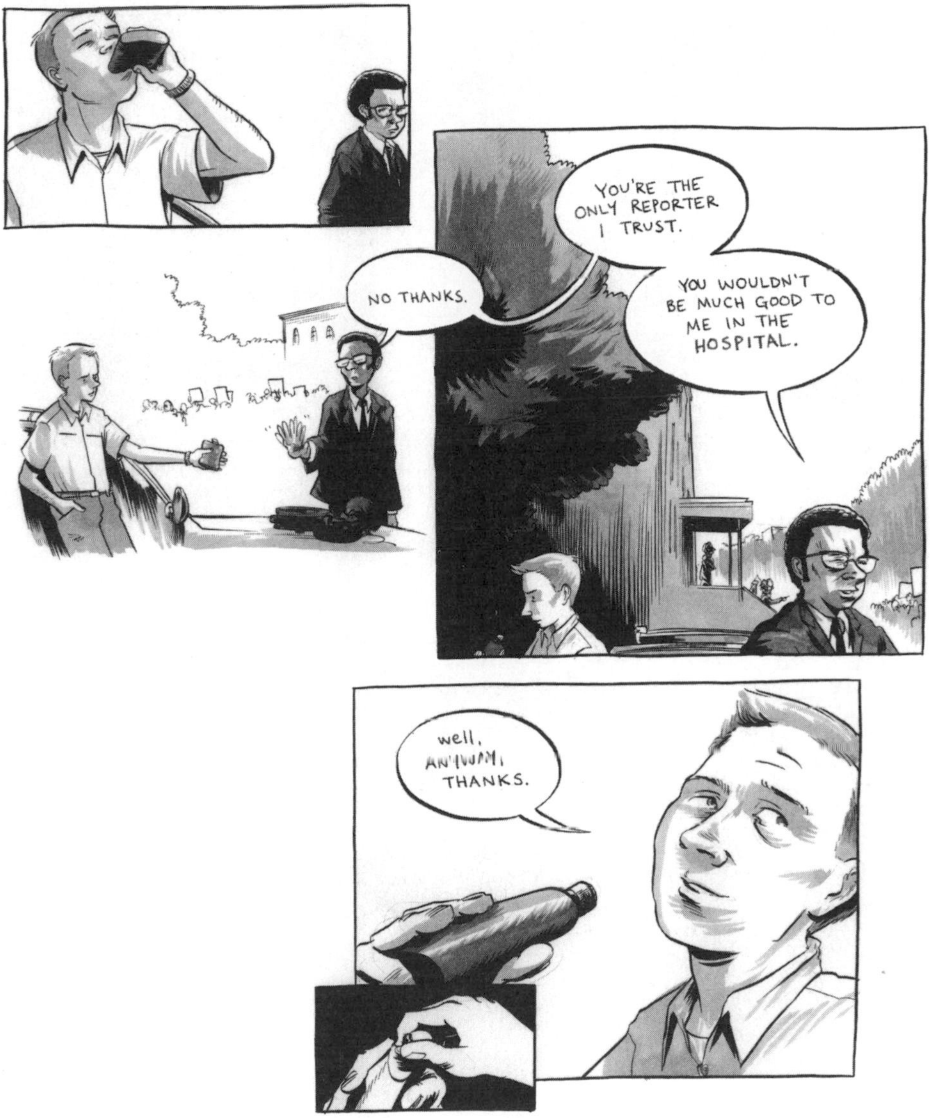
NO THANKS.
YOU'RE THE ONLY REPORTER I TRUST.
YOU WOULDN'T BE MUCH GOOD TO ME IN THE HOSPITAL.
well, AN'YWAY, THANKS.

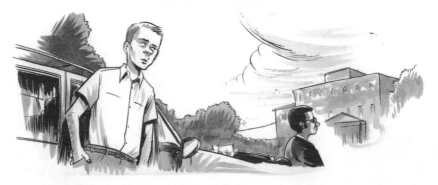

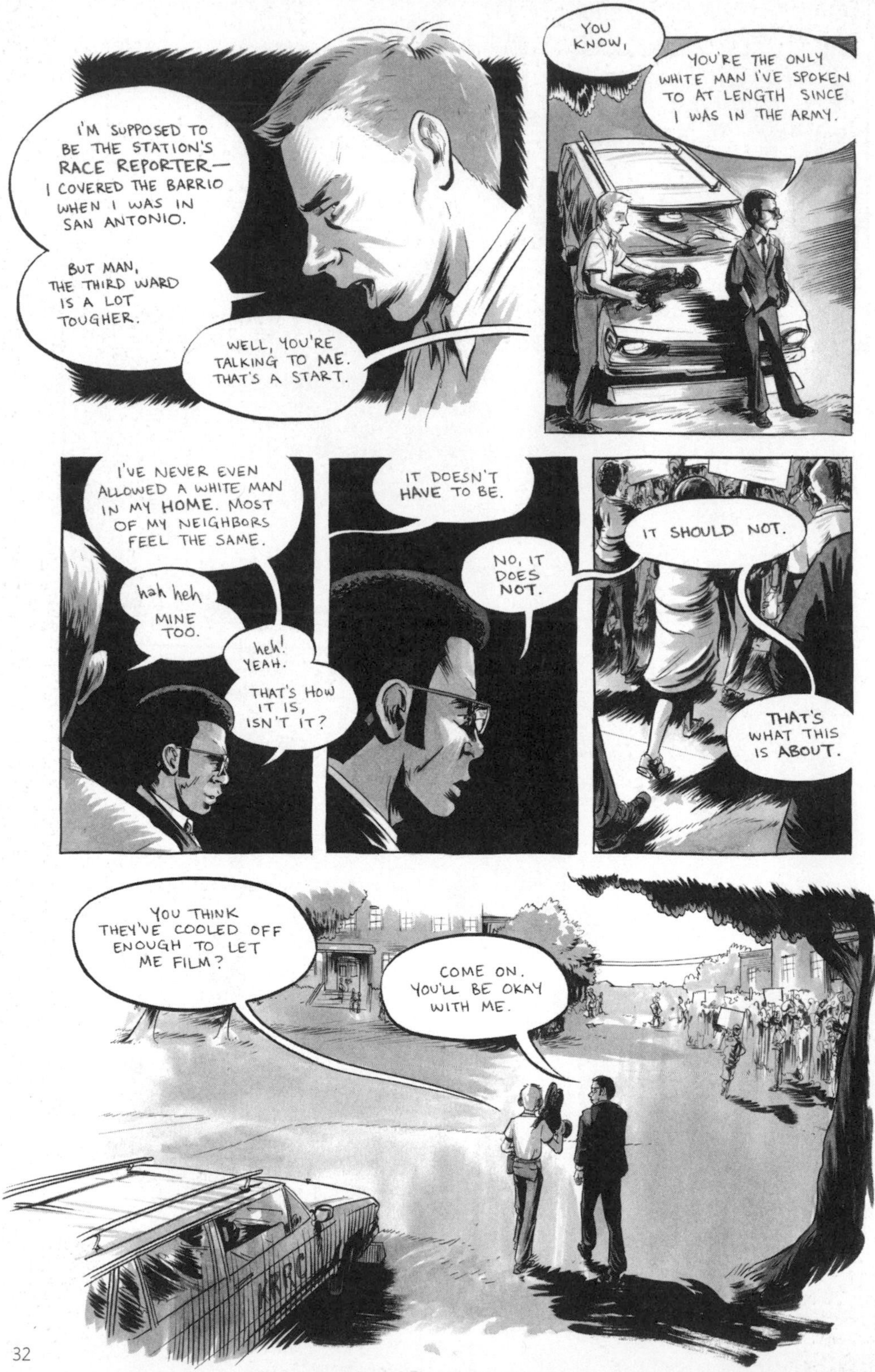
I'M SUPPOSED TO BE THE STATION'S RACE REPORTER— I COVERED THE BARRIO WHEN I WAS IN SAN ANTONIO.
BUT MAN, THE THIRD WARD IS A LOT TOUGHER.
WELL, YOU'RE TALKING TO ME. THAT'S A START.
YOU KNOW,
YOU'RE THE ONLY WHITE MAN I'VE SPOKEN TO AT LENGTH SINCE I WAS IN THE ARMY.
I'VE NEVER EVEN ALLOWED A WHITE MAN IN MY HOME. MOST OF MY NEIGHBORS FEEL THE SAME.
hah heh
MINE TOO.
heh! YEAH.
THAT'S HOW IT IS, ISN'T IT?
IT DOESN'T HAVE TO BE.
NO, IT DOES NOT.
IT SHOULD NOT.
THAT'S WHAT THIS IS ABOUT.
YOU THINK THEY'VE COOLED OFF ENOUGH TO LET ME FILM?
COME ON. YOU'LL BE OKAY WITH ME.
KPRC

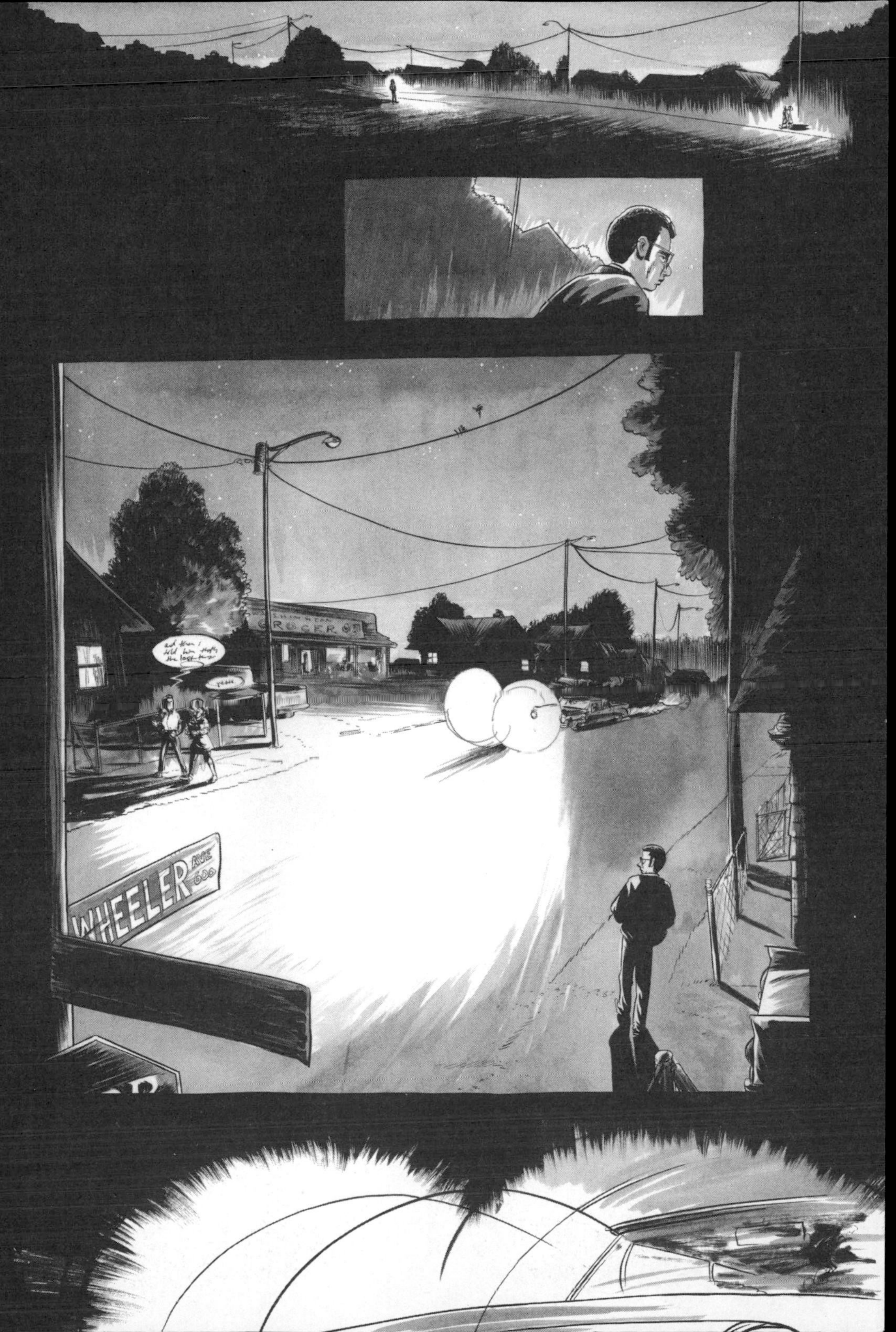
WHEELER AVE 600

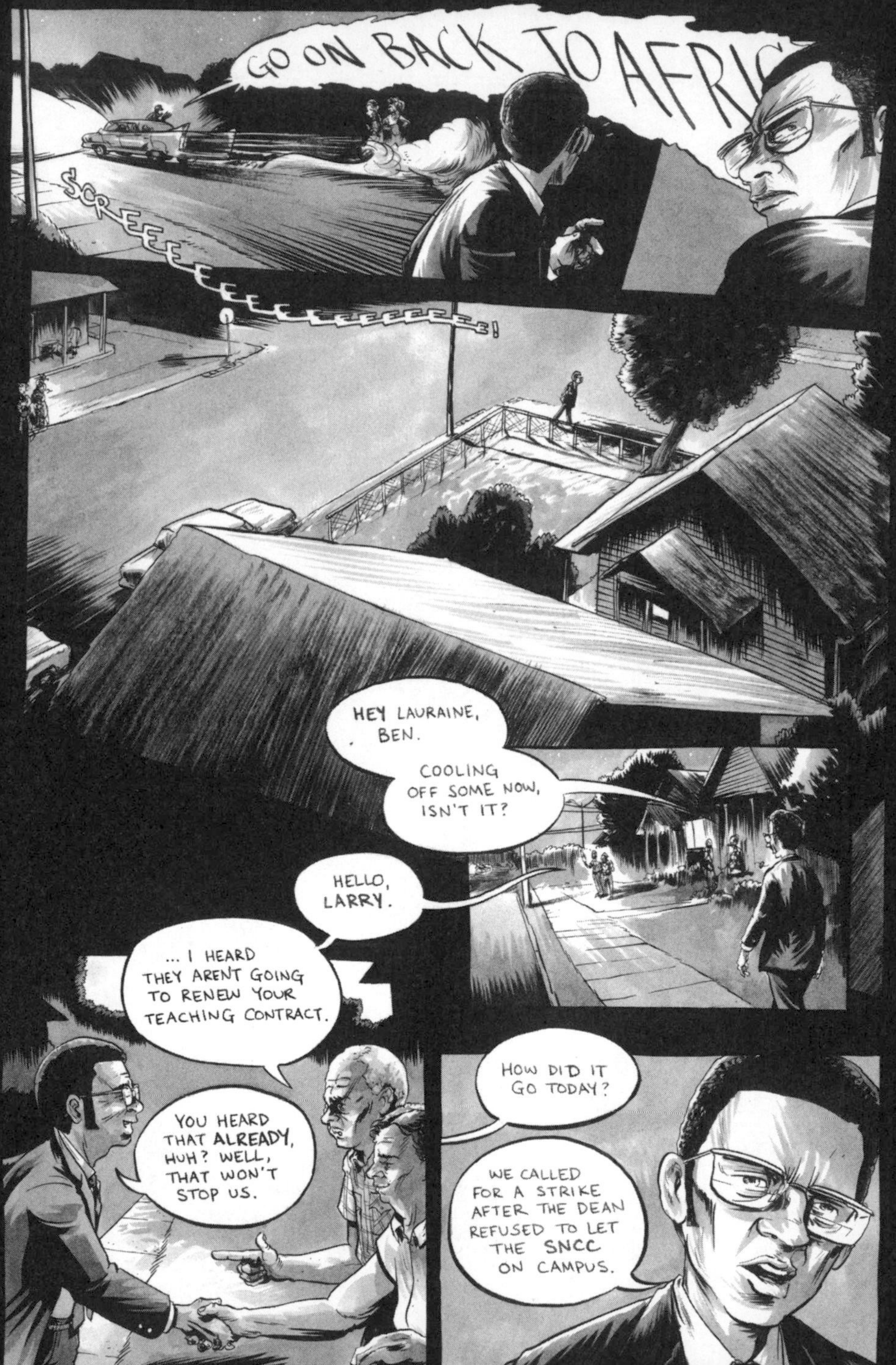
GO ON BACK TO AFRIC
SCREEEEEEEEEEEEEEEEEEEE!
HEY LAURAINE, BEN.
COOLING OFF SOME NOW, ISN'T IT?
HELLO, LARRY.
... I HEARD THEY AREN'T GOING TO RENEW YOUR TEACHING CONTRACT.
YOU HEARD THAT ALREADY, HUH? WELL, THAT WON'T STOP US.
HOW DID IT GO TODAY?
WE CALLED FOR A STRIKE AFTER THE DEAN REFUSED TO LET THE SNCC ON CAMPUS.

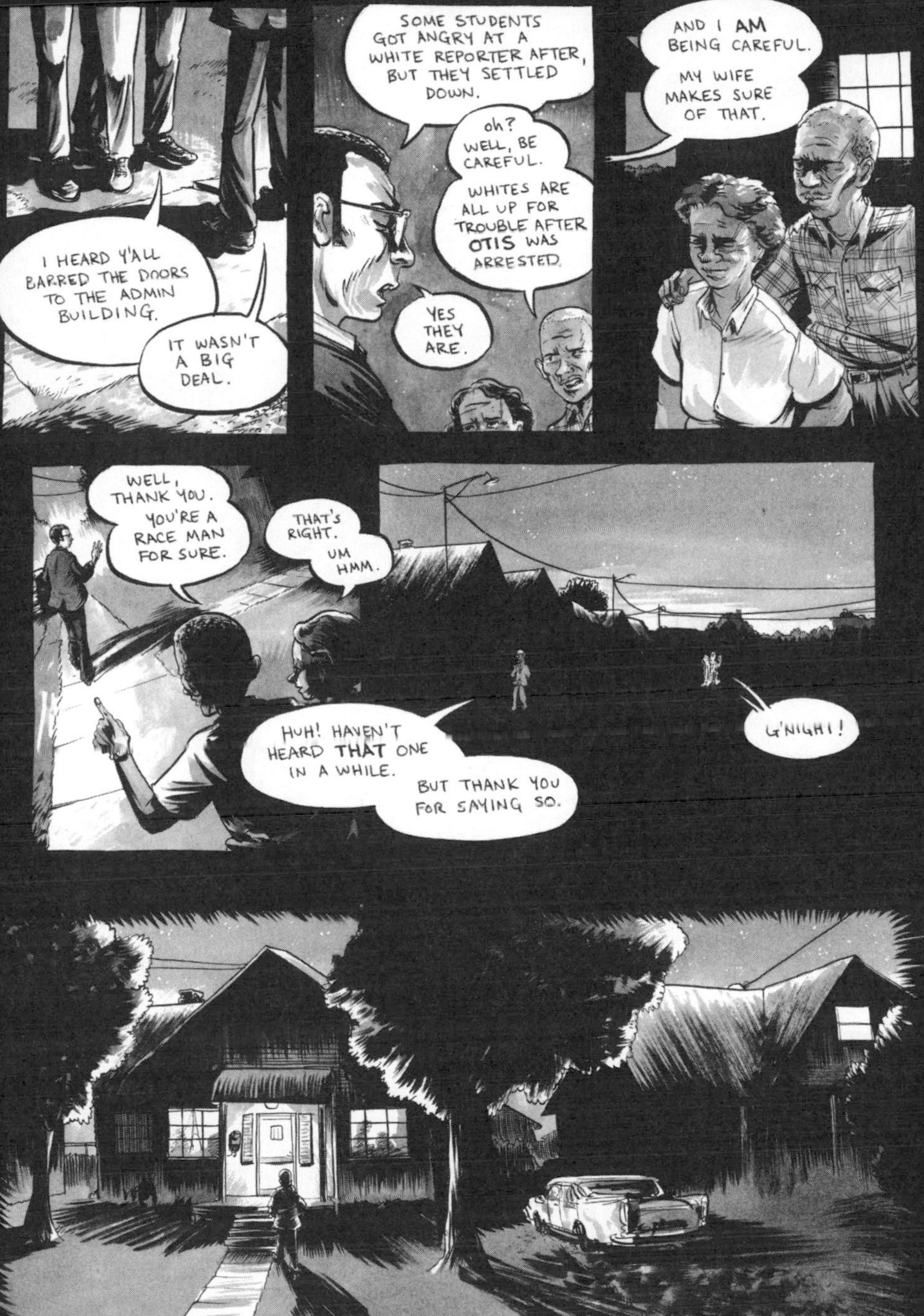
I HEARD Y'ALL BARRED THE DOORS TO THE ADMIN BUILDING.
IT WASN'T A BIG DEAL.
SOME STUDENTS GOT ANGRY AT A WHITE REPORTER AFTER, BUT THEY SETTLED DOWN.
oh? WELL, BE CAREFUL.
WHITES ARE ALL UP FOR TROUBLE AFTER OTIS WAS ARRESTED.
YES THEY ARE.
AND I AM BEING CAREFUL.
MY WIFE MAKES SURE OF THAT.
WELL, THANK YOU.
YOU'RE A RACE MAN FOR SURE.
THAT'S RIGHT.
UM HMM.
HUH! HAVEN'T HEARD THAT ONE IN A WHILE.
BUT THANK YOU FOR SAYING SO.
G'NIGHT!

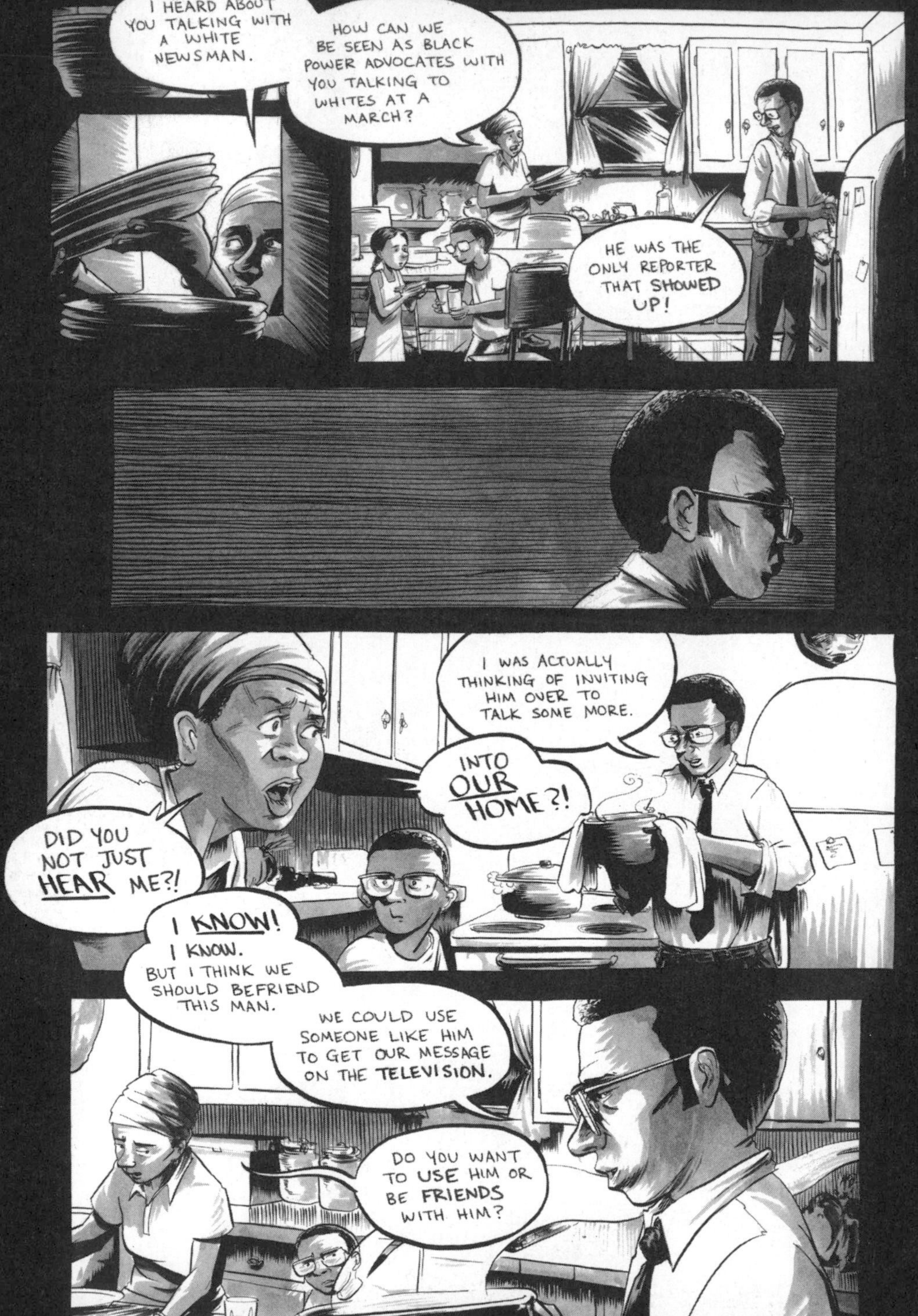
I HEARD ABOUT YOU TALKING WITH A WHITE NEWSMAN.
HOW CAN WE BE SEEN AS BLACK POWER ADVOCATES WITH YOU TALKING TO WHITES AT A MARCH?
HE WAS THE ONLY REPORTER THAT SHOWED UP!
I WAS ACTUALLY THINKING OF INVITING HIM OVER TO TALK SOME MORE.
INTO OUR HOME?!
DID YOU NOT JUST HEAR ME?!
I KNOW! I KNOW. BUT I THINK WE SHOULD BEFRIEND THIS MAN.
WE COULD USE SOMEONE LIKE HIM TO GET OUR MESSAGE ON THE TELEVISION.
DO YOU WANT TO USE HIM OR BE FRIENDS WITH HIM?

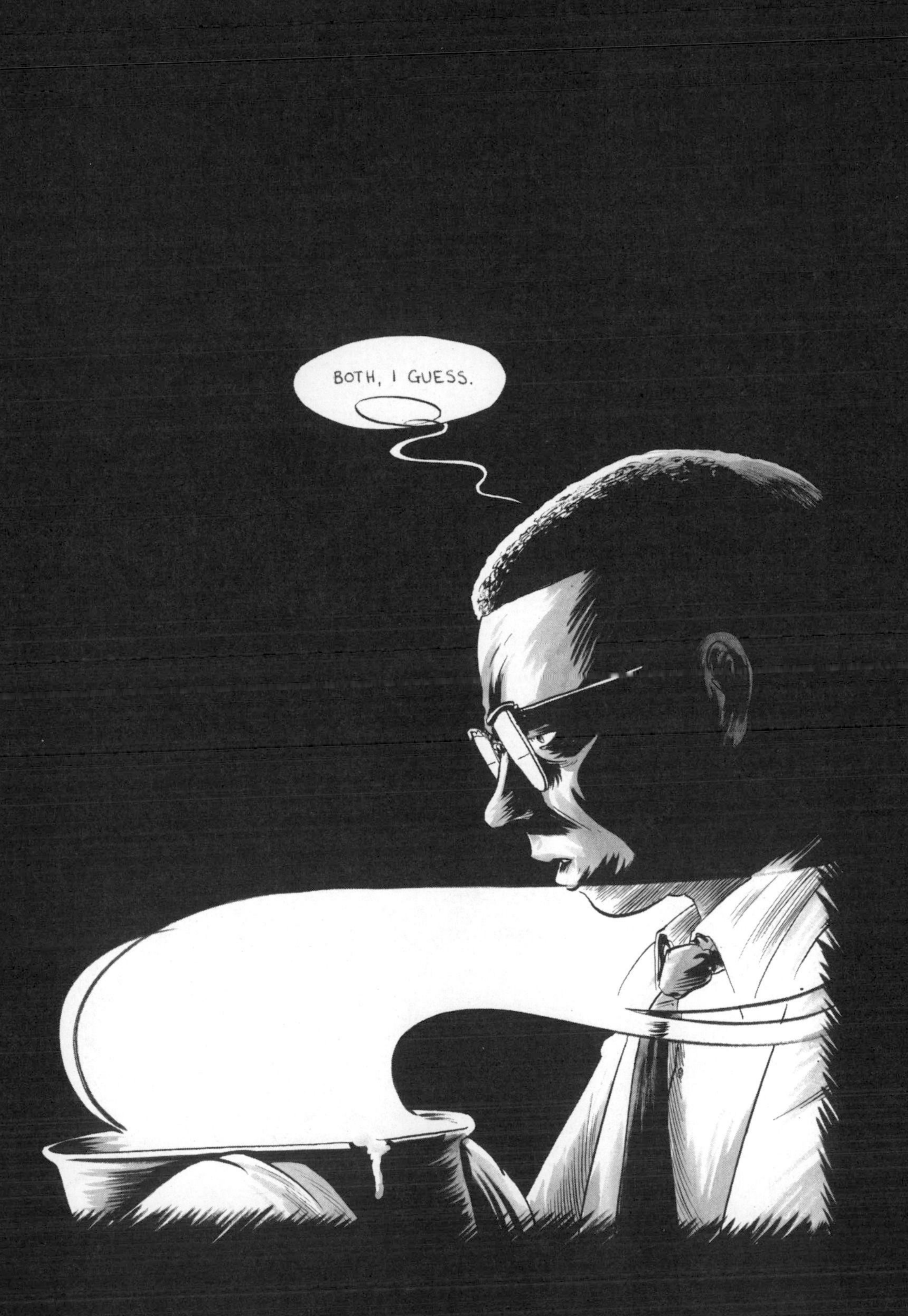
BOTH, I GUESS.

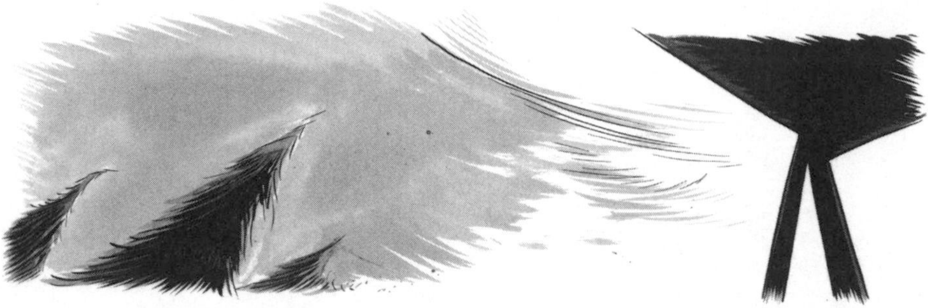

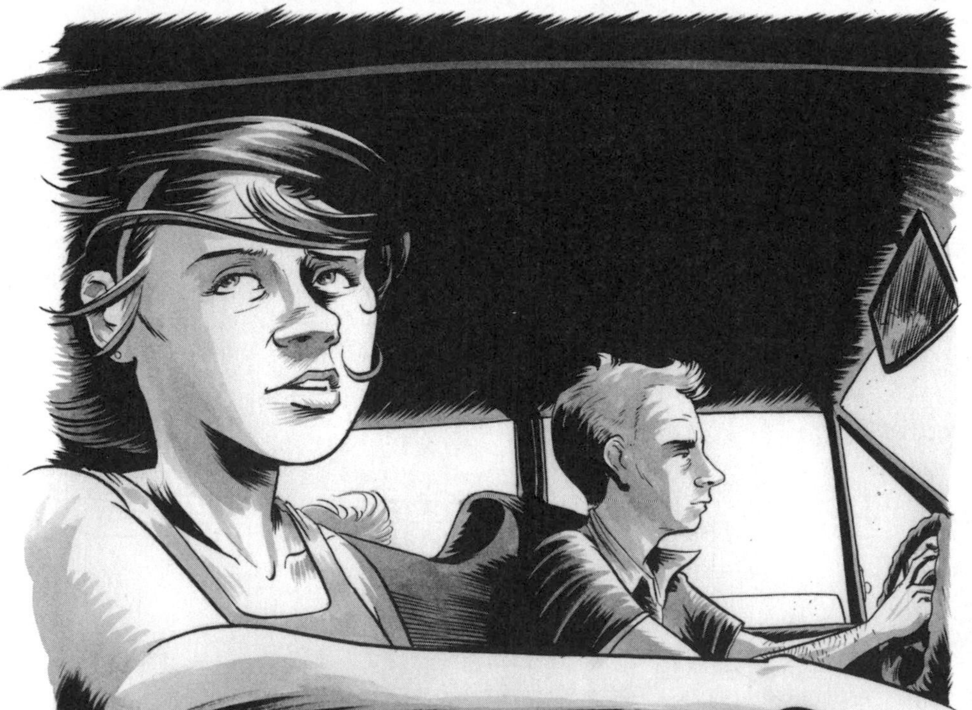

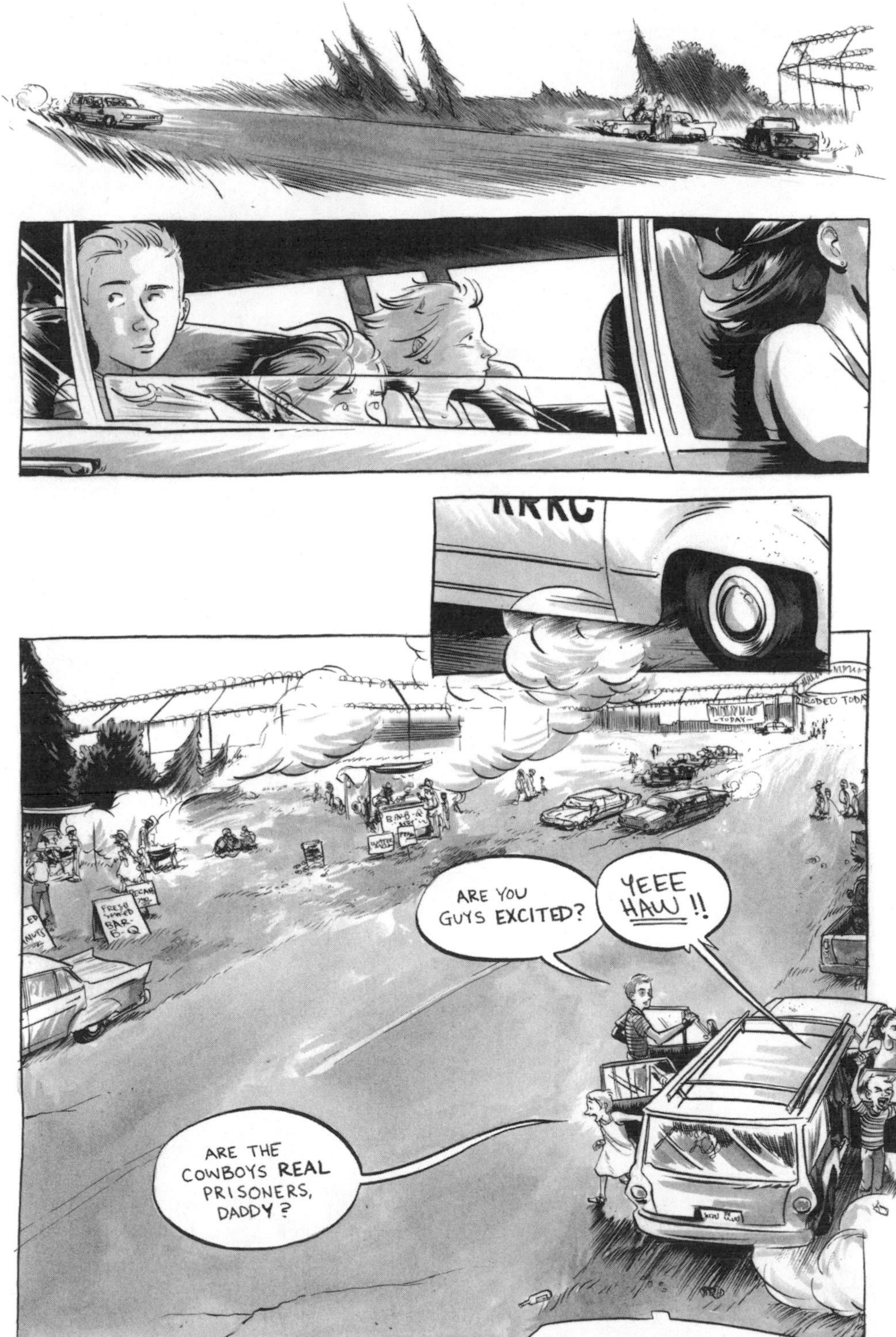
KRKC
ARE YOU GUYS EXCITED?
YEEE HAW !!
ARE THE COWBOYS REAL PRISONERS, DADDY?

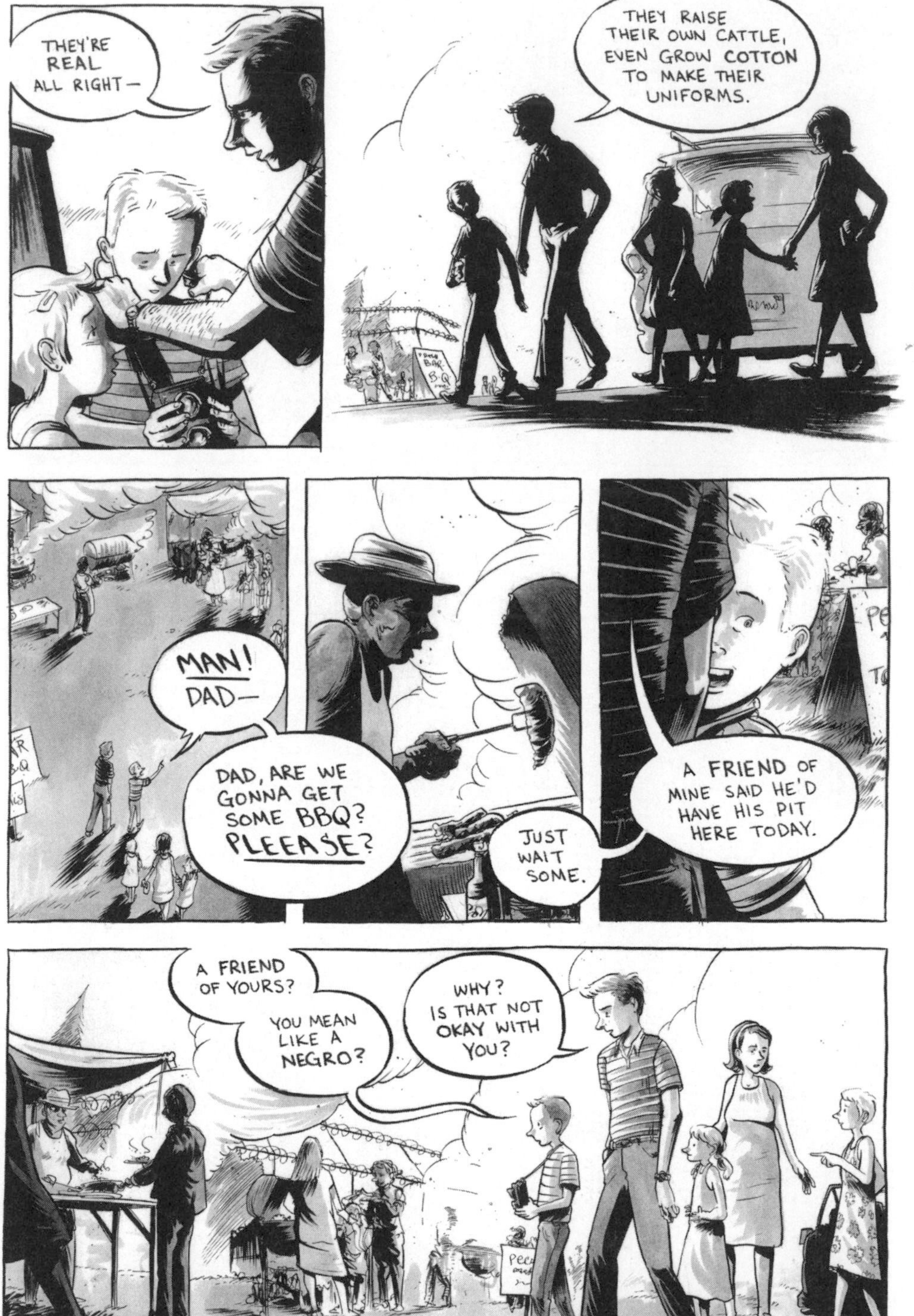
THEY'RE REAL ALL RIGHT—
THEY RAISE THEIR OWN CATTLE, EVEN GROW COTTON TO MAKE THEIR UNIFORMS.
MAN! DAD—
DAD, ARE WE GONNA GET SOME BBQ? PLEEA$E?
JUST WAIT SOME.
A FRIEND OF MINE SAID HE'D HAVE HIS PIT HERE TODAY.
A FRIEND OF YOURS?
YOU MEAN LIKE A NEGRO?
WHY? IS THAT NOT OKAY WITH YOU?

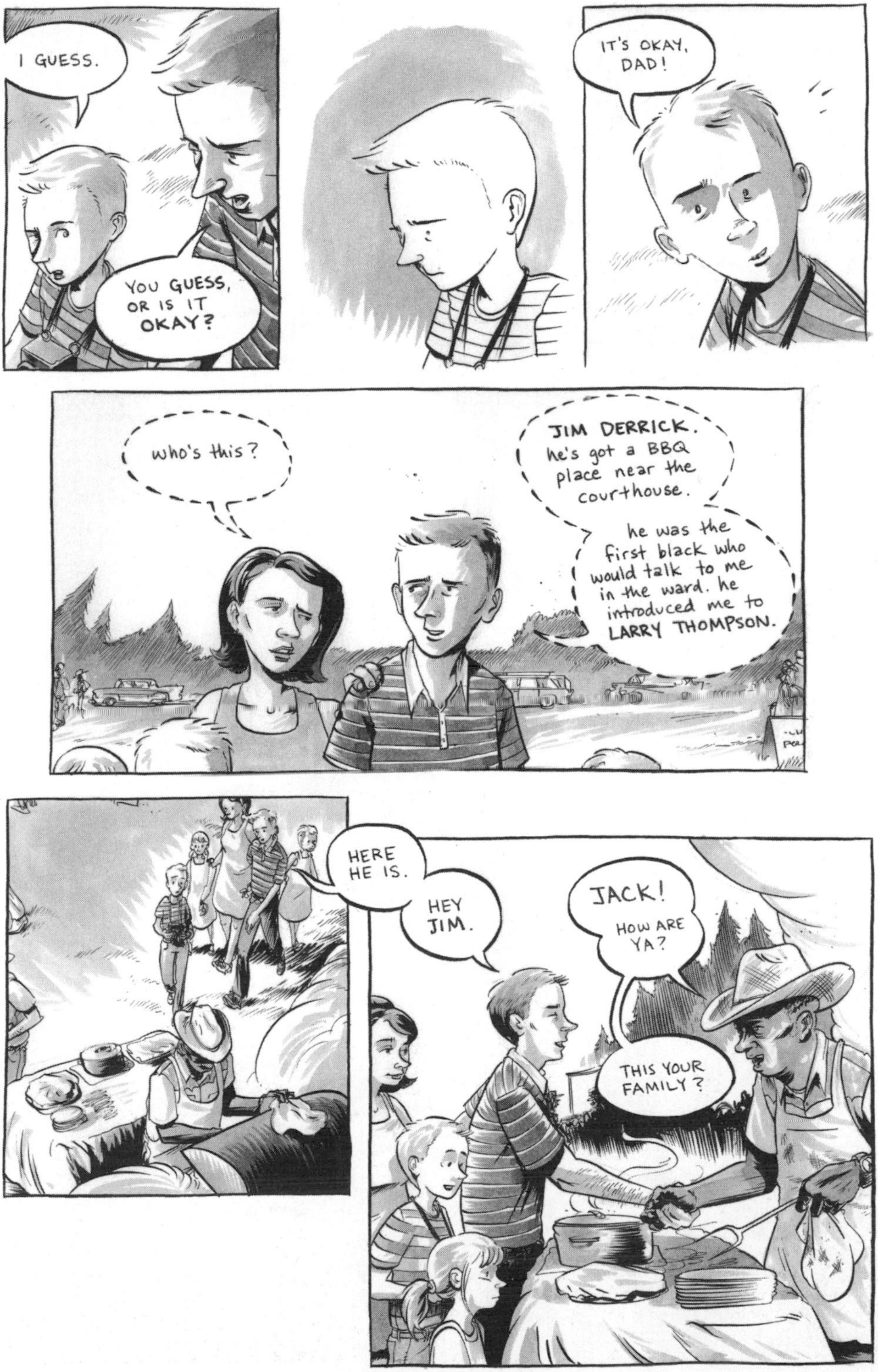
I GUESS.
YOU GUESS, OR IS IT OKAY?
IT'S OKAY, DAD!
who's this?
JIM DERRICK. he's got a BBQ place near the courthouse.
he was the first black who would talk to me in the ward. he introduced me to LARRY THOMPSON.
HERE HE IS.
HEY JIM.
JACK! HOW ARE YA?
THIS YOUR FAMILY?

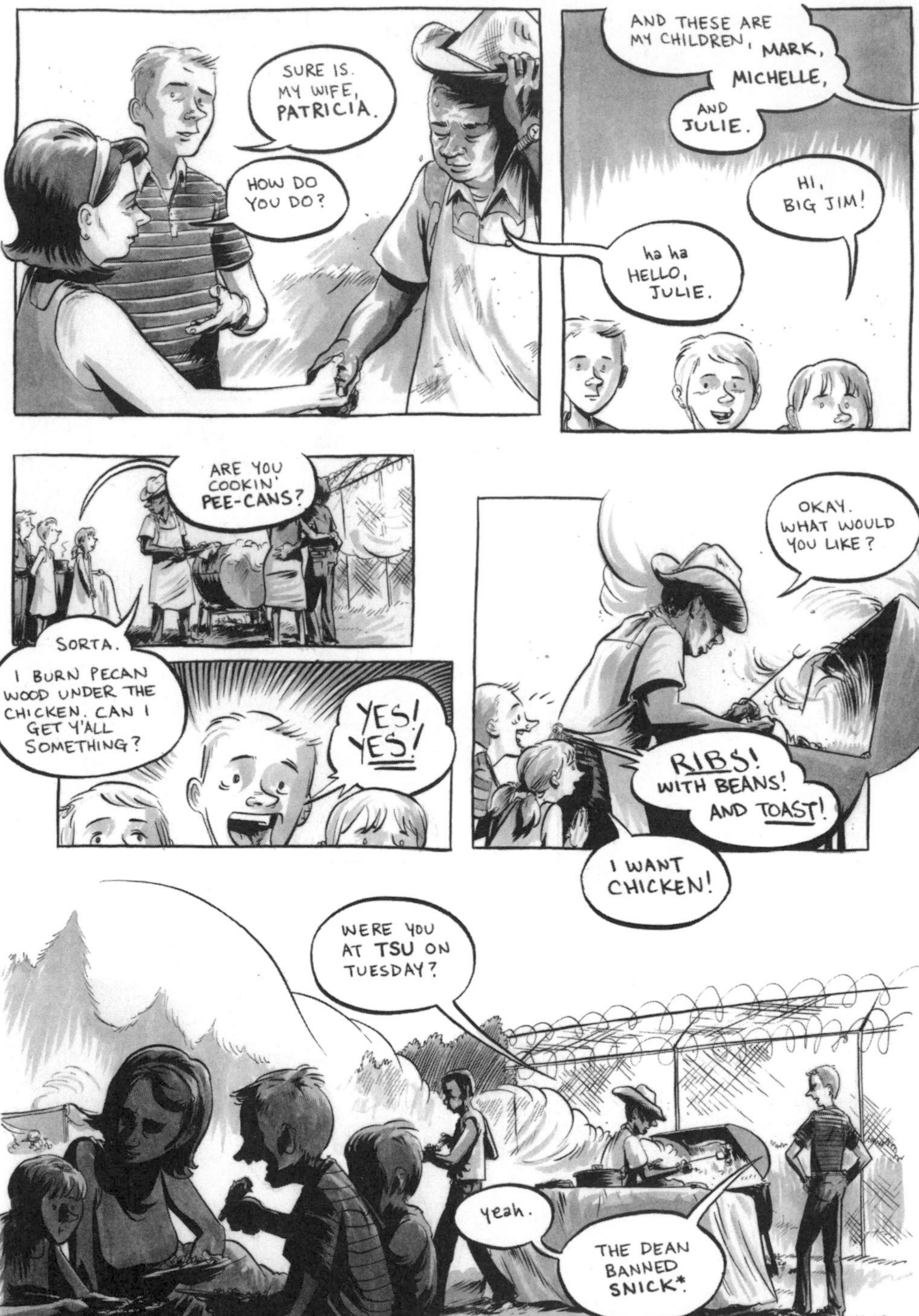
SURE IS. MY WIFE, PATRICIA.
HOW DO YOU DO?
AND THESE ARE MY CHILDREN, MARK, MICHELLE, AND JULIE.
HI, BIG JIM!
ha ha HELLO, JULIE.
ARE YOU COOKIN' PEE-CANS?
SORTA.
I BURN PECAN WOOD UNDER THE CHICKEN. CAN I GET Y'ALL SOMETHING?
YES! YES!
OKAY. WHAT WOULD YOU LIKE?
RIBS! WITH BEANS! AND TOAST!
I WANT CHICKEN!
WERE YOU AT TSU ON TUESDAY?
yeah.
THE DEAN BANNED SNICK*.

*SNCC

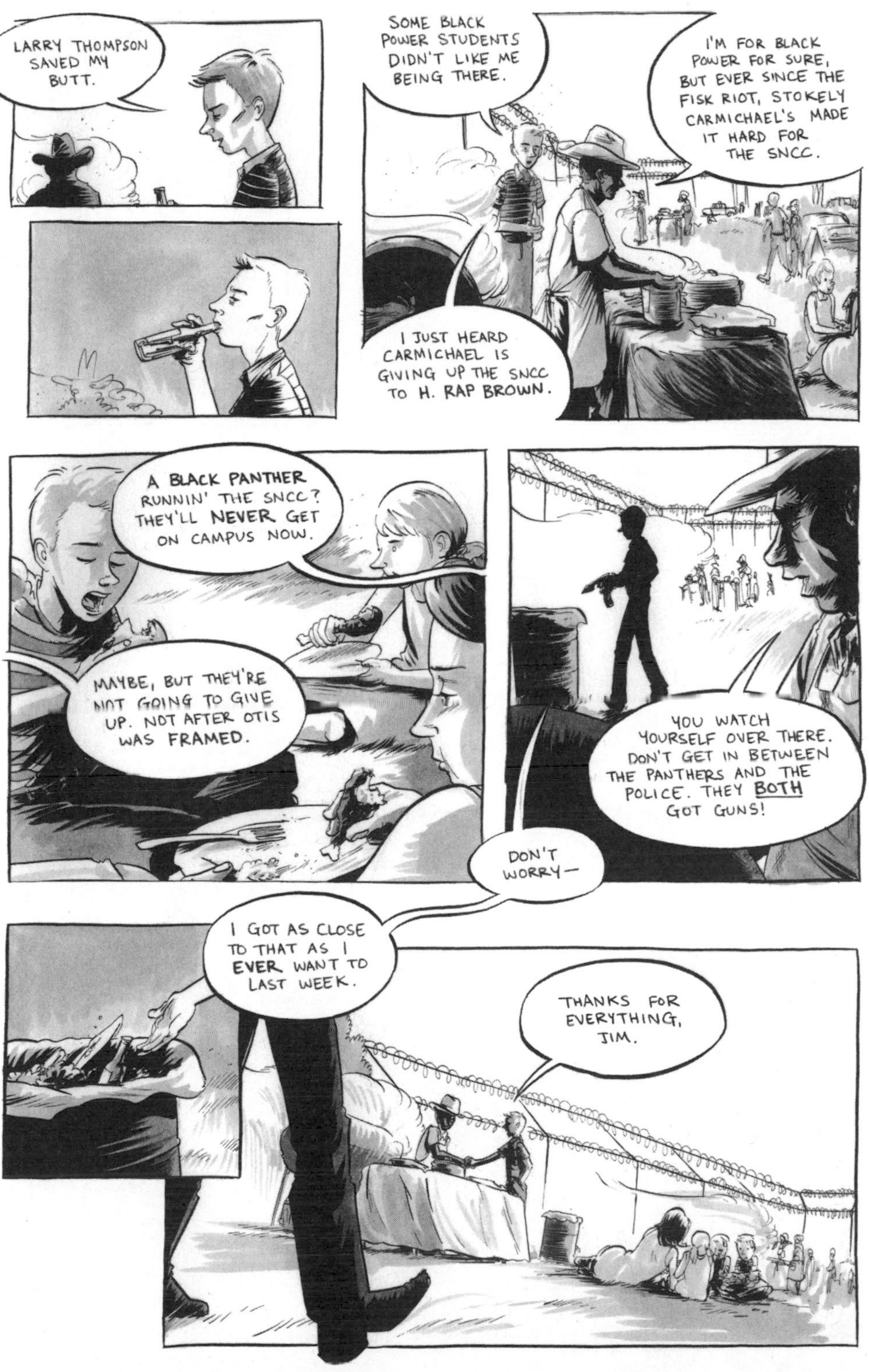
LARRY THOMPSON SAVED MY BUTT.
SOME BLACK POWER STUDENTS DIDN'T LIKE ME BEING THERE.
I'M FOR BLACK POWER FOR SURE, BUT EVER SINCE THE FISK RIOT, STOKELY CARMICHAEL'S MADE IT HARD FOR THE SNCC.
I JUST HEARD CARMICHAEL IS GIVING UP THE SNCC TO H. RAP BROWN.
A BLACK PANTHER RUNNIN' THE SNCC? THEY'LL NEVER GET ON CAMPUS NOW.
MAYBE, BUT THEY'RE NOT GOING TO GIVE UP. NOT AFTER OTIS WAS FRAMED.
YOU WATCH YOURSELF OVER THERE. DON'T GET IN BETWEEN THE PANTHERS AND THE POLICE. THEY BOTH GOT GUNS!
DON'T WORRY—
I GOT AS CLOSE TO THAT AS I EVER WANT TO LAST WEEK.
THANKS FOR EVERYTHING, JIM.

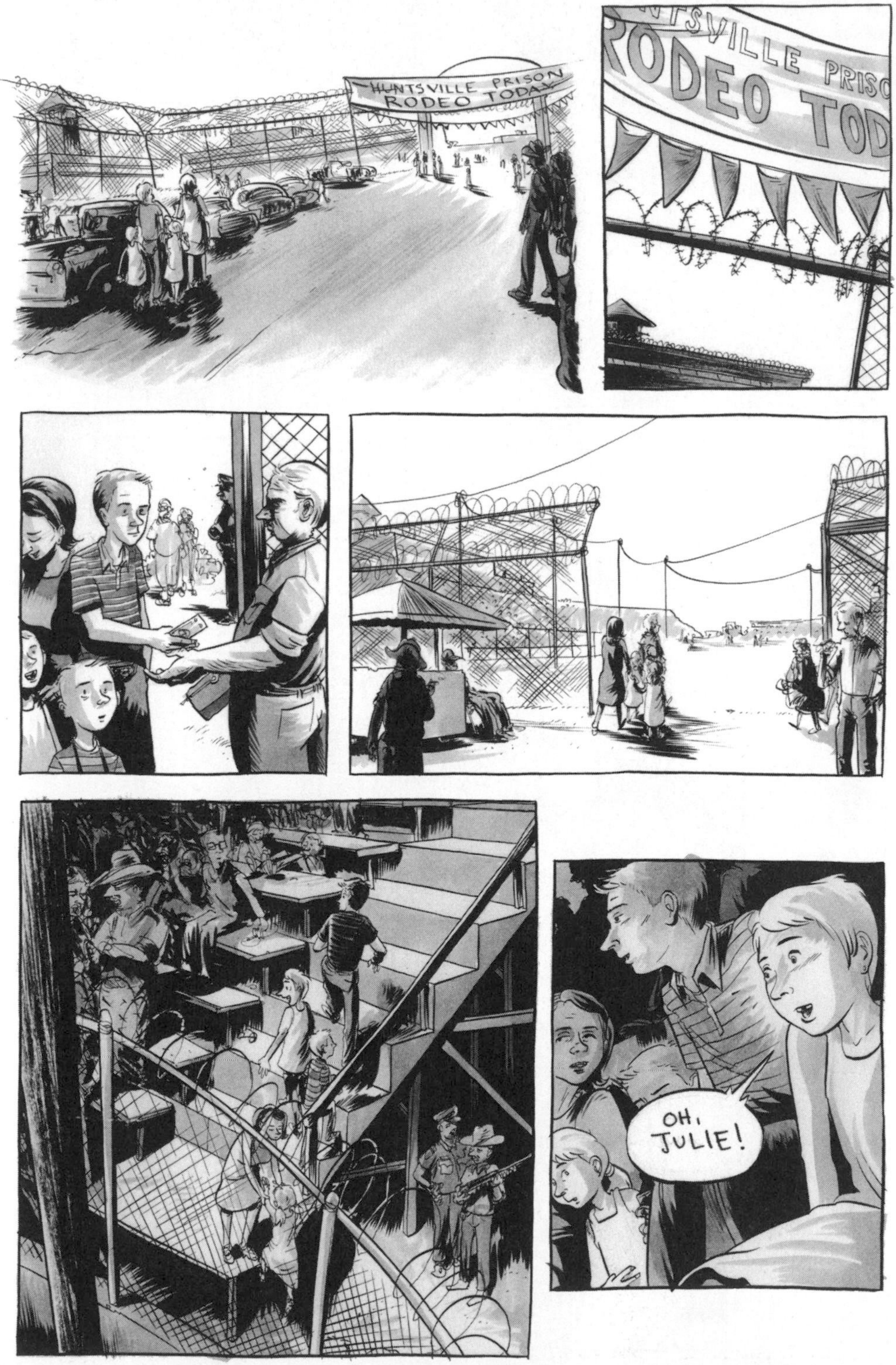
HUNTSVILLE PRISON
RODEO TODAY
RODEO TOD
OH, JULIE!

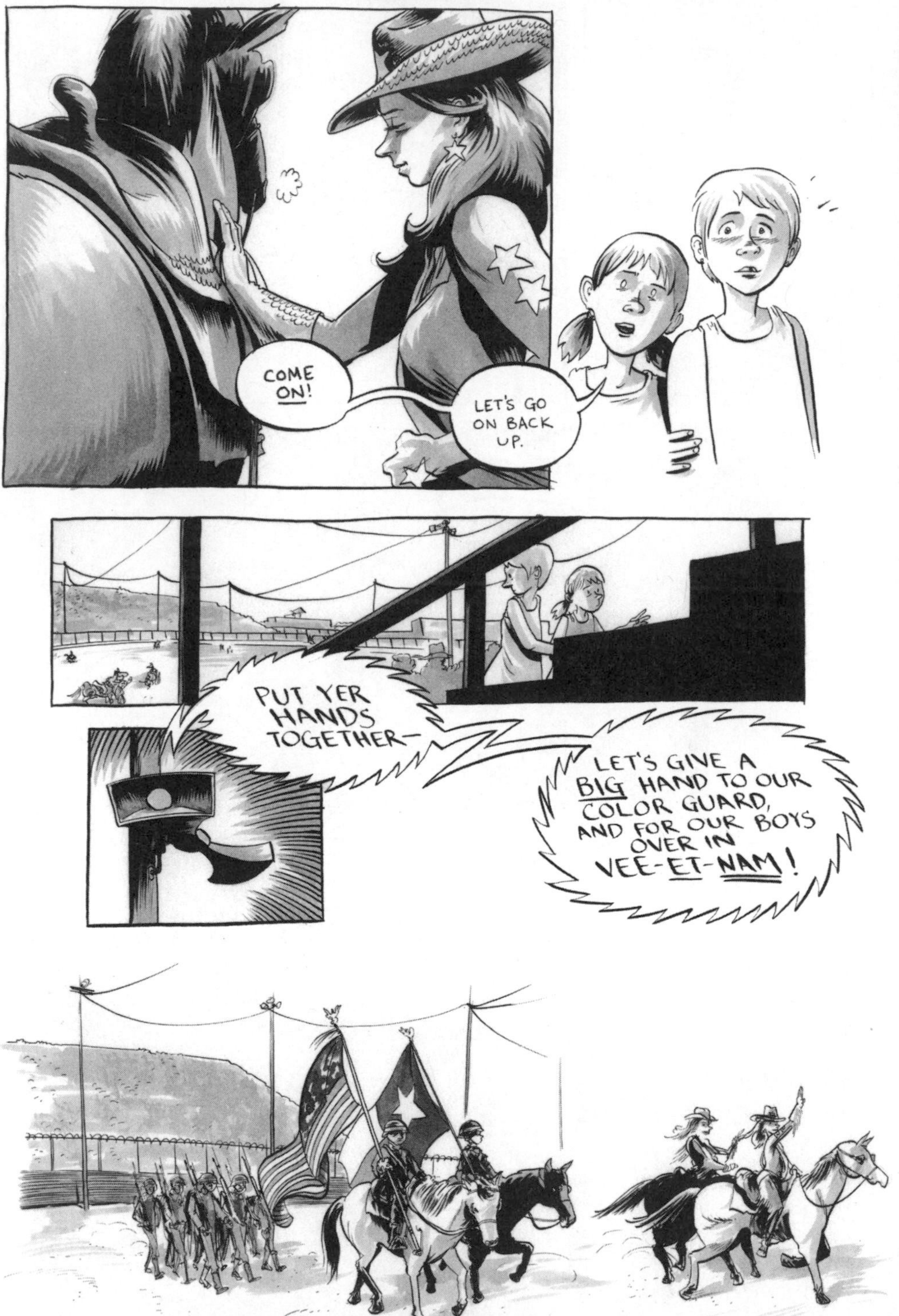
COME ON!
LET'S GO ON BACK UP.
PUT YER HANDS TOGETHER—
LET'S GIVE A BIG HAND TO OUR COLOR GUARD, AND FOR OUR BOYS OVER IN VEE-ET-NAM!

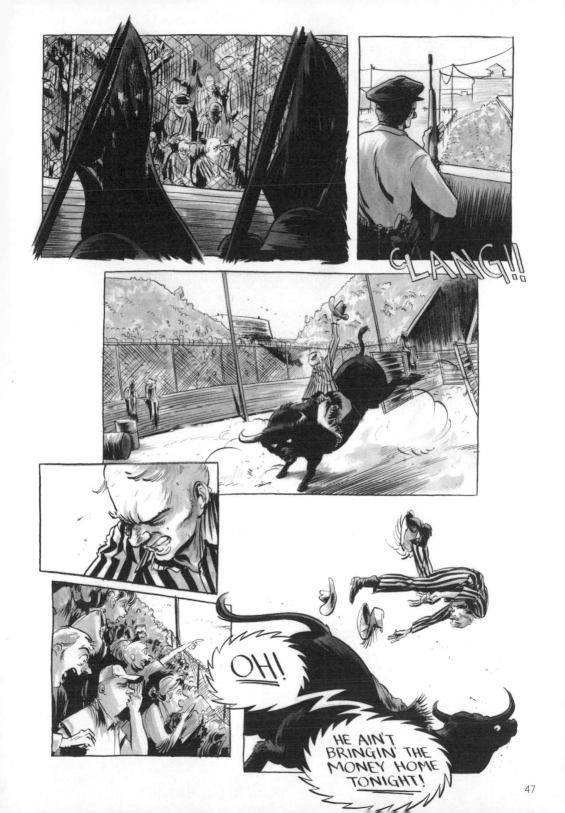

CLANG!!

OH!

HE AIN'T
BRINGIN' THE
MONEY HOME
TONIGHT!

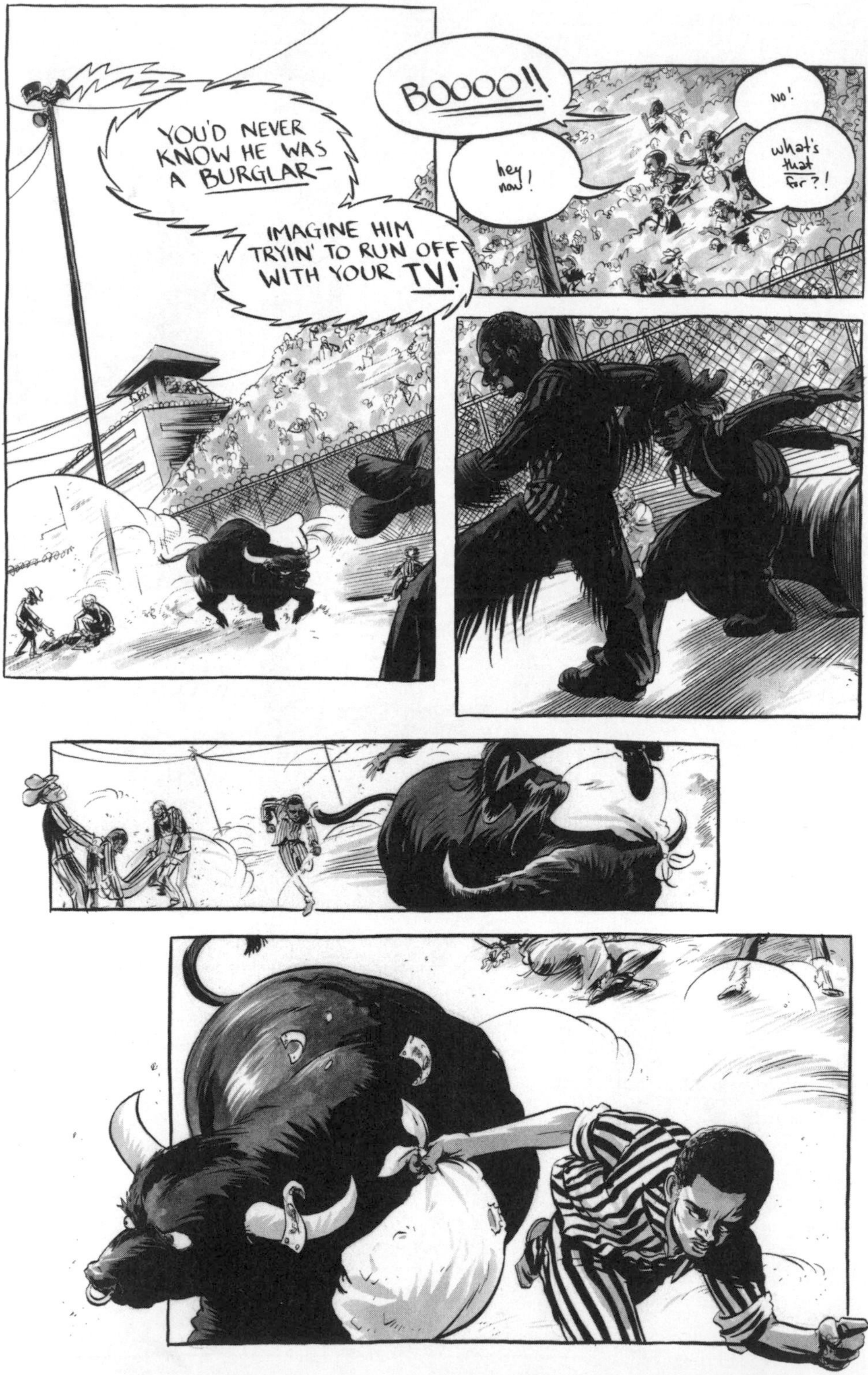
YOU'D NEVER KNOW HE WAS A BURGLAR—
IMAGINE HIM TRYIN' TO RUN OFF WITH YOUR TV!
BOOOO!!
hey now!
no!
what's that for?!

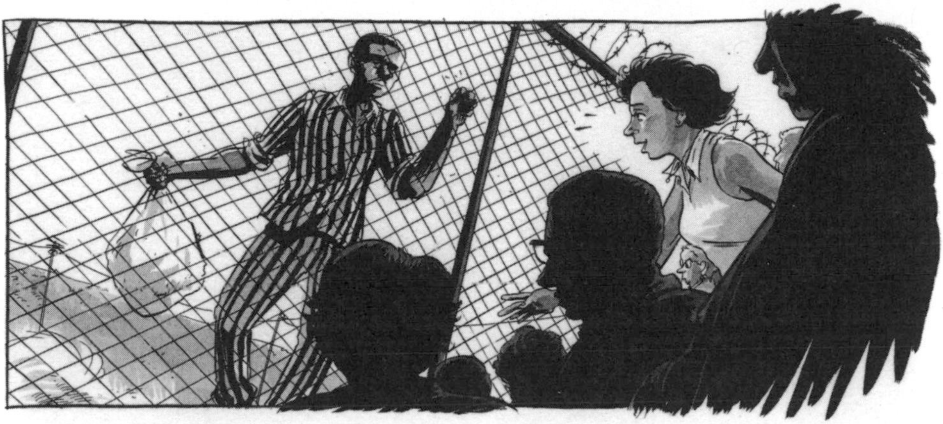

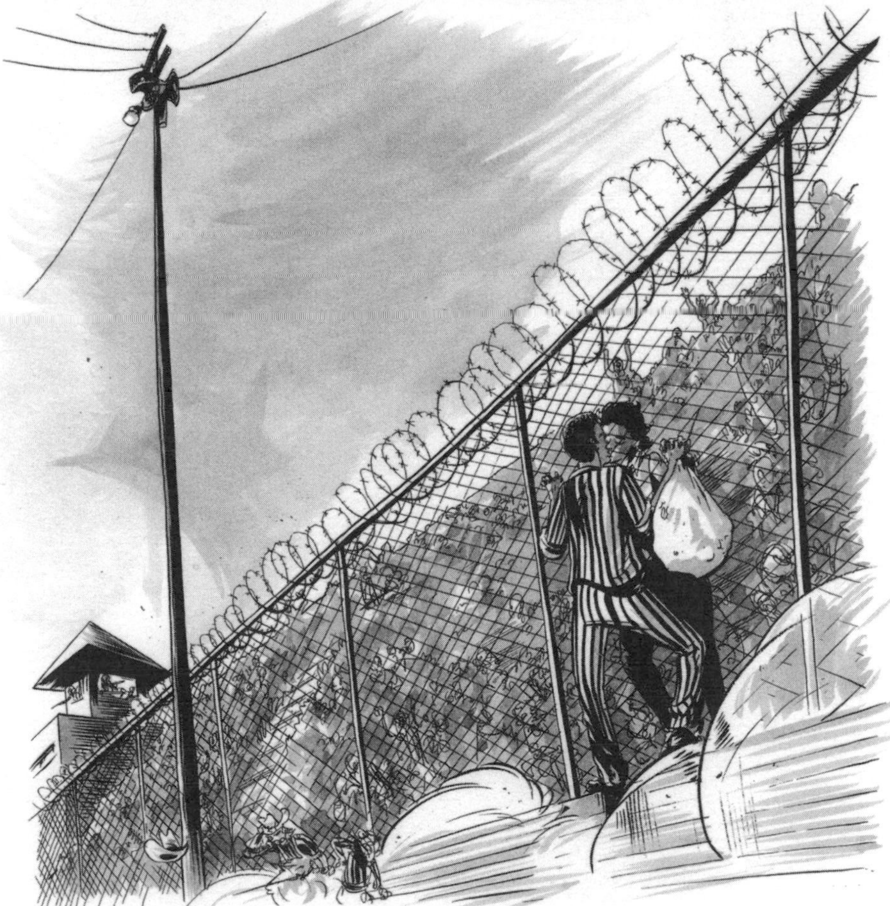

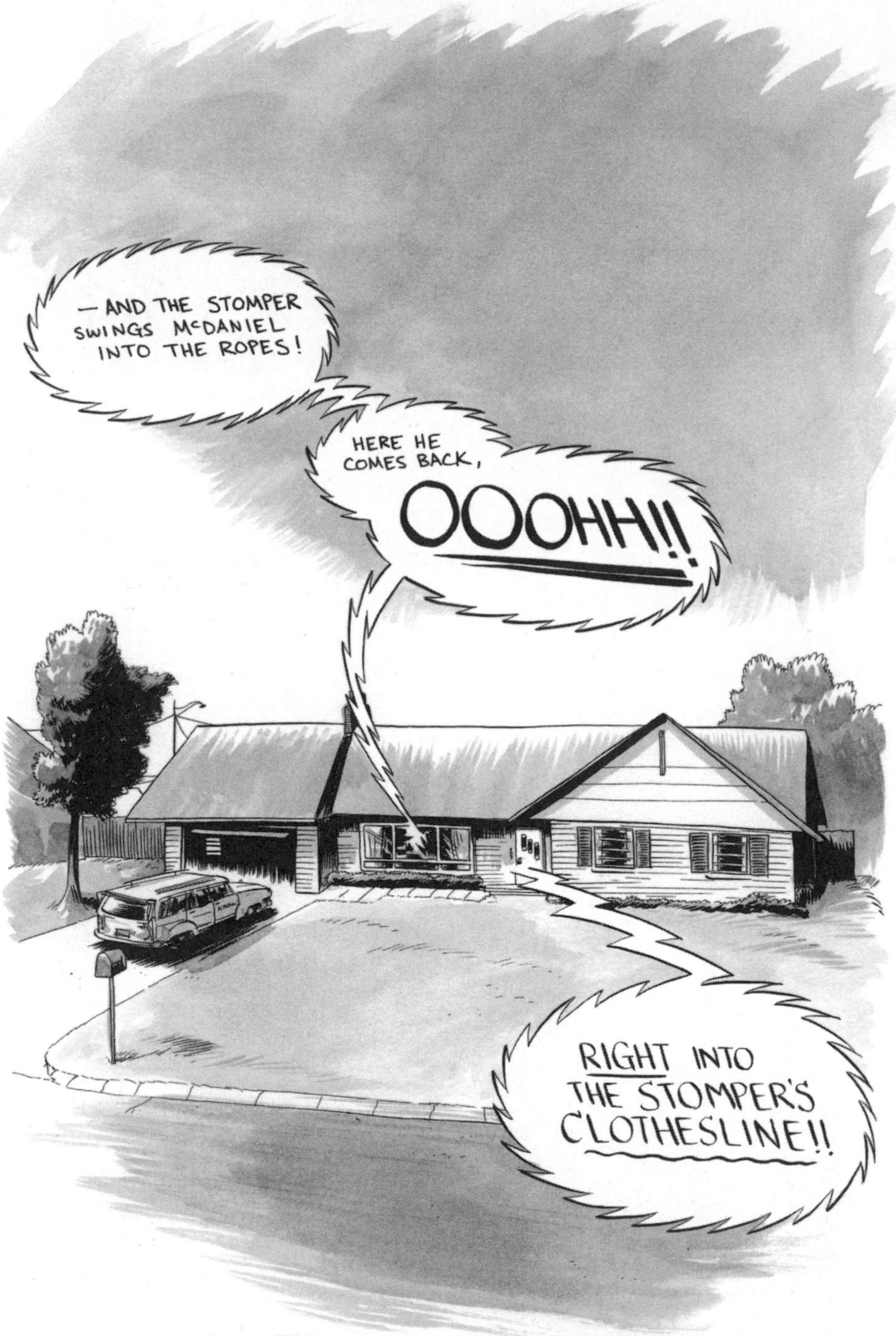
—AND THE STOMPER SWINGS McDANIEL INTO THE ROPES!
HERE HE COMES BACK, OOOHH!!
RIGHT INTO THE STOMPER'S CLOTHESLINE!!

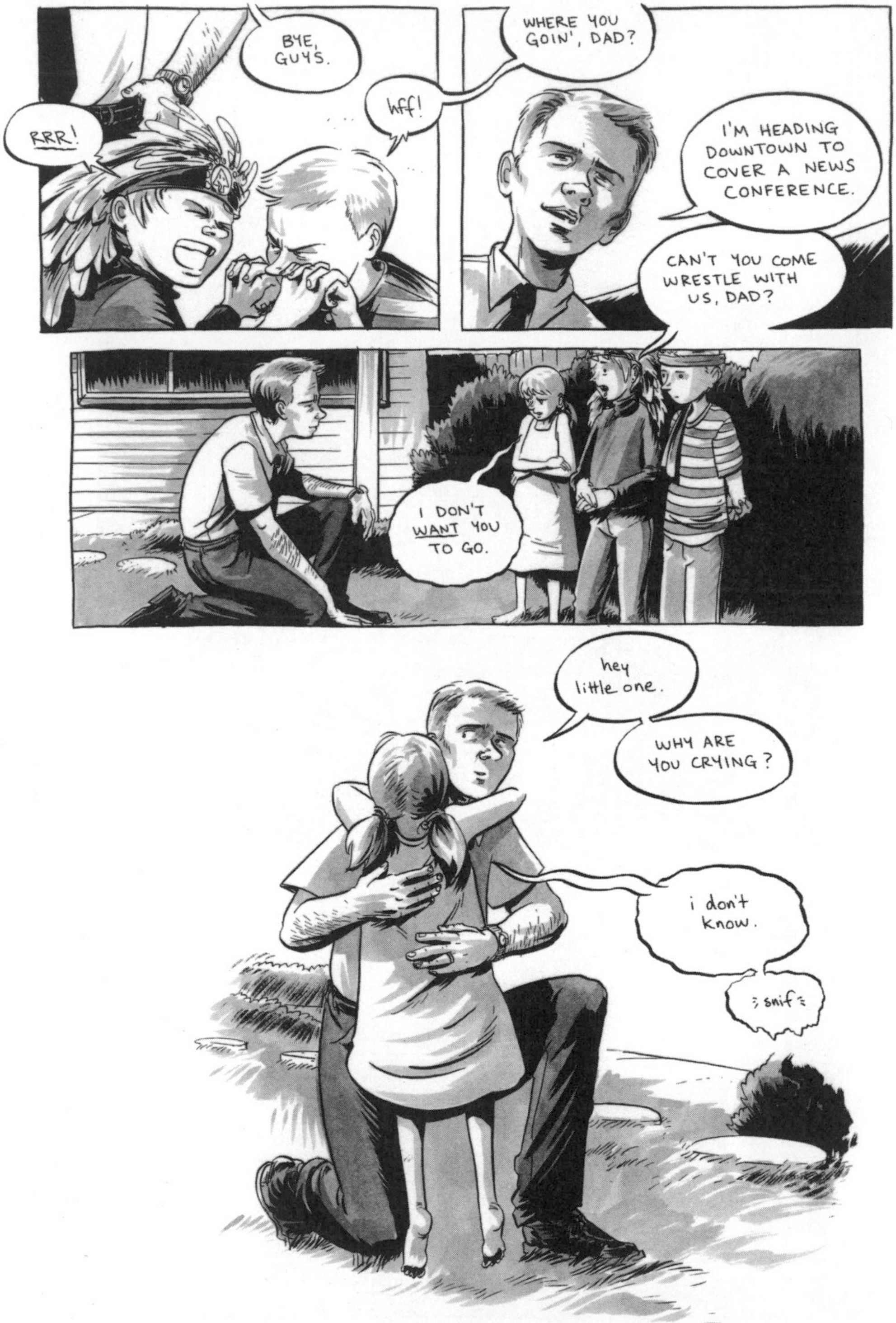
RRR!
BYE, GUYS.
hff!
WHERE YOU GOIN', DAD?
I'M HEADING DOWNTOWN TO COVER A NEWS CONFERENCE.
CAN'T YOU COME WRESTLE WITH US, DAD?
I DON'T WANT YOU TO GO.
hey little one.
WHY ARE YOU CRYING?
i don't know.
snif

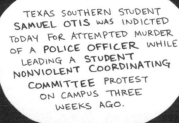

TEXAS SOUTHERN STUDENT SAMUEL OTIS WAS INDICTED TODAY FOR ATTEMPTED MURDER OF A POLICE OFFICER WHILE LEADING A STUDENT NONVIOLENT COORDINATING COMMITTEE PROTEST ON CAMPUS THREE WEEKS AGO.

ahem

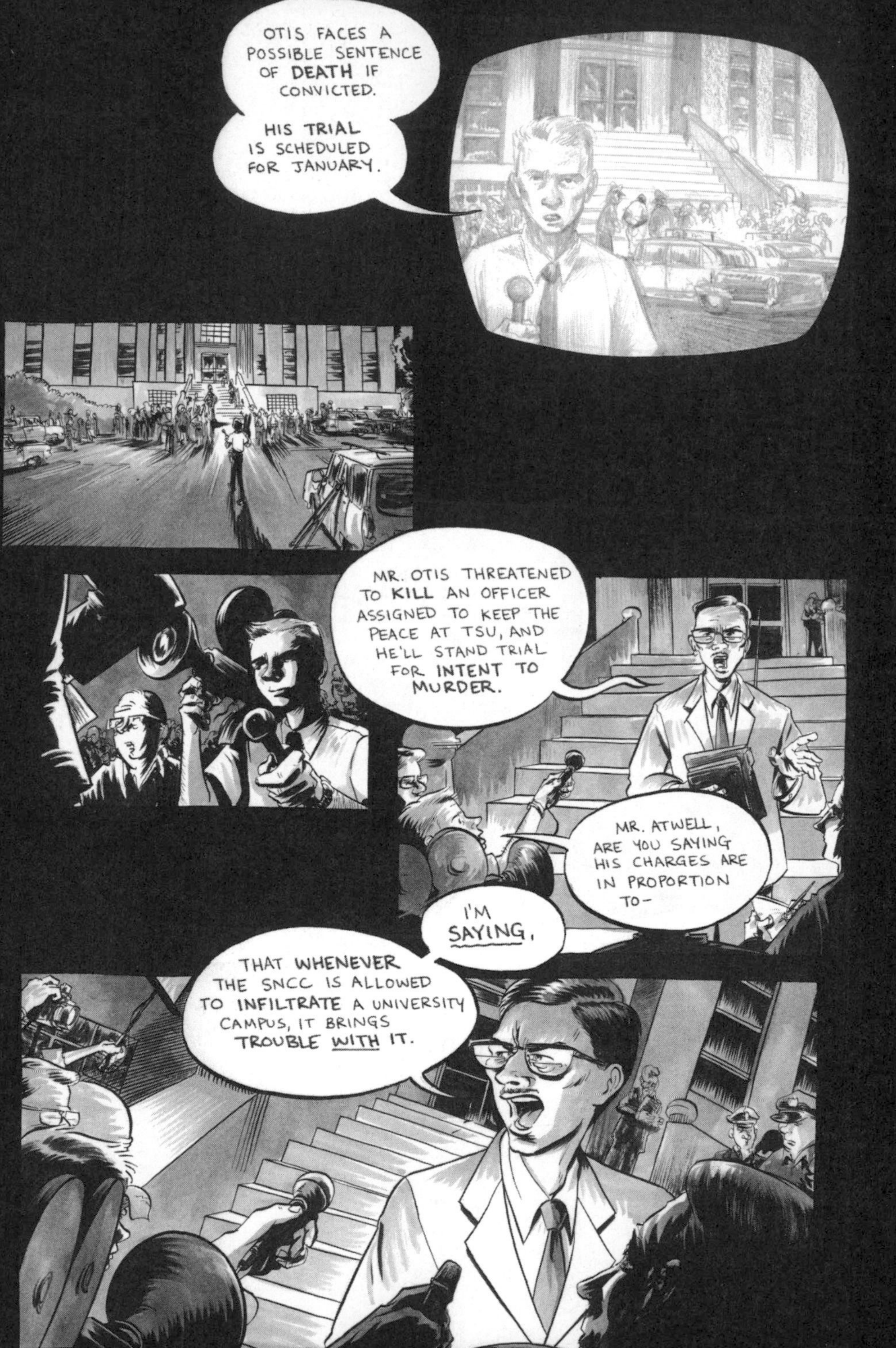
OTIS FACES A POSSIBLE SENTENCE OF **DEATH** IF CONVICTED.
HIS **TRIAL** IS SCHEDULED FOR JANUARY.
MR. OTIS THREATENED TO **KILL** AN OFFICER ASSIGNED TO KEEP THE PEACE AT TSU, AND HE'LL STAND TRIAL FOR **INTENT TO MURDER.**
MR. ATWELL, ARE YOU SAYING HIS CHARGES ARE IN PROPORTION TO–
I'M SAYING,
THAT **WHENEVER** THE SNCC IS ALLOWED TO **INFILTRATE** A UNIVERSITY CAMPUS, IT BRINGS **TROUBLE WITH IT.**

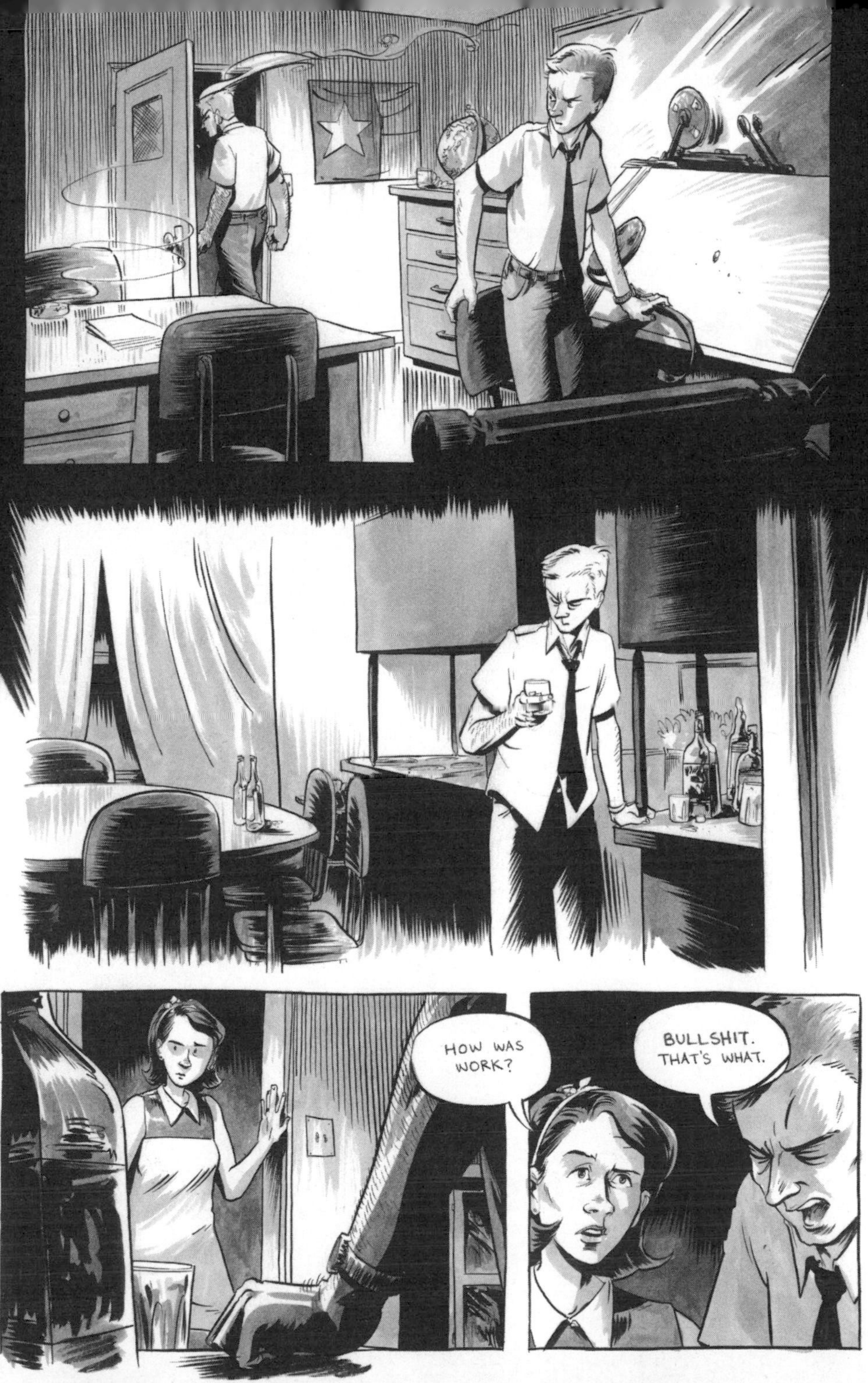
HOW WAS WORK?
BULLSHIT. THAT'S WHAT.

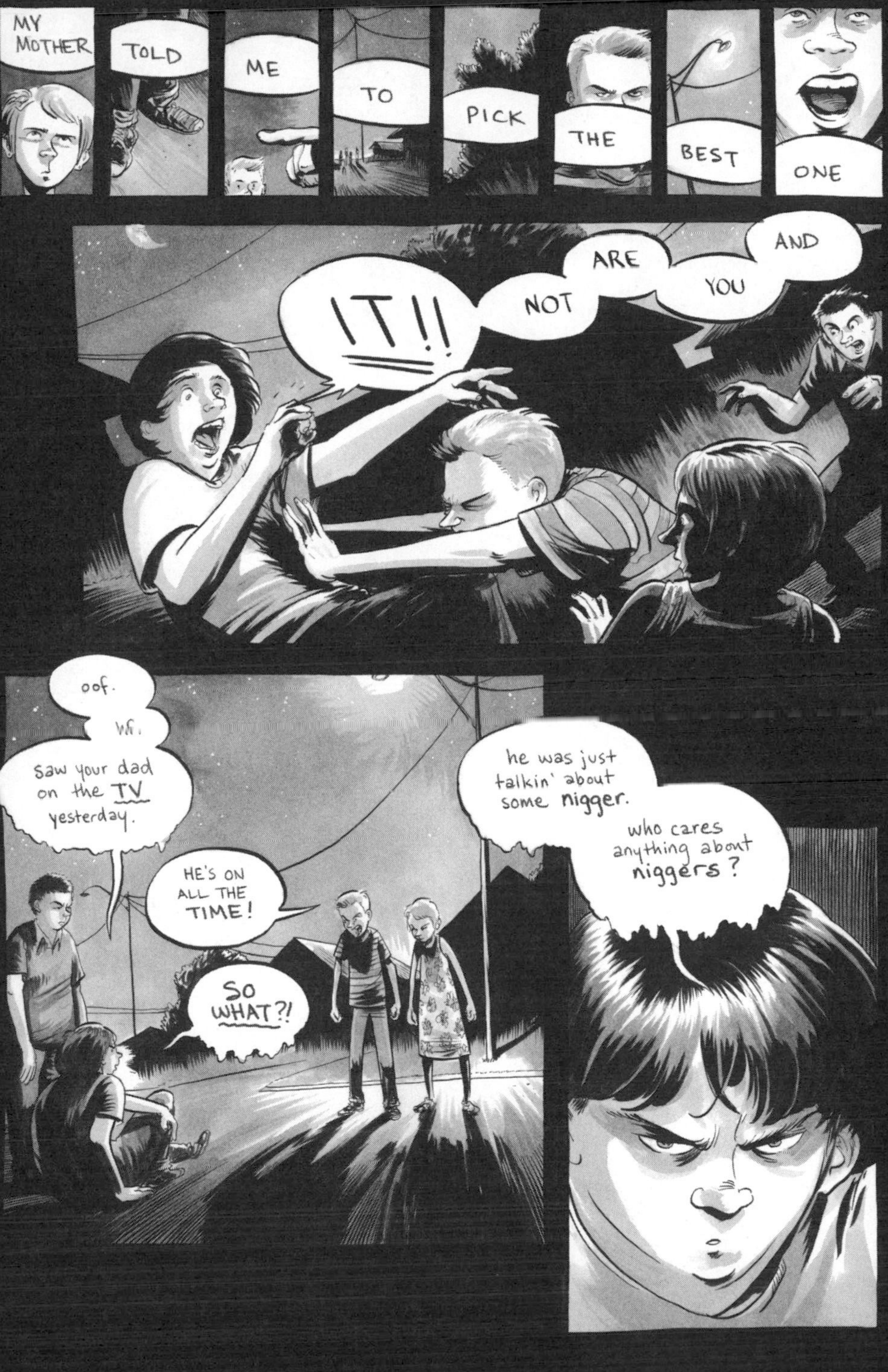
MY MOTHER
TOLD
ME
TO
PICK
THE
BEST
ONE
AND
YOU
ARE
NOT
IT!!
oof.
saw your dad on the TV yesterday.
HE'S ON ALL THE TIME!
SO WHAT?!
he was just talkin' about some nigger.
who cares anything about niggers?

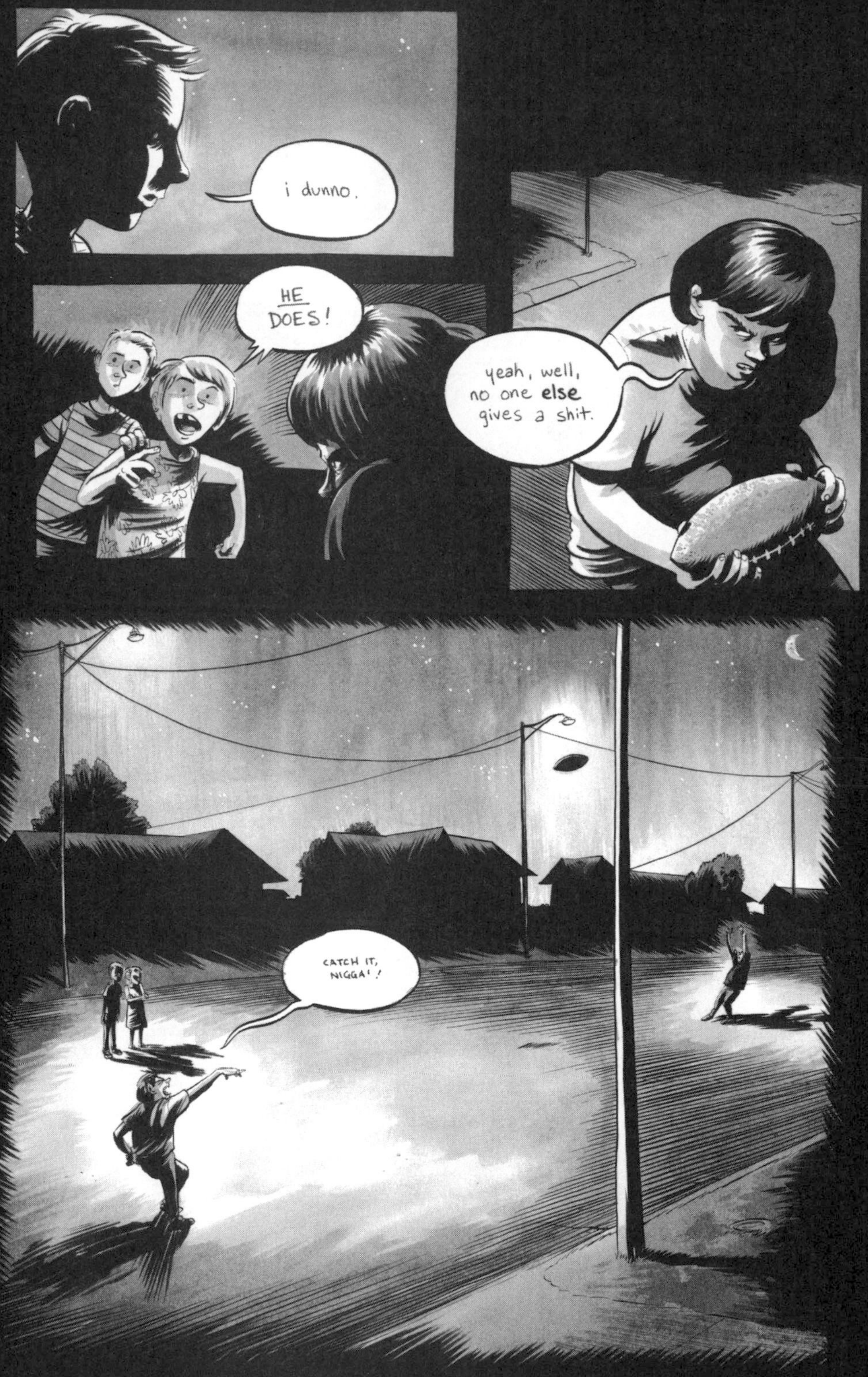
i dunno.
HE DOES!
yeah, well, no one else gives a shit.
CATCH IT, NIGGA!

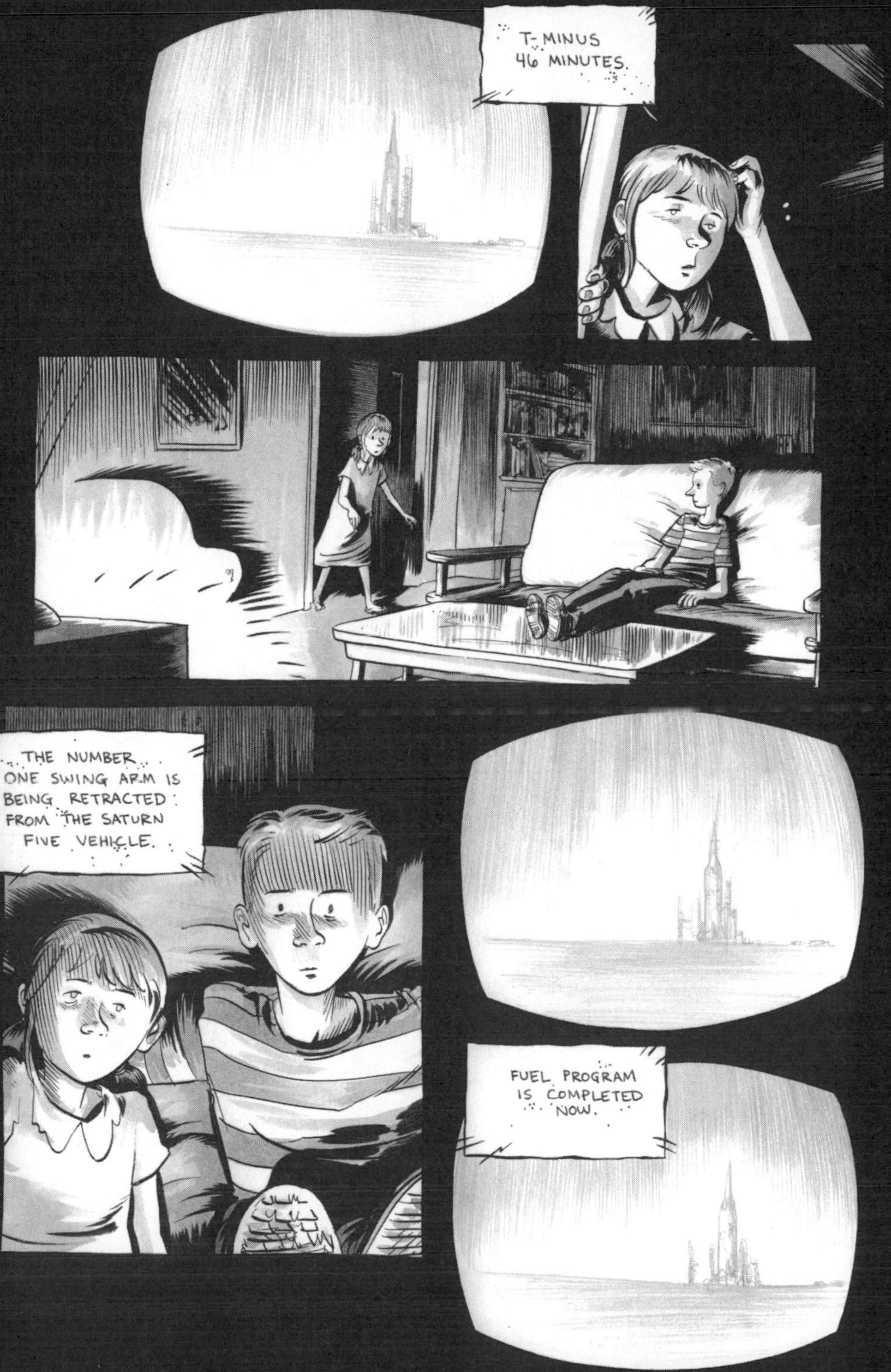

T-MINUS 46 MINUTES.
THE NUMBER ONE SWING ARM IS BEING RETRACTED FROM THE SATURN FIVE VEHICLE.
FUEL PROGRAM IS COMPLETED NOW.

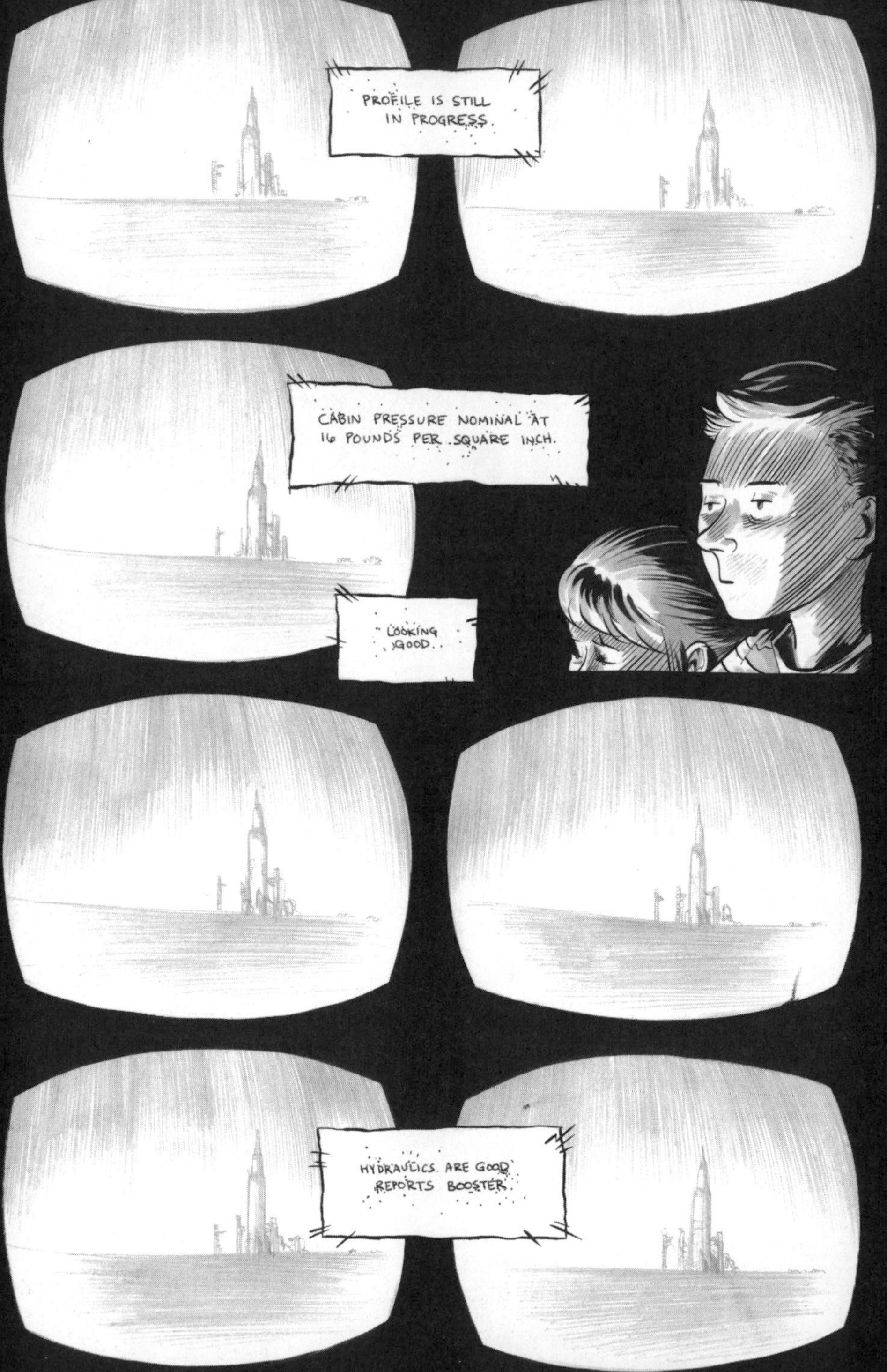
PROFILE IS STILL IN PROGRESS.
CABIN PRESSURE NOMINAL AT 16 POUNDS PER SQUARE INCH.
LOOKING GOOD.
HYDRAULICS ARE GOOD REPORTS BOOSTER.

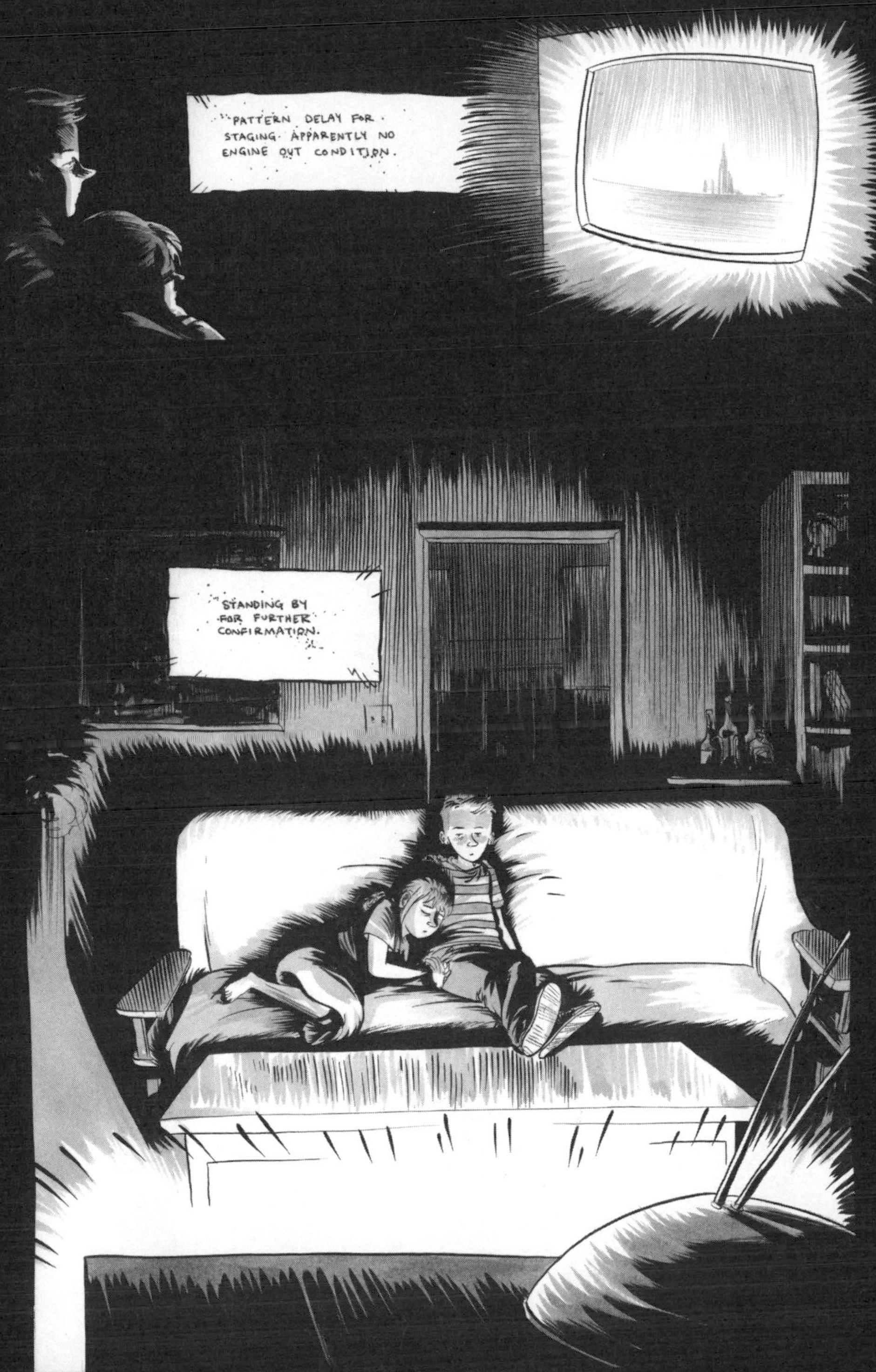
"PATTERN DELAY FOR STAGING. APPARENTLY NO ENGINE OUT CONDITION.
"STANDING BY FOR FURTHER CONFIRMATION.

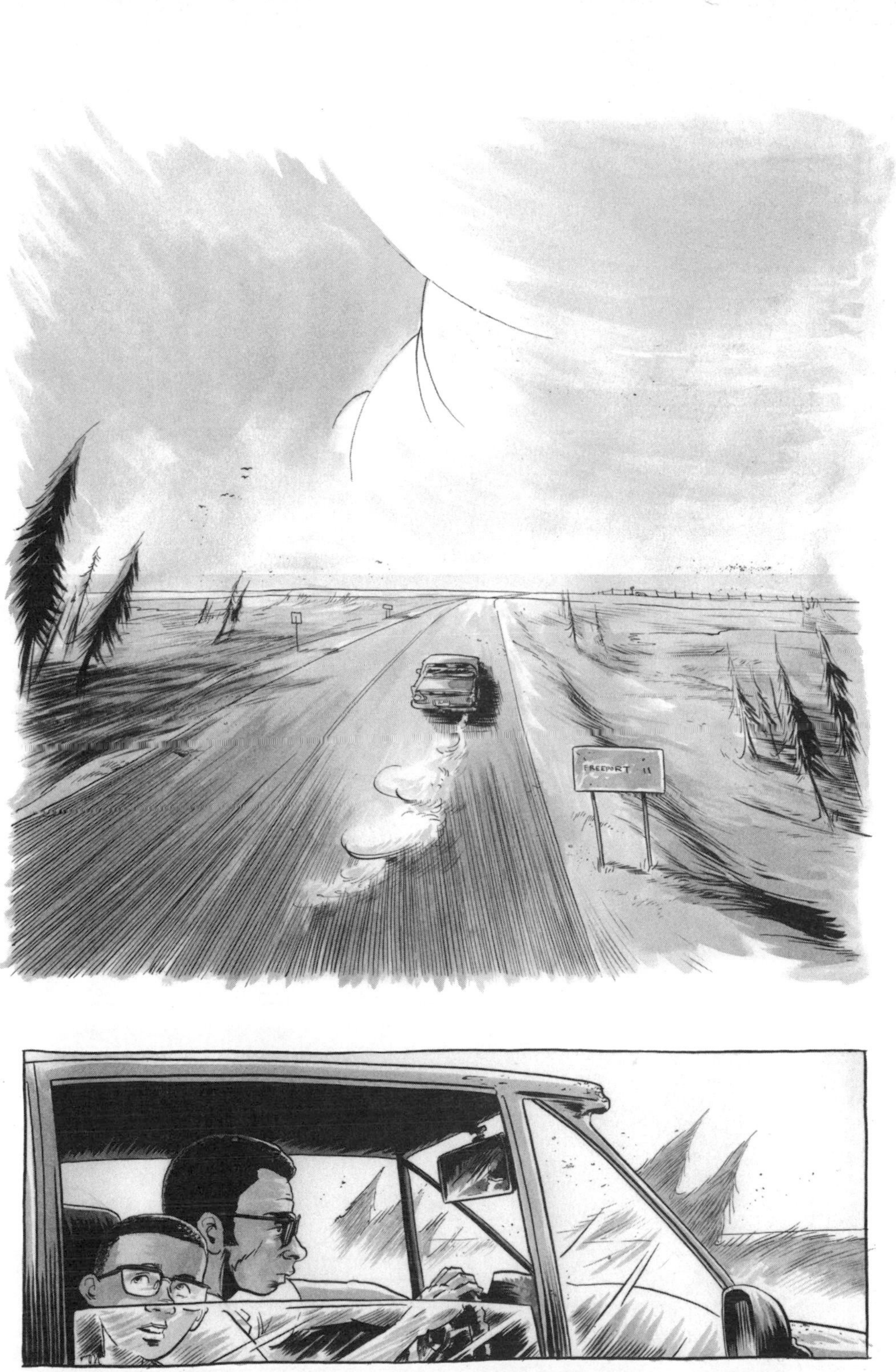
FREEPORT 11

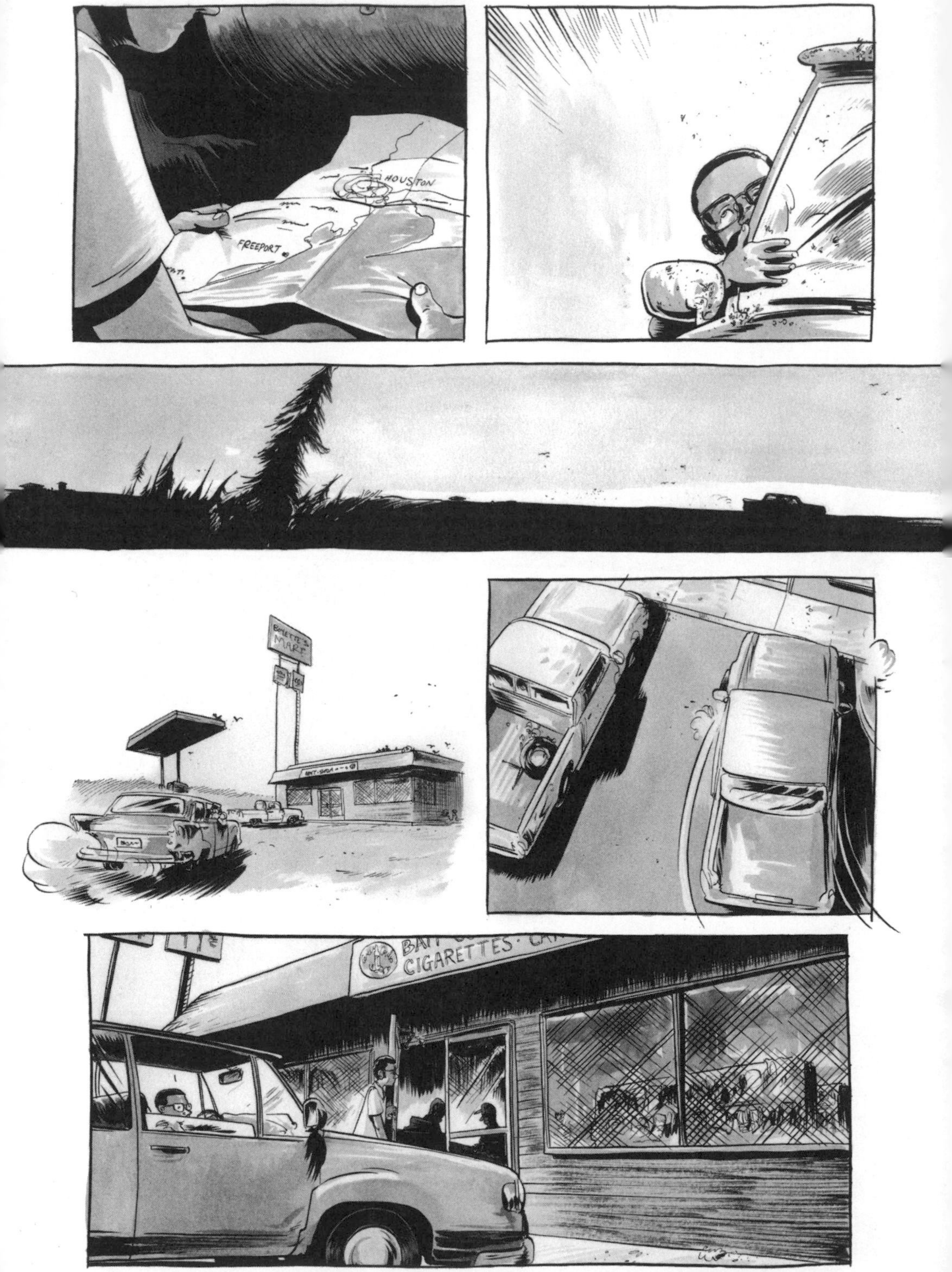
HOUSTON
FREEPORT
CIGARETTES

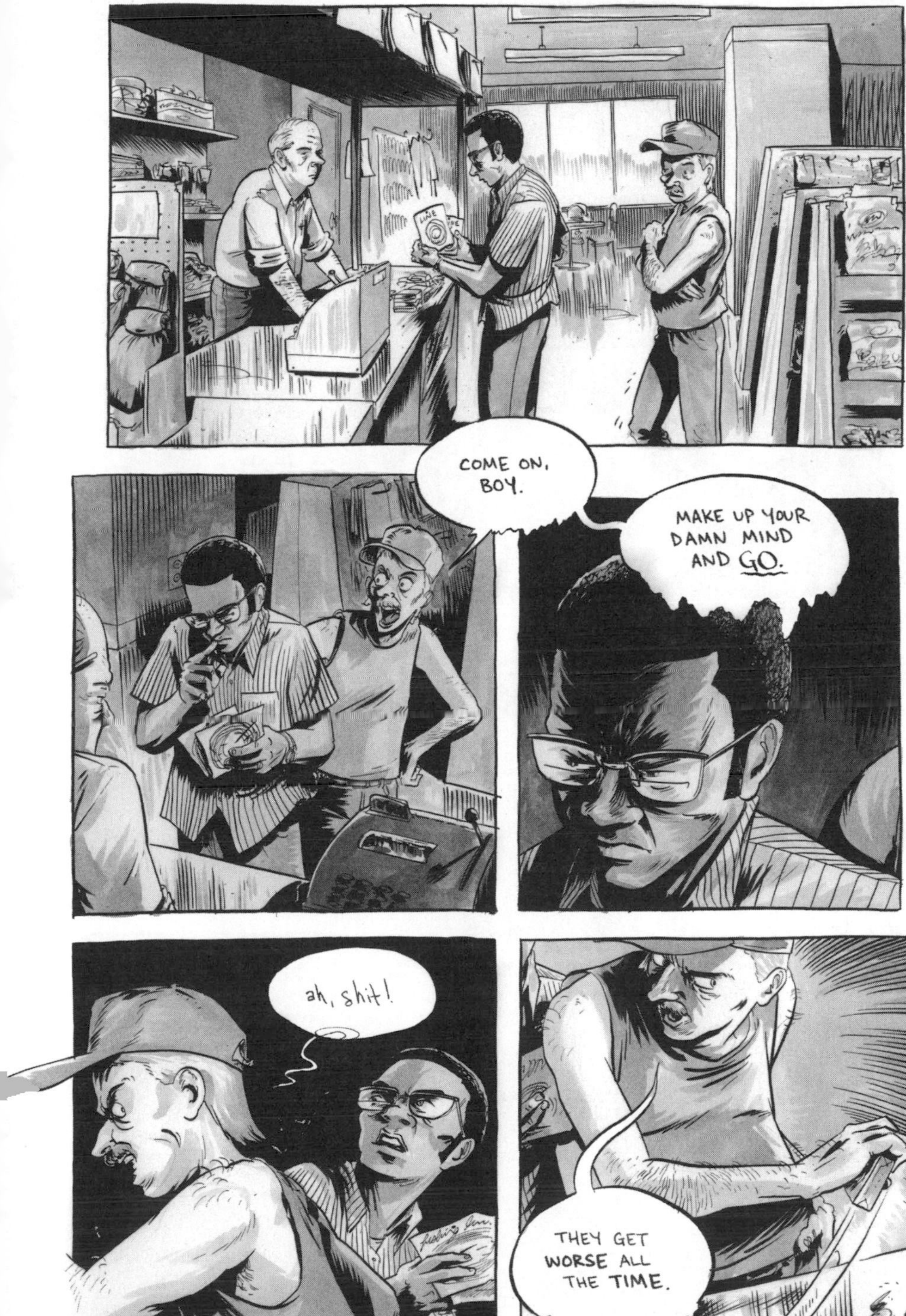
COME ON, BOY.
MAKE UP YOUR DAMN MIND AND GO.
ah, shit!
THEY GET WORSE ALL THE TIME.

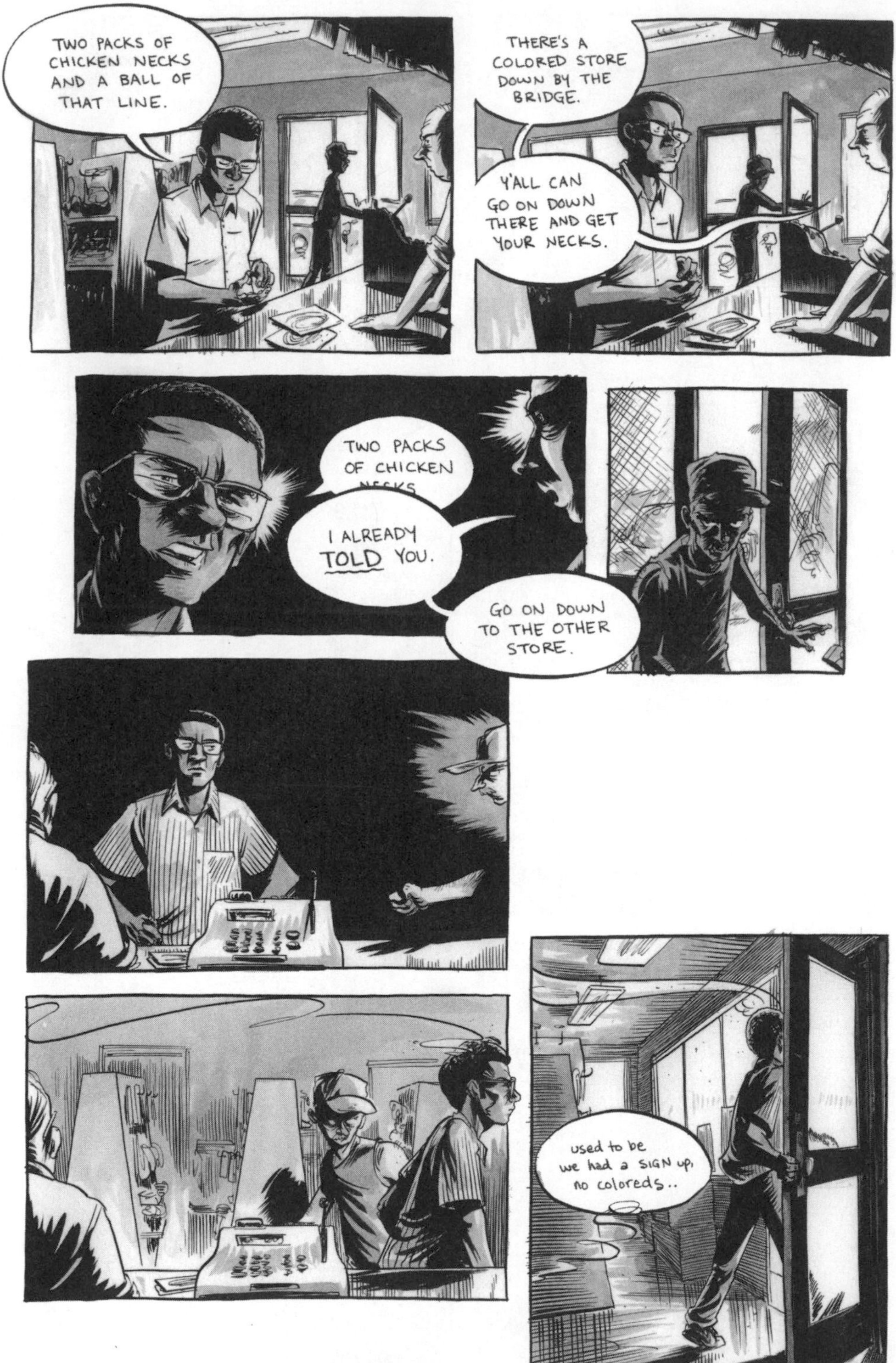
TWO PACKS OF CHICKEN NECKS AND A BALL OF THAT LINE.
THERE'S A COLORED STORE DOWN BY THE BRIDGE.
Y'ALL CAN GO ON DOWN THERE AND GET YOUR NECKS.
TWO PACKS OF CHICKEN
I ALREADY TOLD YOU.
GO ON DOWN TO THE OTHER STORE.
used to be we had a SIGN up, no coloreds..

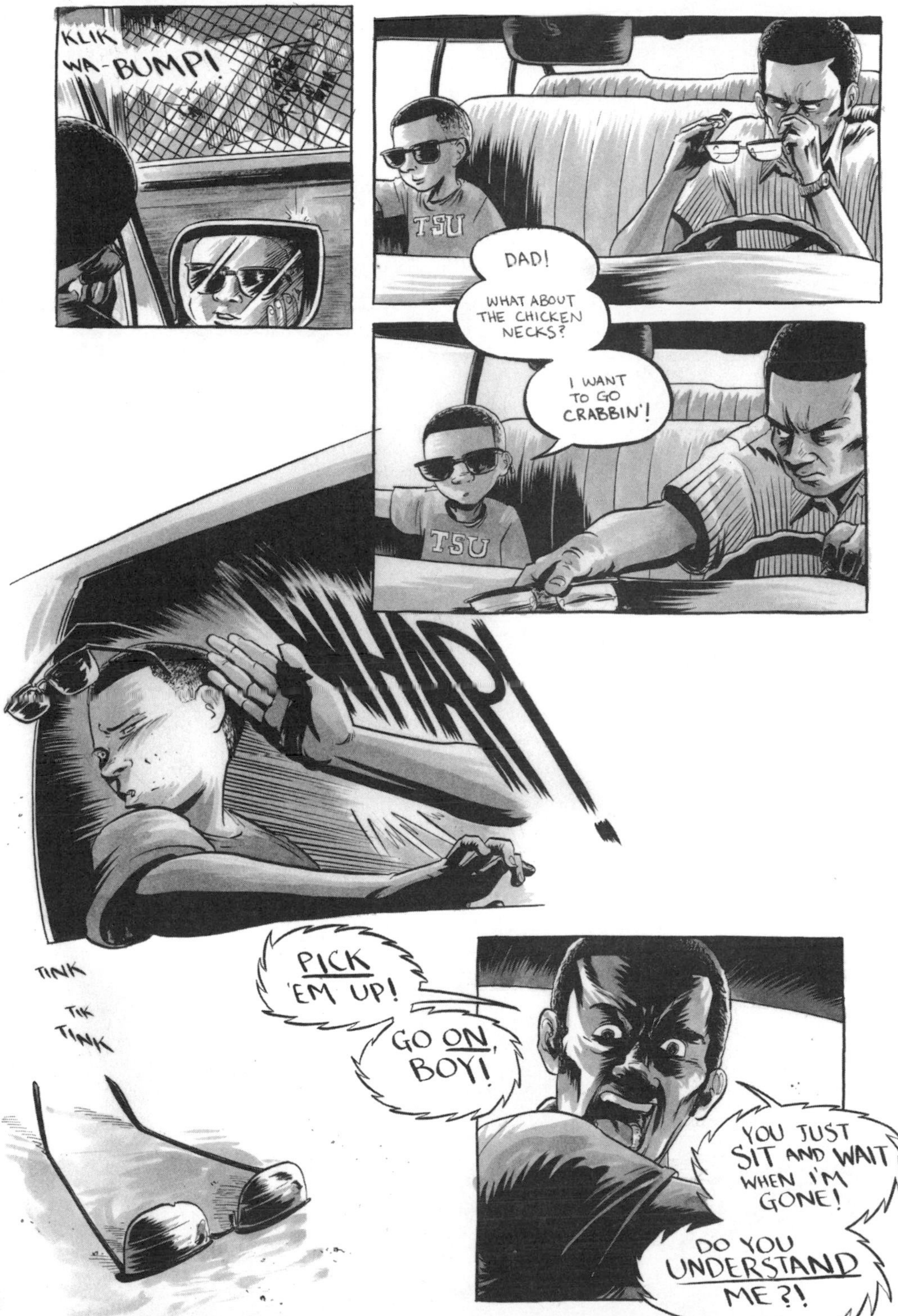

KLIK
WA-BUMP!
DAD!
WHAT ABOUT THE CHICKEN NECKS?
I WANT TO GO CRABBIN'!
WHAP!
TINK
TIK
TINK
PICK 'EM UP!
GO ON, BOY!
YOU JUST SIT AND WAIT WHEN I'M GONE!
DO YOU UNDERSTAND ME?!

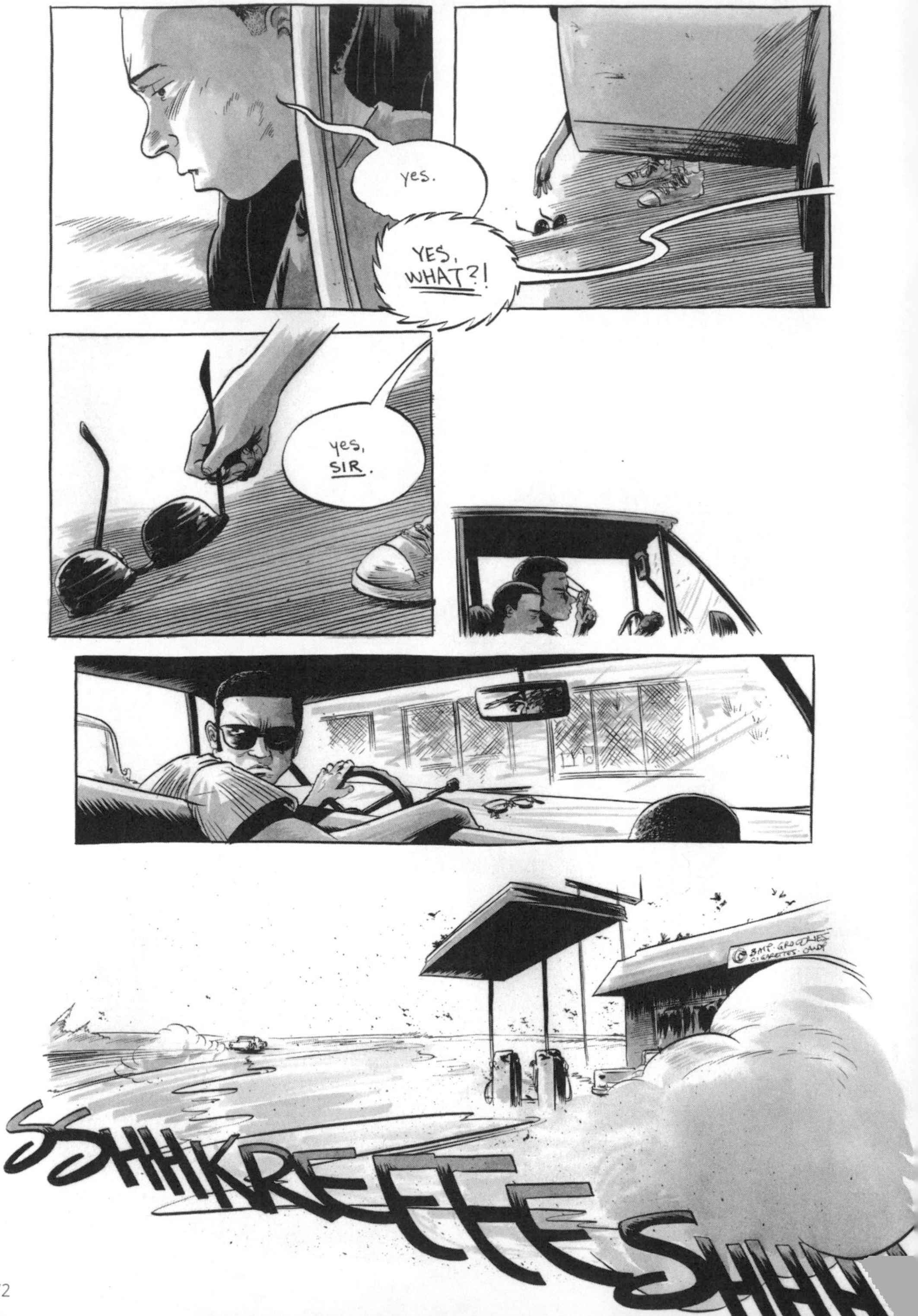
yes.
YES, WHAT?!
yes, SIR.
SSHHKREEEESHHH

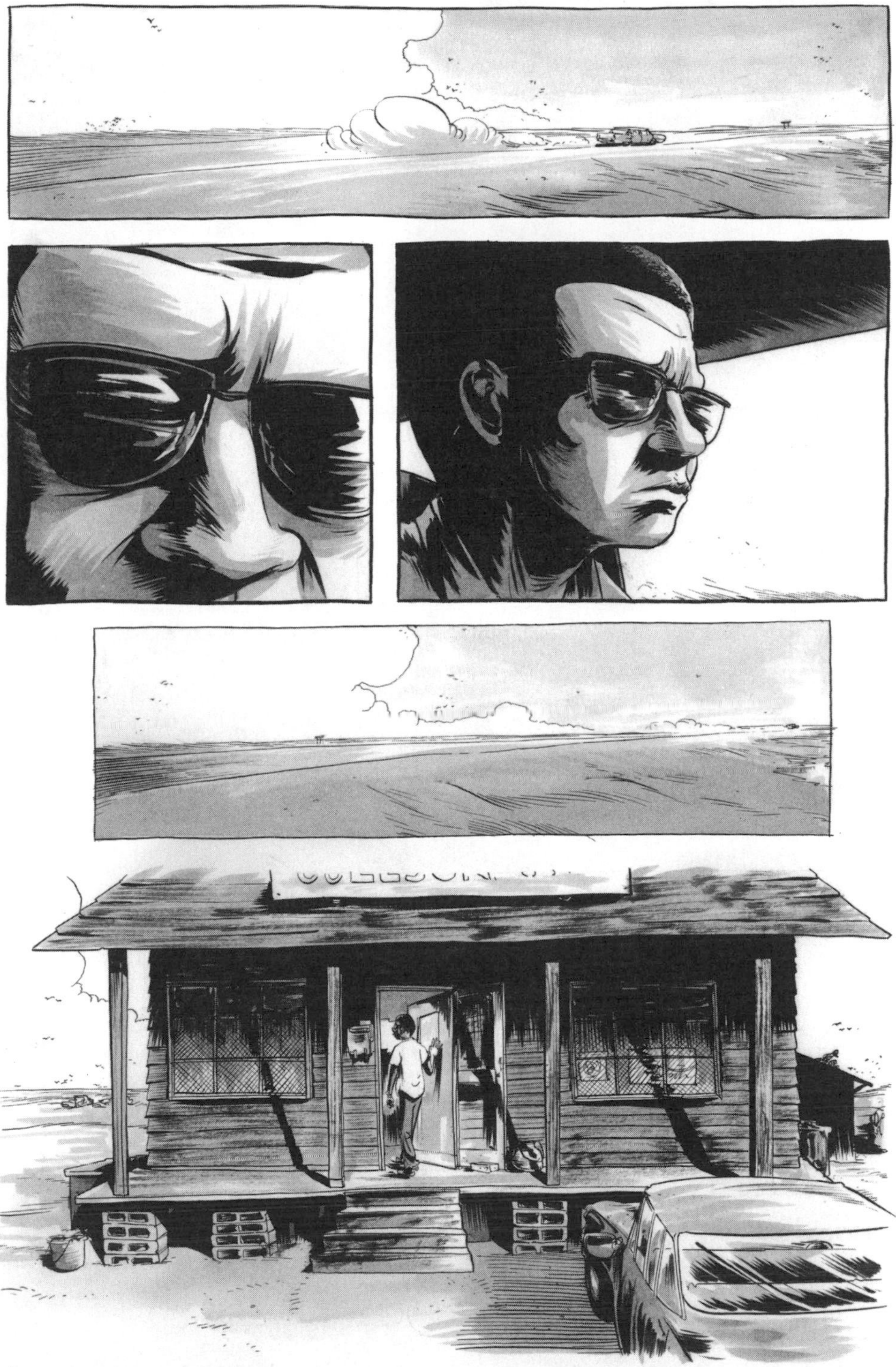

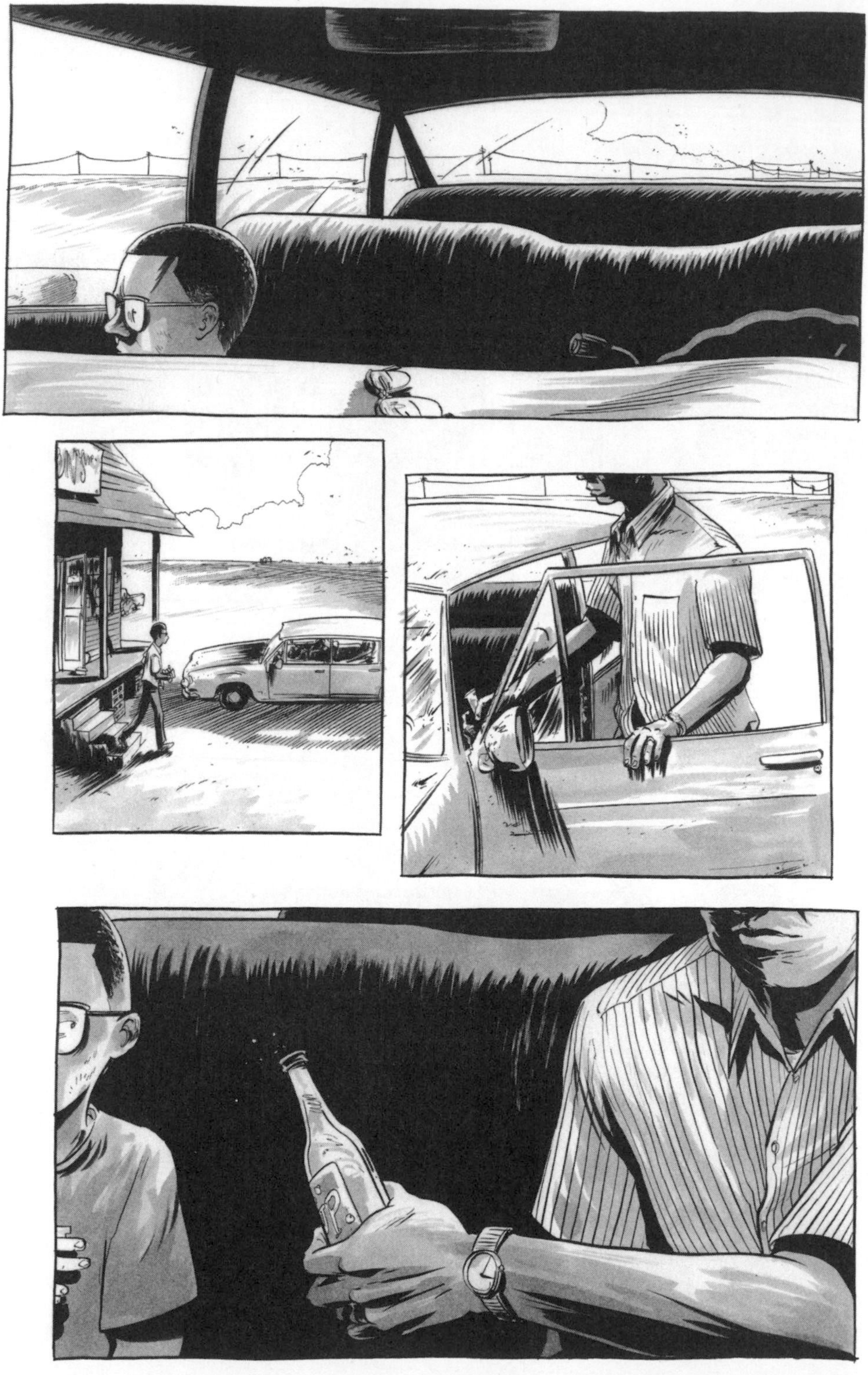

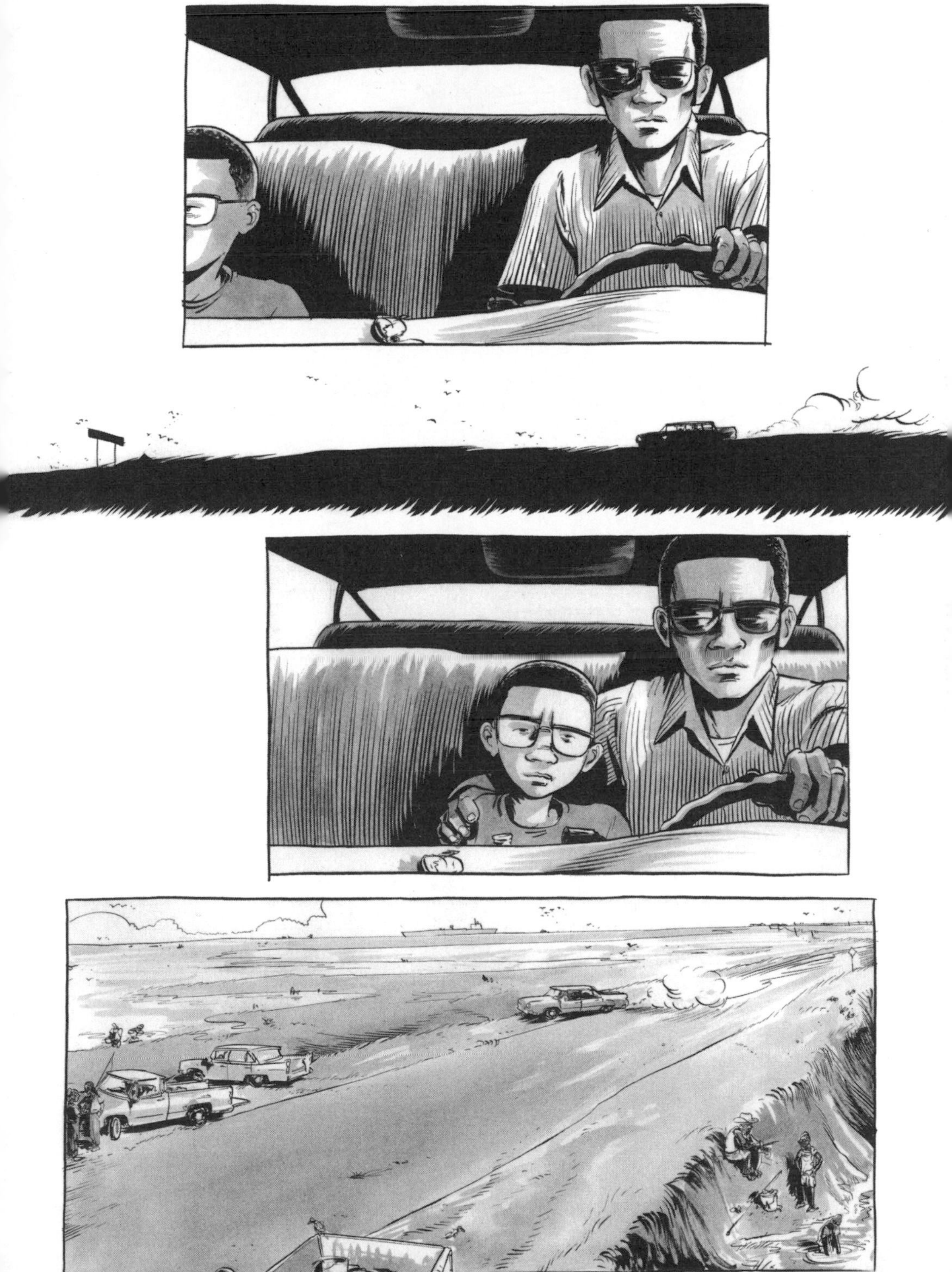

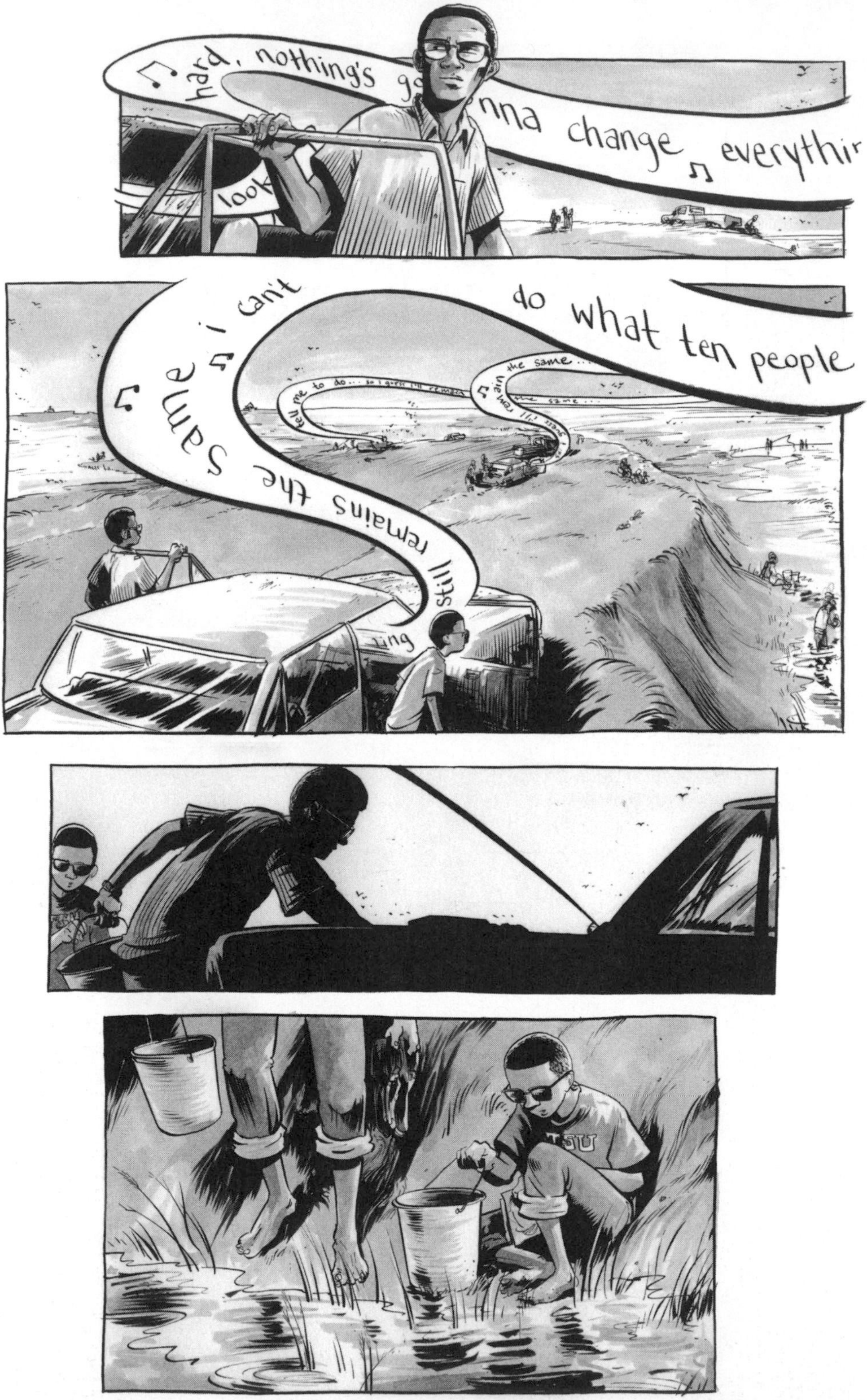

hard, nothing's go
nna change everythi
look
i can't
do what ten people
tell me to do...
remain the same...
same the same
remains the same
still

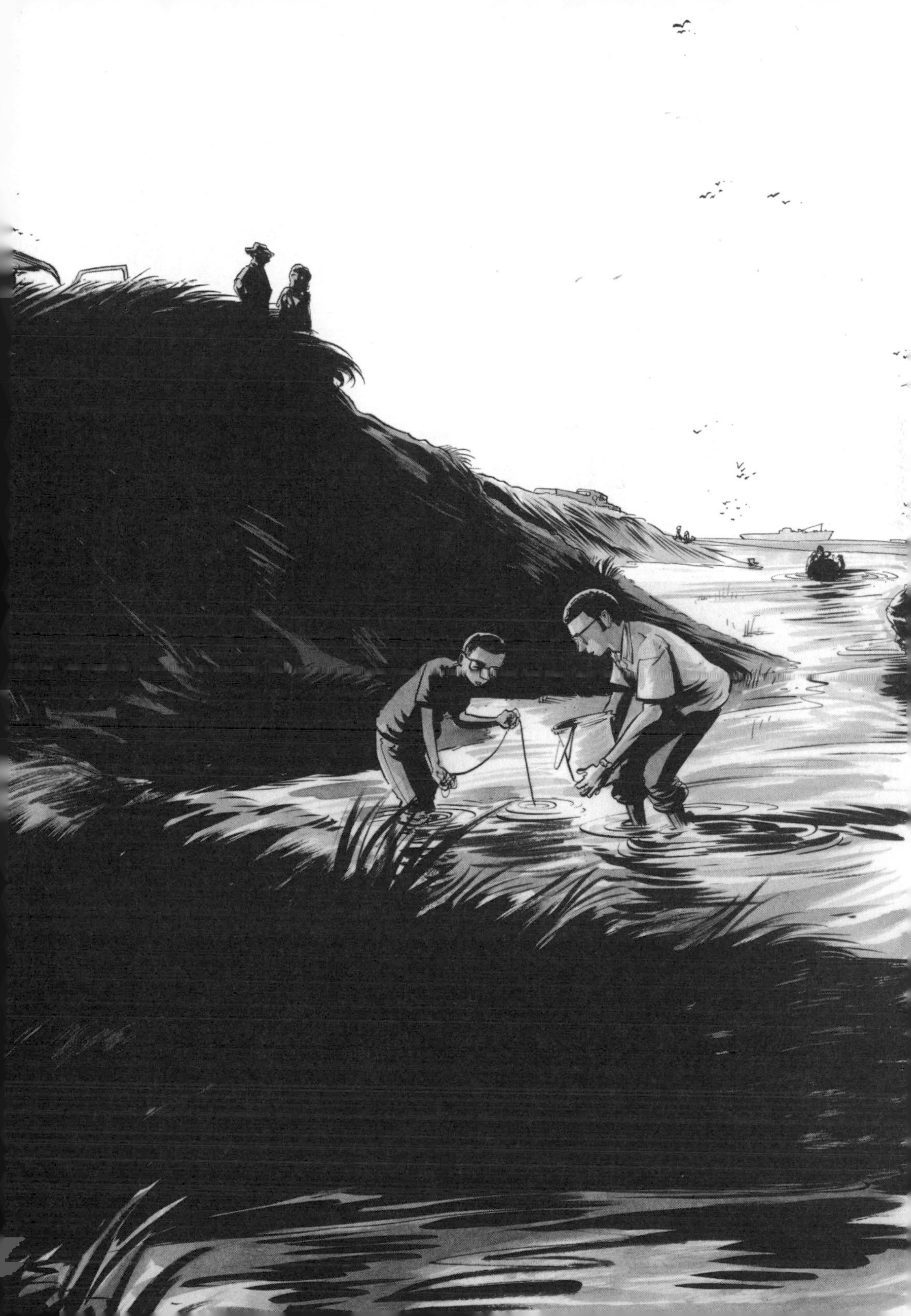

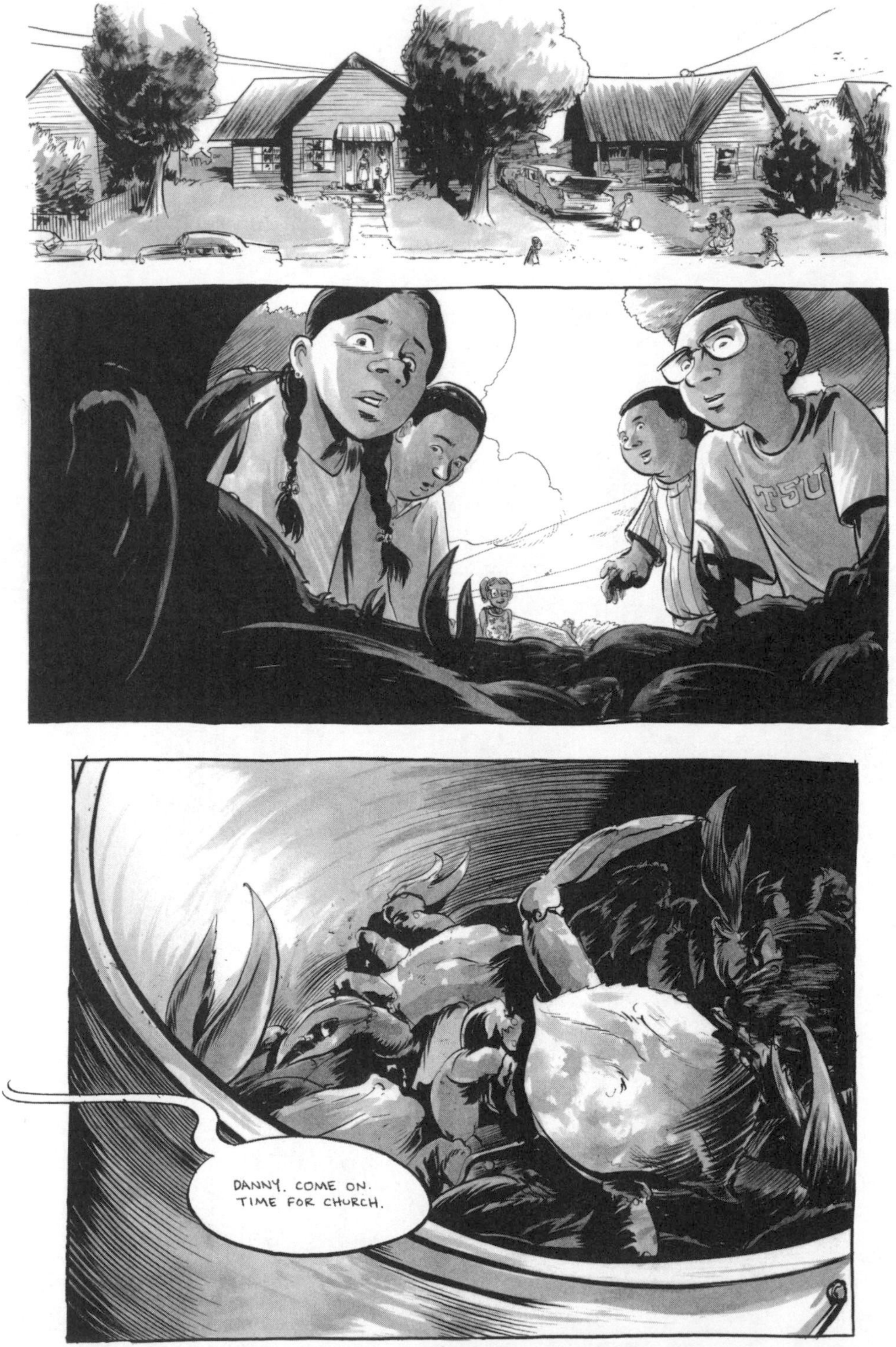
TSU
DANNY. COME ON. TIME FOR CHURCH.

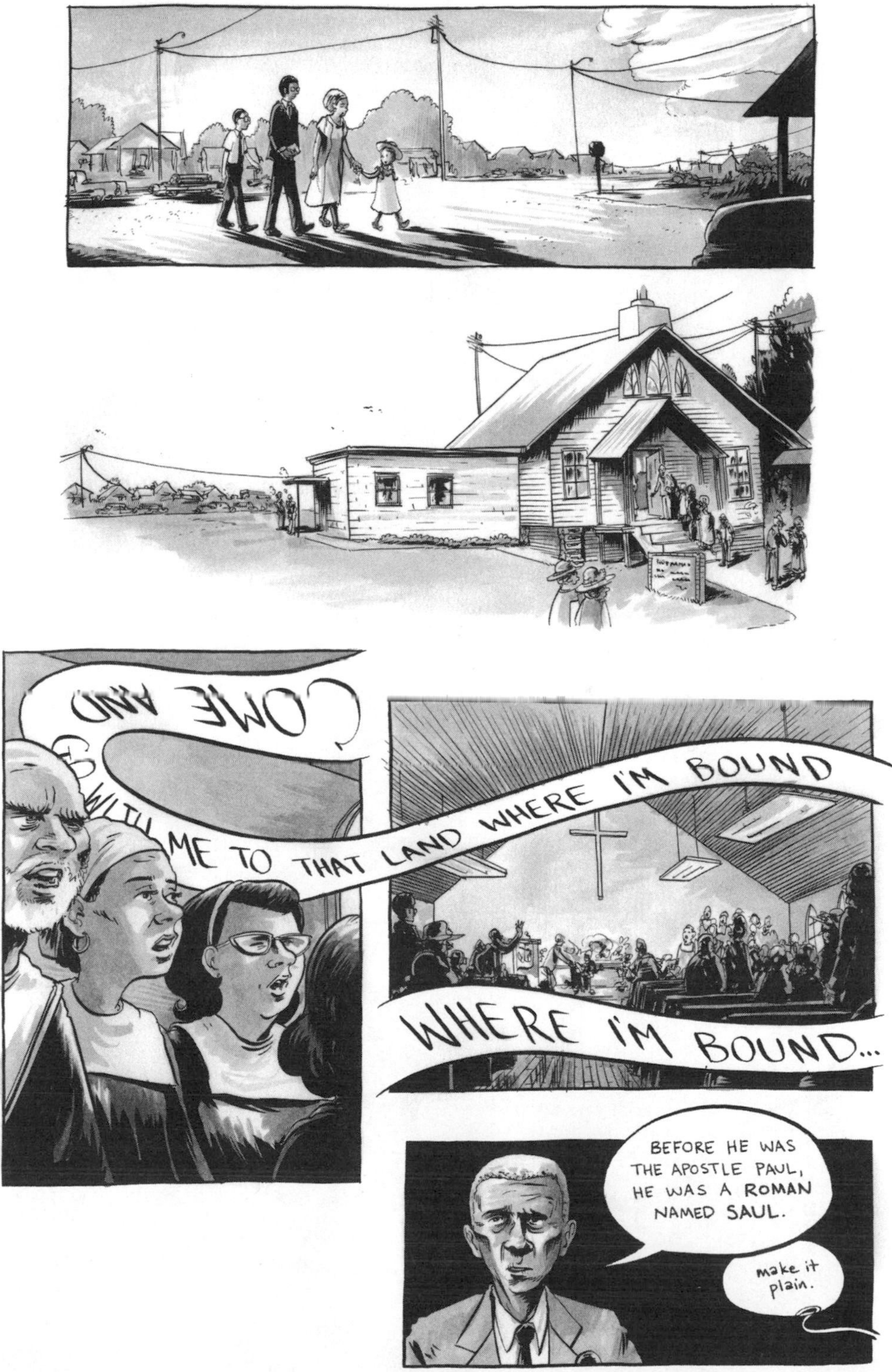
COME AND GO WITH ME TO THAT LAND WHERE I'M BOUND
WHERE I'M BOUND...
BEFORE HE WAS THE APOSTLE PAUL, HE WAS A ROMAN NAMED SAUL.
make it plain.

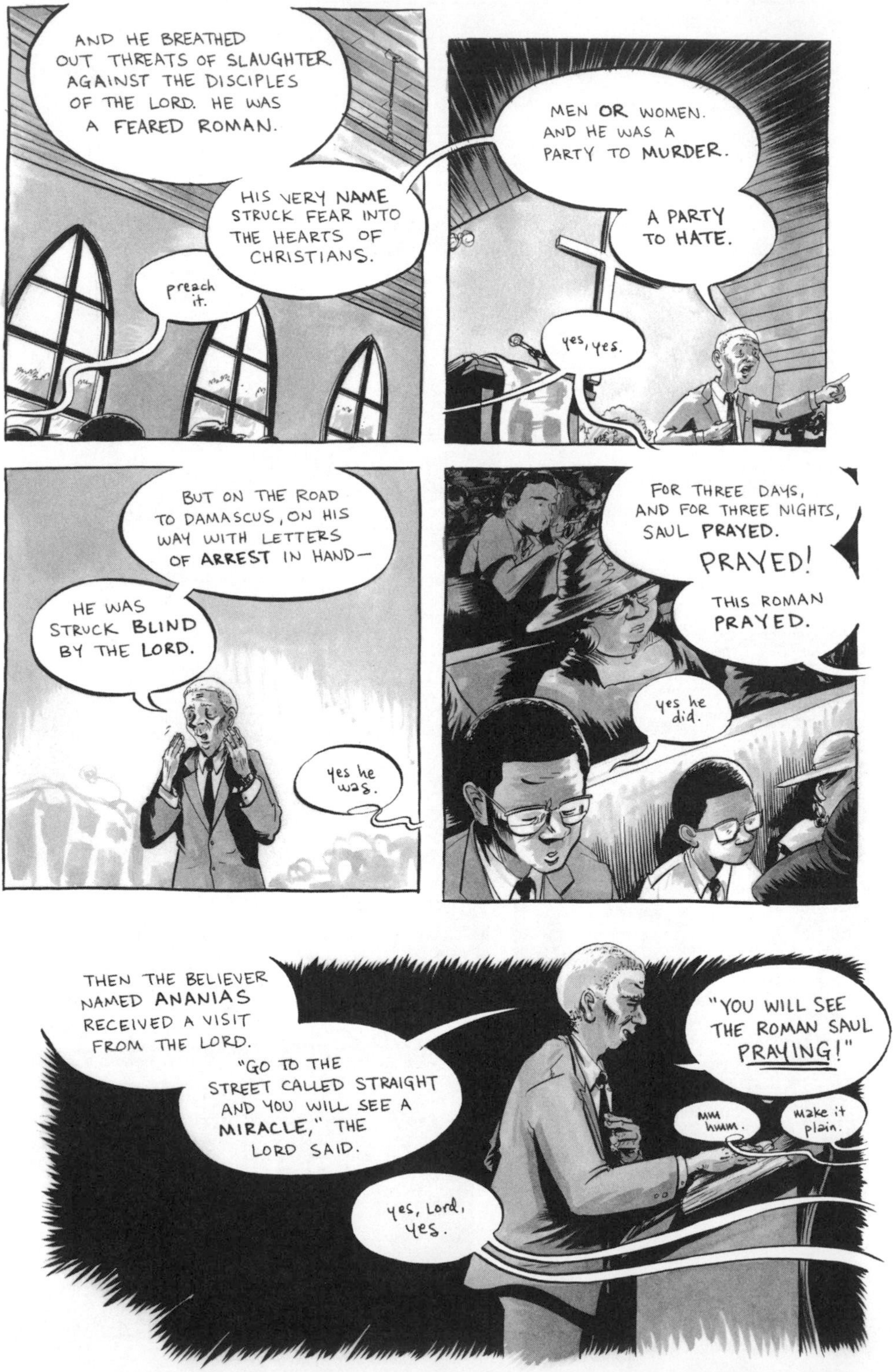
AND HE BREATHED OUT THREATS OF SLAUGHTER AGAINST THE DISCIPLES OF THE LORD. HE WAS A FEARED ROMAN.
HIS VERY NAME STRUCK FEAR INTO THE HEARTS OF CHRISTIANS.
preach it.
MEN OR WOMEN. AND HE WAS A PARTY TO MURDER.
A PARTY TO HATE.
yes, yes.
BUT ON THE ROAD TO DAMASCUS, ON HIS WAY WITH LETTERS OF ARREST IN HAND—
HE WAS STRUCK BLIND BY THE LORD.
yes he was.
FOR THREE DAYS, AND FOR THREE NIGHTS, SAUL PRAYED.
PRAYED!
THIS ROMAN PRAYED.
yes he did.
THEN THE BELIEVER NAMED ANANIAS RECEIVED A VISIT FROM THE LORD.
"GO TO THE STREET CALLED STRAIGHT AND YOU WILL SEE A MIRACLE," THE LORD SAID.
"YOU WILL SEE THE ROMAN SAUL PRAYING!"
mm hmm.
make it plain.
yes, Lord, yes.

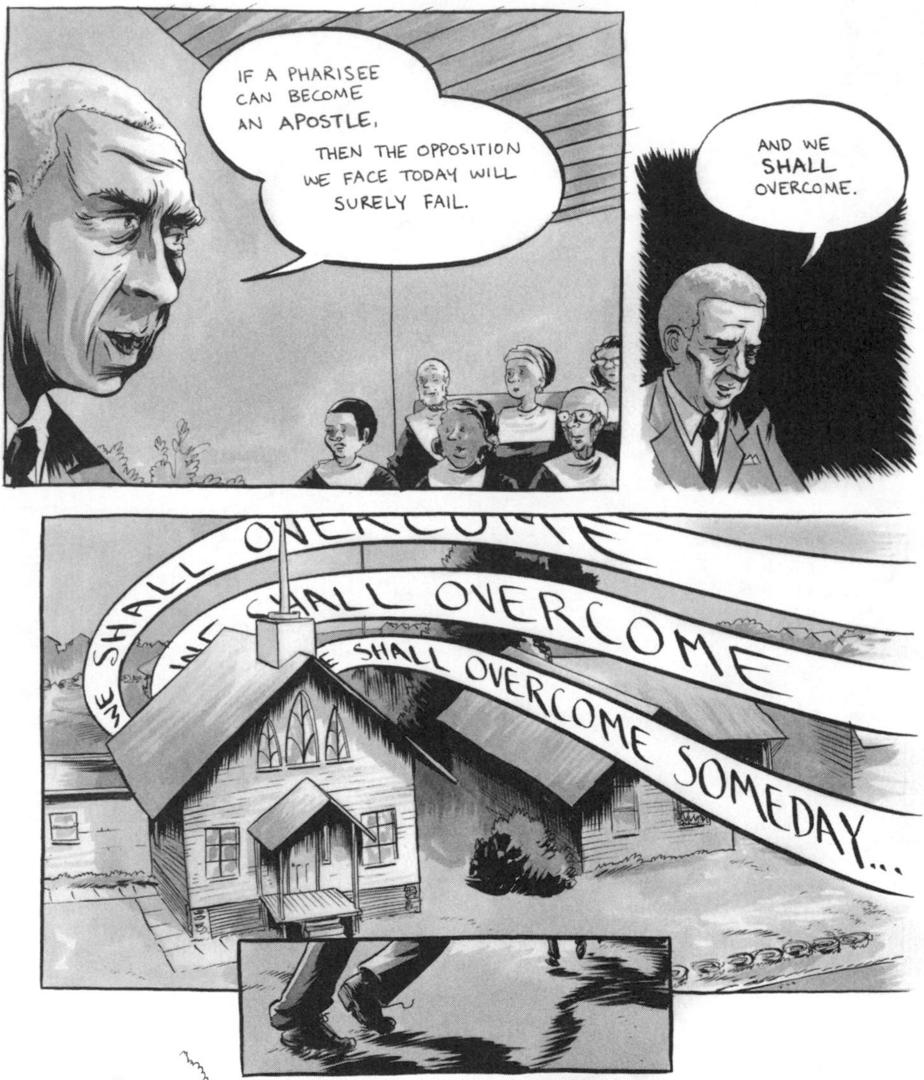
IF A PHARISEE CAN BECOME AN APOSTLE,
THEN THE OPPOSITION WE FACE TODAY WILL SURELY FAIL.
AND WE SHALL OVERCOME.
WE SHALL OVERCOME
SHALL OVERCOME
SHALL OVERCOME
OVERCOME SOMEDAY...

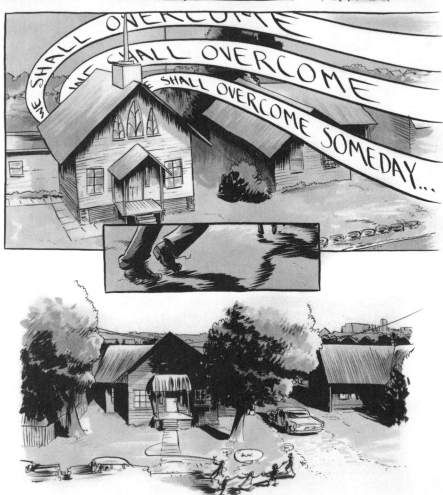

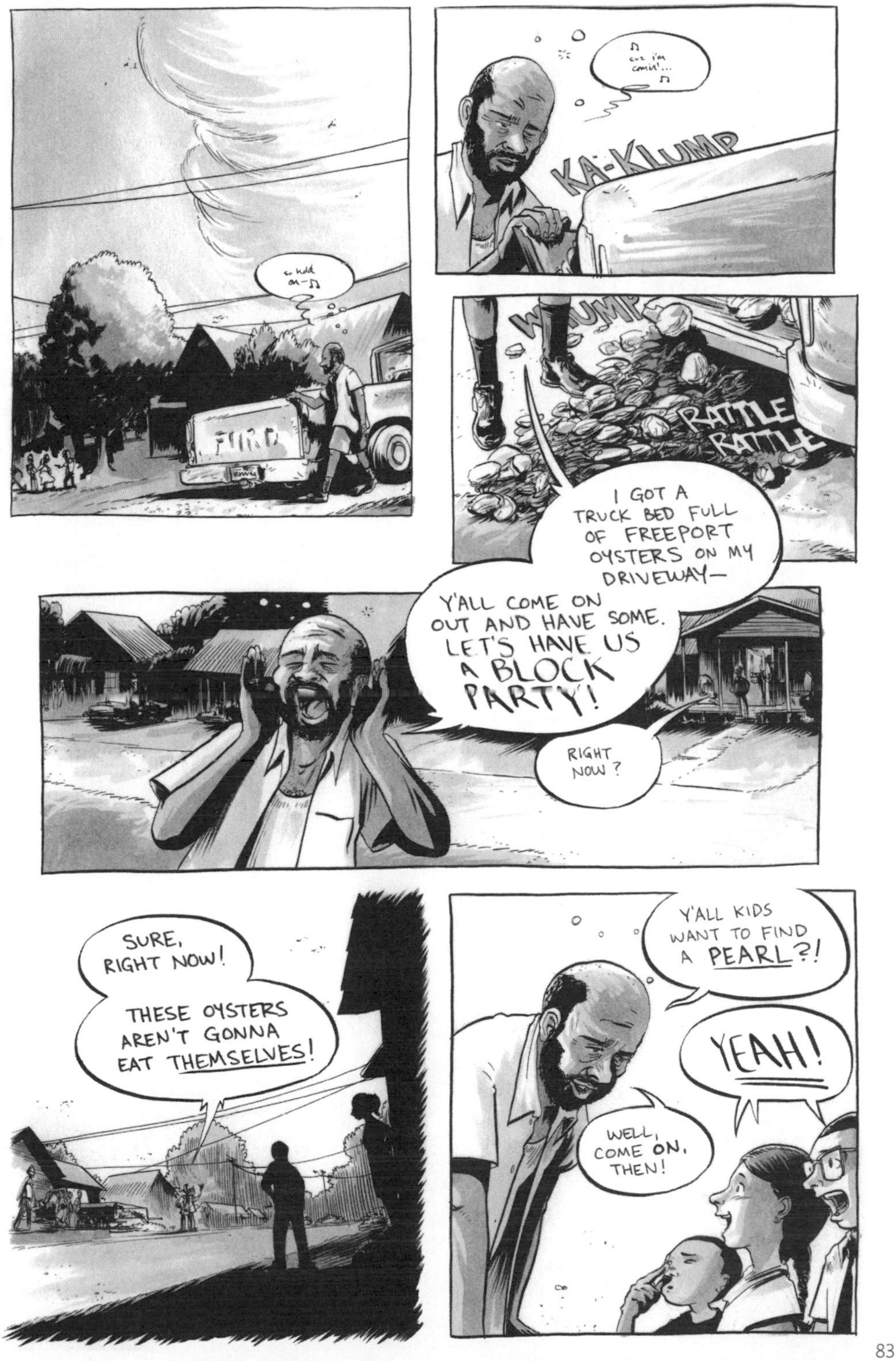

so hold on—
cuz i'm comin'...
KA-KLUMP
WUMP
RATTLE RATTLE
I GOT A TRUCK BED FULL OF FREEPORT OYSTERS ON MY DRIVEWAY—
Y'ALL COME ON OUT AND HAVE SOME. LET'S HAVE US A BLOCK PARTY!
RIGHT NOW?
SURE, RIGHT NOW!
THESE OYSTERS AREN'T GONNA EAT THEMSELVES!
Y'ALL KIDS WANT TO FIND A PEARL?!
YEAH!
WELL, COME ON, THEN!

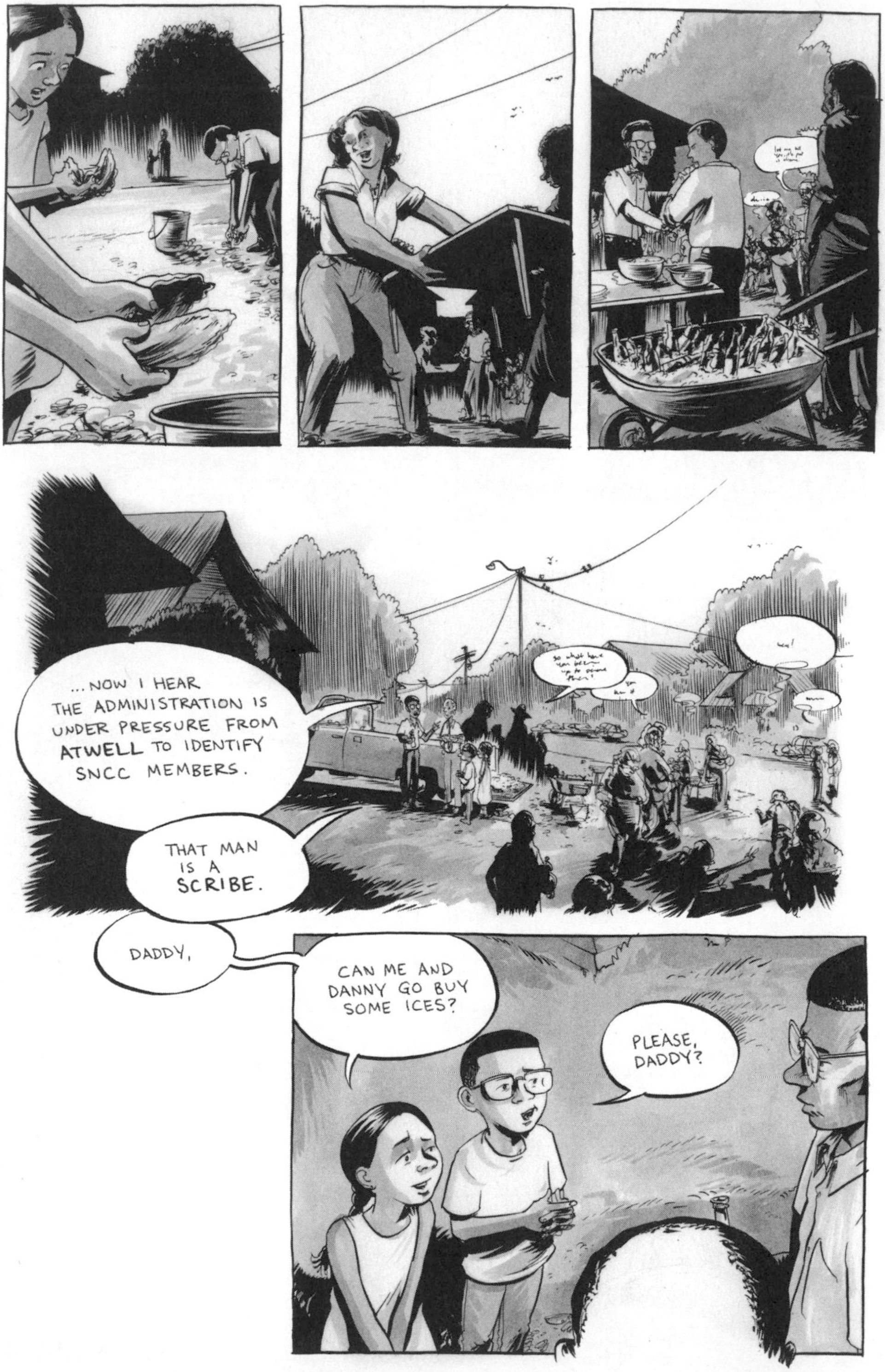
...NOW I HEAR THE ADMINISTRATION IS UNDER PRESSURE FROM ATWELL TO IDENTIFY SNCC MEMBERS.
THAT MAN IS A SCRIBE.
DADDY,
CAN ME AND DANNY GO BUY SOME ICES?
PLEASE, DADDY?

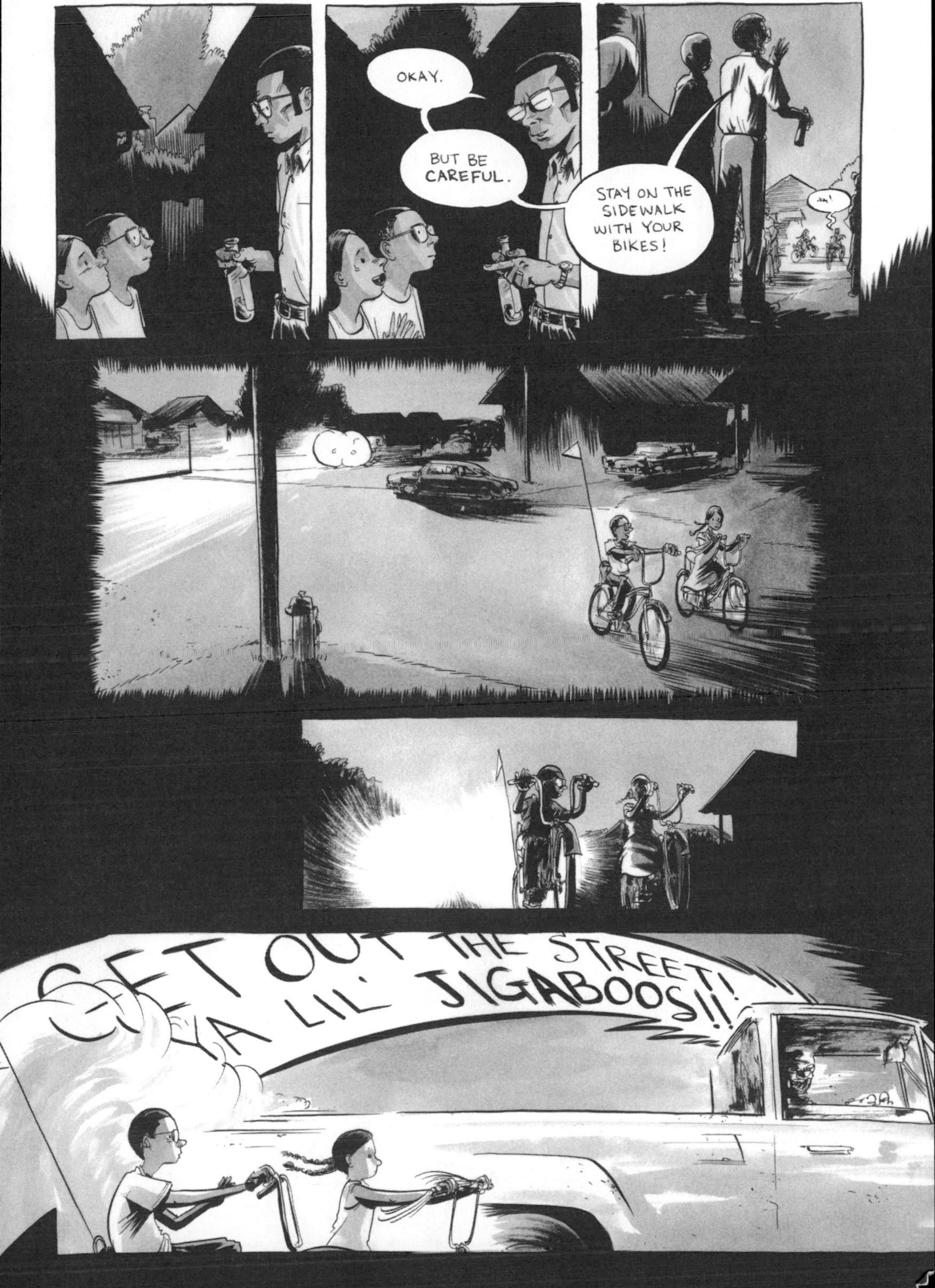
OKAY.
BUT BE CAREFUL.
STAY ON THE SIDEWALK WITH YOUR BIKES!
GET OUT THE STREET! YA LIL' JIGABOOS!!

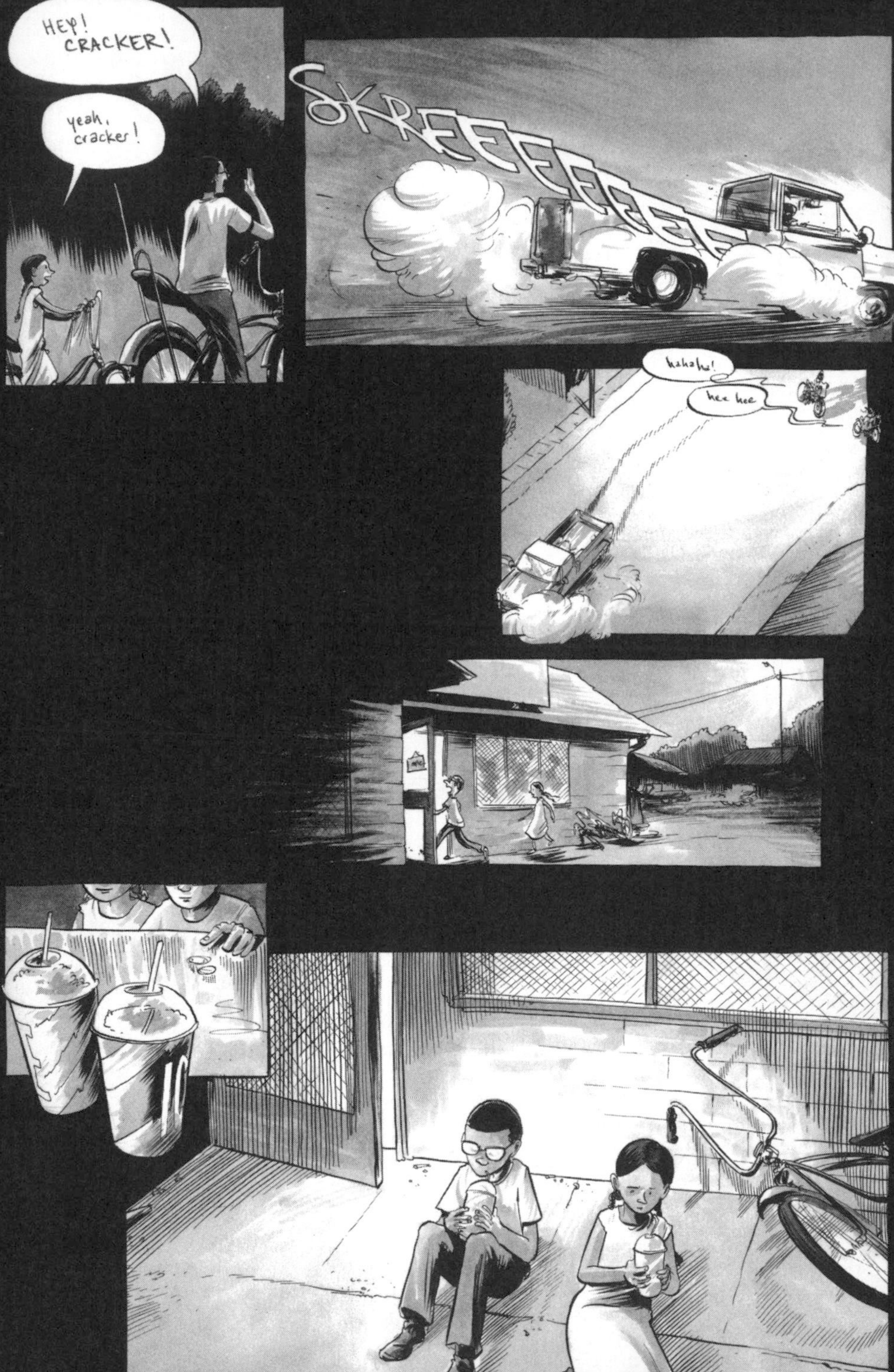
HEY! CRACKER!
yeah, cracker!
SKREEEEEEEE
hahaha!
hee hee

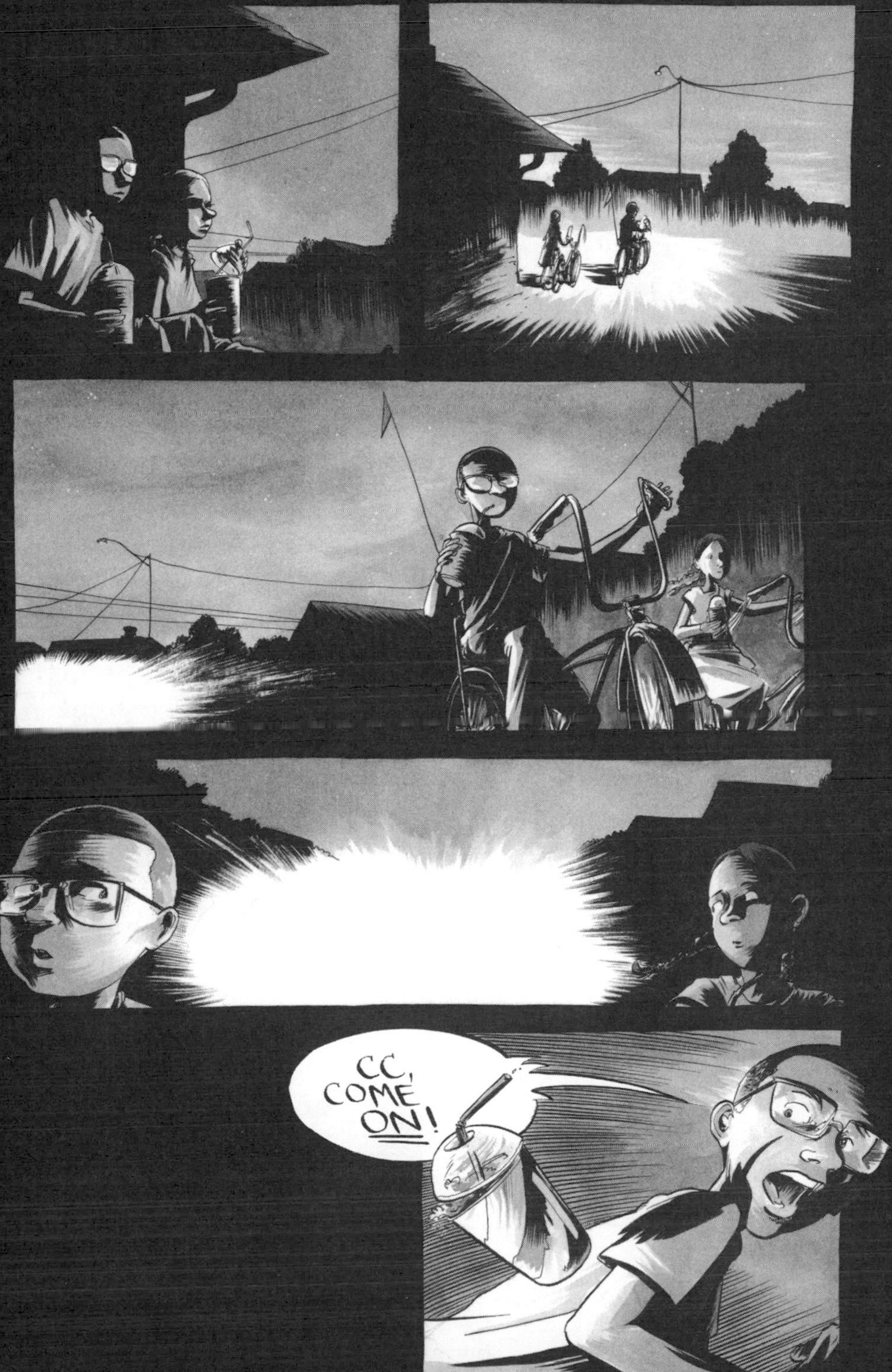
CC, COME ON!

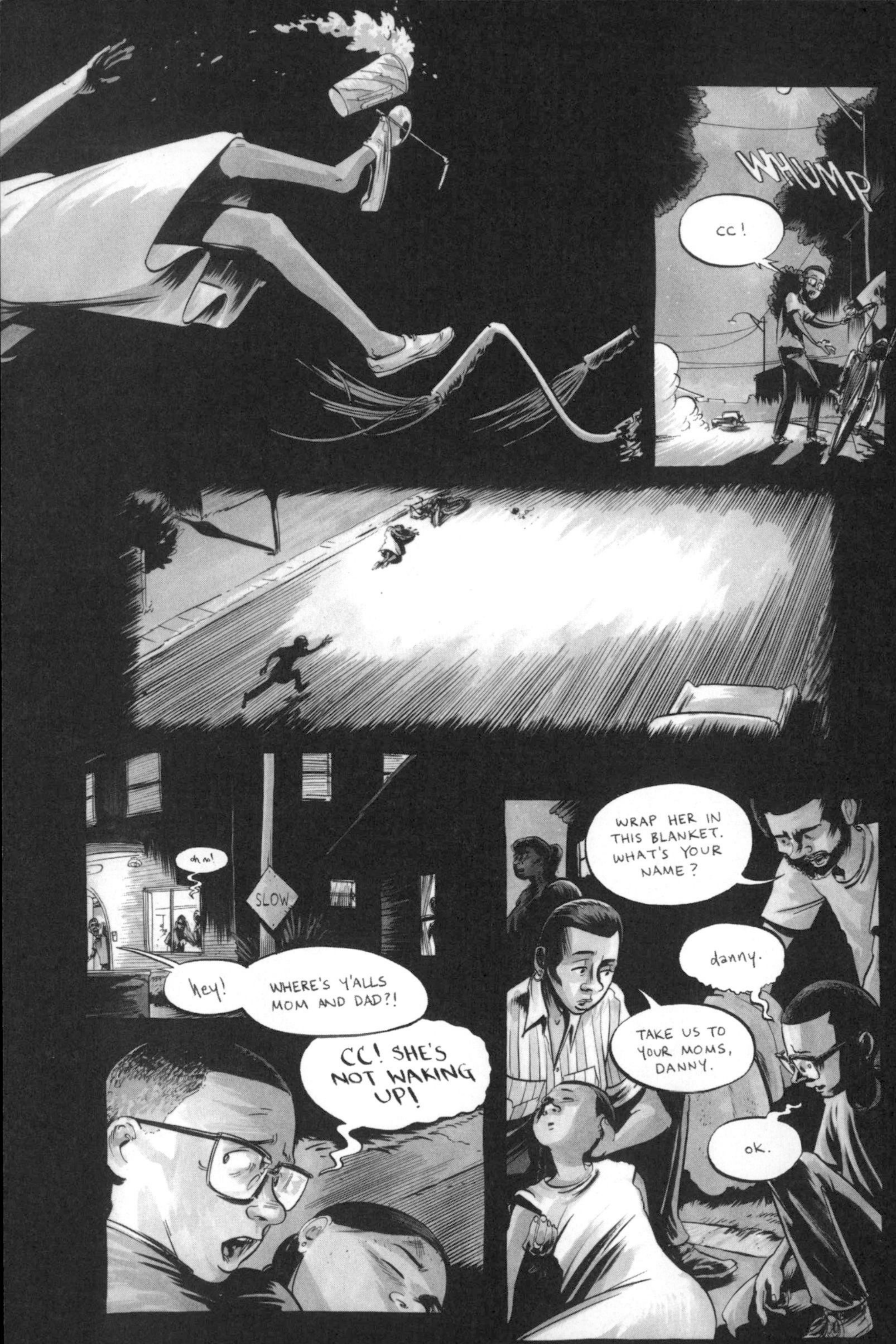
WHUMP
CC!
oh no!
SLOW
hey!
WHERE'S Y'ALLS MOM AND DAD?!
CC! SHE'S NOT WAKING UP!
WRAP HER IN THIS BLANKET. WHAT'S YOUR NAME?
danny.
TAKE US TO YOUR MOMS, DANNY.
ok.

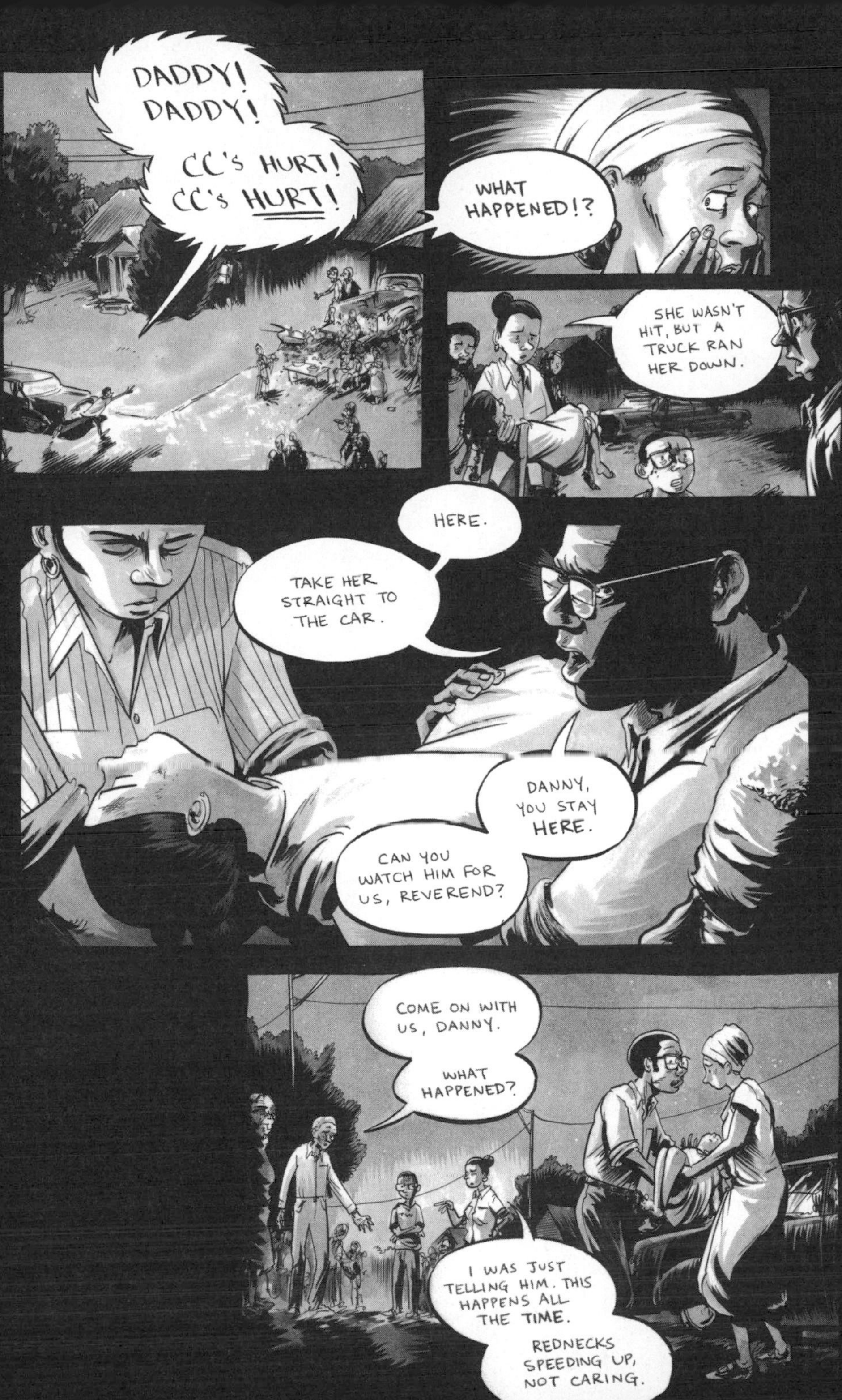
DADDY! DADDY!
CC's HURT! CC's HURT!
WHAT HAPPENED!?
SHE WASN'T HIT, BUT A TRUCK RAN HER DOWN.
HERE.
TAKE HER STRAIGHT TO THE CAR.
DANNY, YOU STAY HERE.
CAN YOU WATCH HIM FOR US, REVEREND?
COME ON WITH US, DANNY.
WHAT HAPPENED?
I WAS JUST TELLING HIM. THIS HAPPENS ALL THE TIME.
REDNECKS SPEEDING UP, NOT CARING.

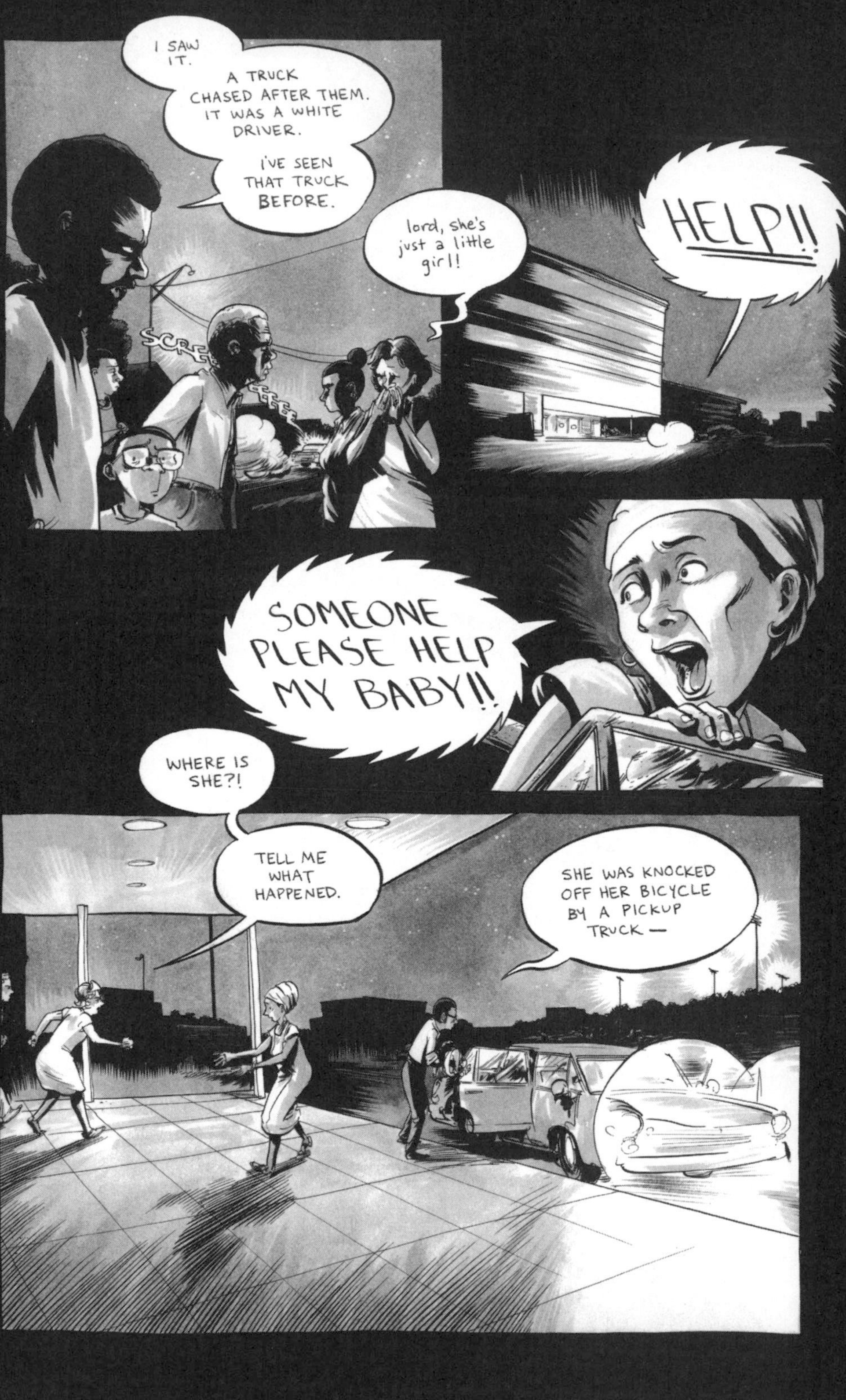

I SAW IT.
A TRUCK CHASED AFTER THEM. IT WAS A WHITE DRIVER.
I'VE SEEN THAT TRUCK BEFORE.
SCREEEE
lord, she's just a little girl!
HELP!!
SOMEONE PLEASE HELP MY BABY!!
WHERE IS SHE?!
TELL ME WHAT HAPPENED.
SHE WAS KNOCKED OFF HER BICYCLE BY A PICKUP TRUCK —

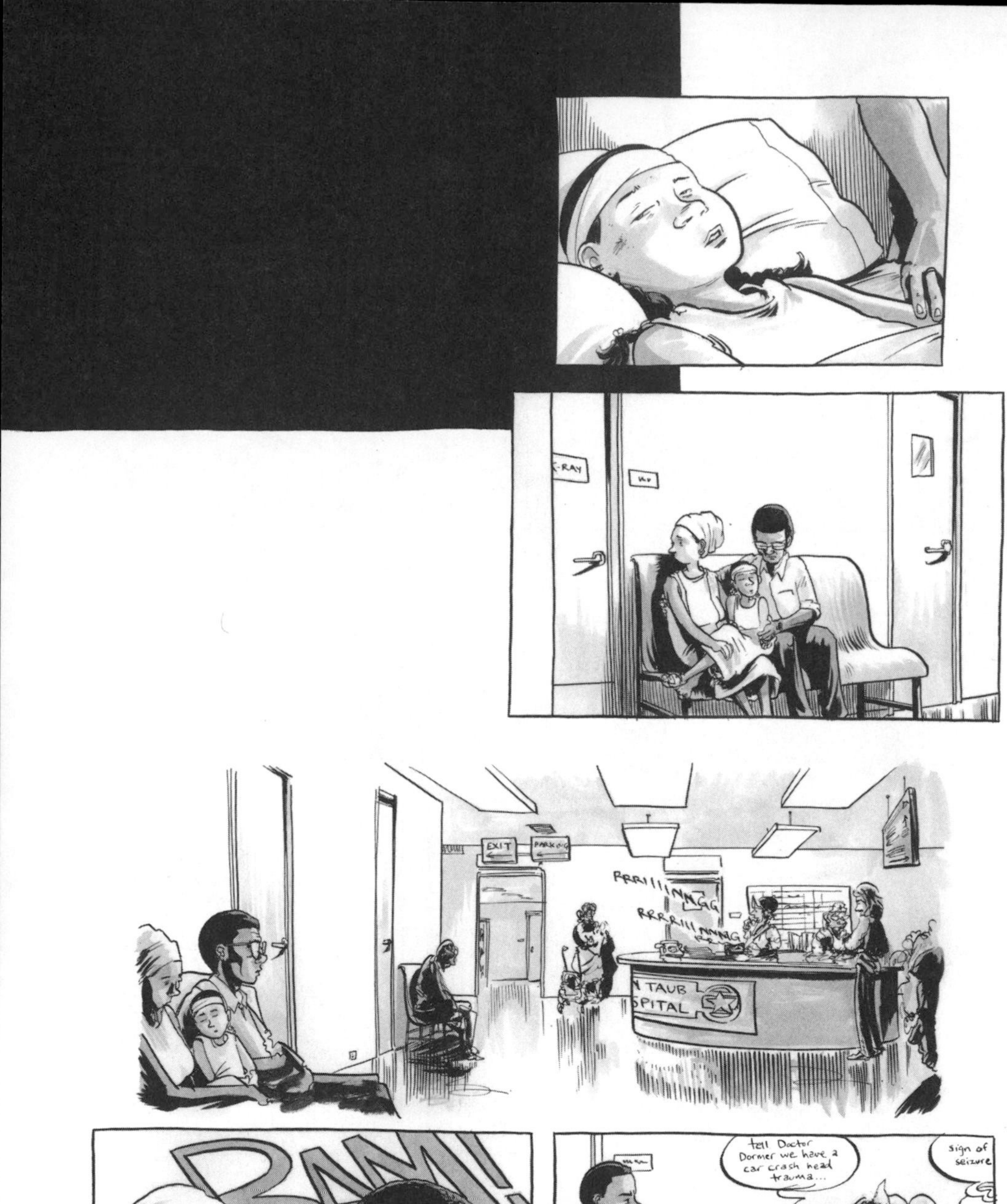
EXIT
RRRIIIINNGG
RRRRIIINNNG
N TAUB
SPITAL
BAM!
tell Doctor Dormer we have a car crash head trauma...
sign of seizure
should I intubate him?
SQUEEE

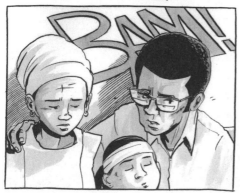

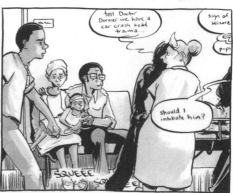

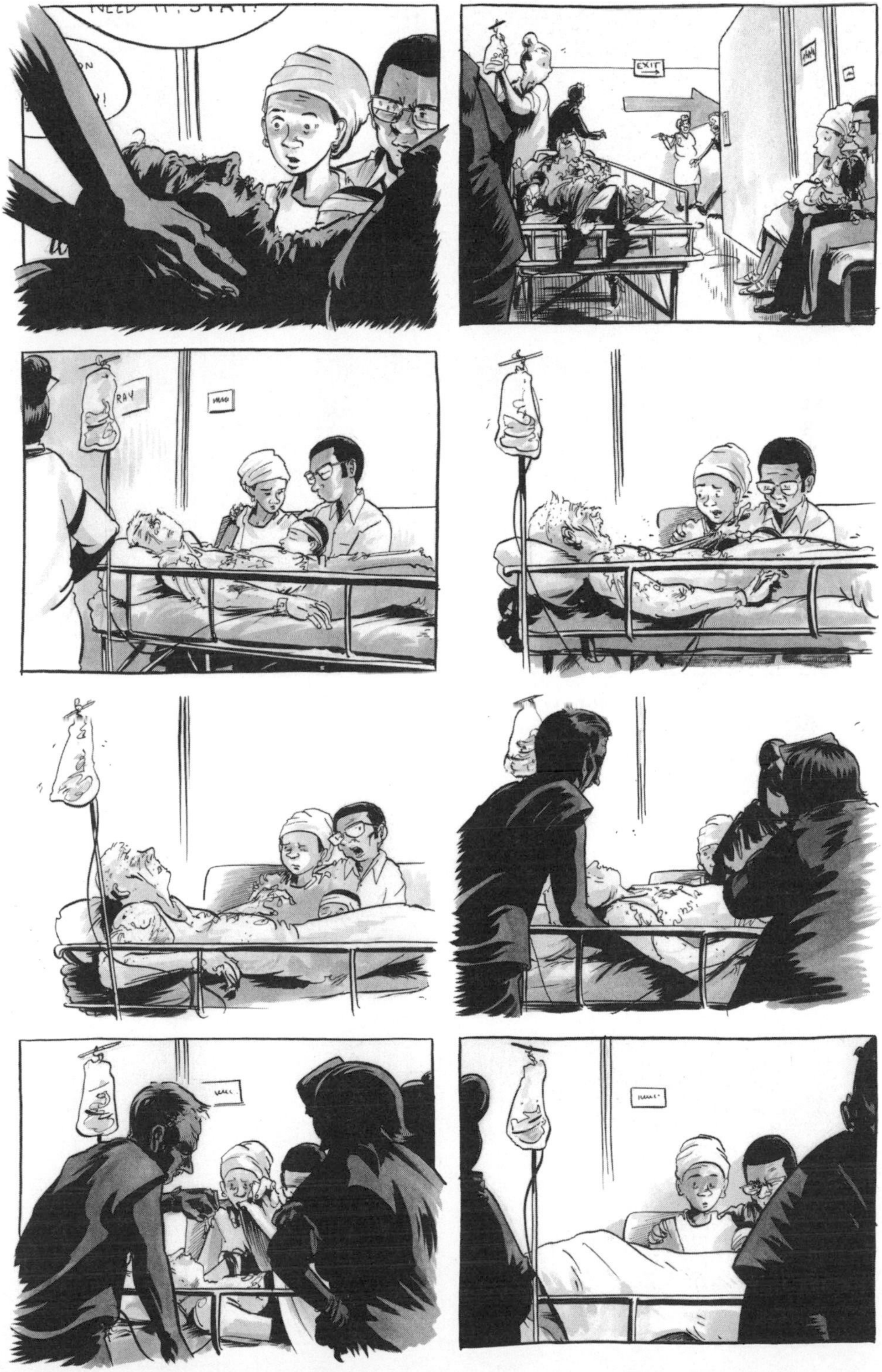
EXIT
RAY

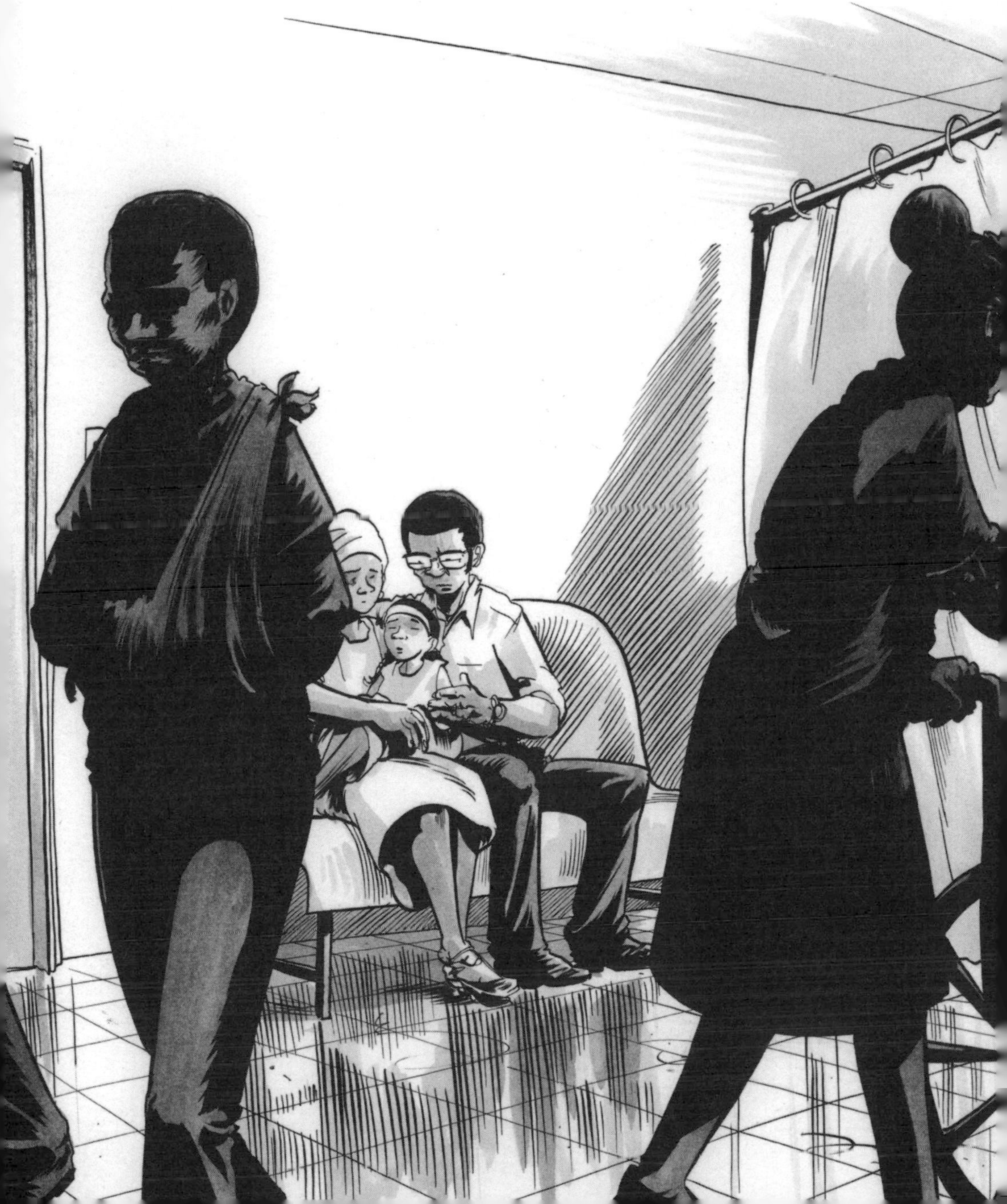

CLINK
CLINK

?

UNH UH.
YOU ARE <u>NOT</u>
WEARING <u>THAT</u>.

YOU EITHER,
CECILIA.

MOM!

I WANT TO!
WHY <u>NOT</u>?

BECAUSE I
<u>SAID</u> SO.

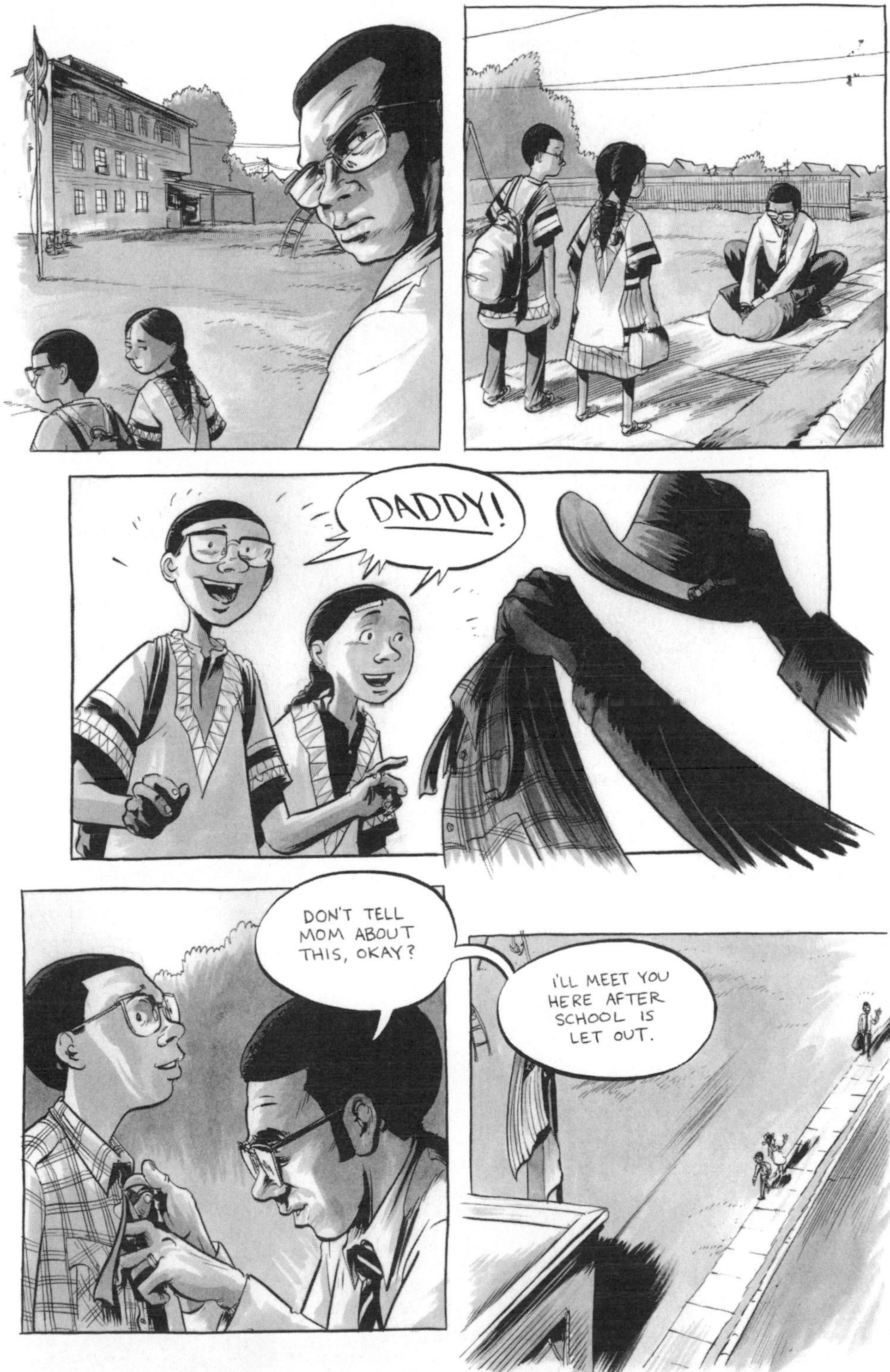
DADDY!
DON'T TELL MOM ABOUT THIS, OKAY?
I'LL MEET YOU HERE AFTER SCHOOL IS LET OUT.

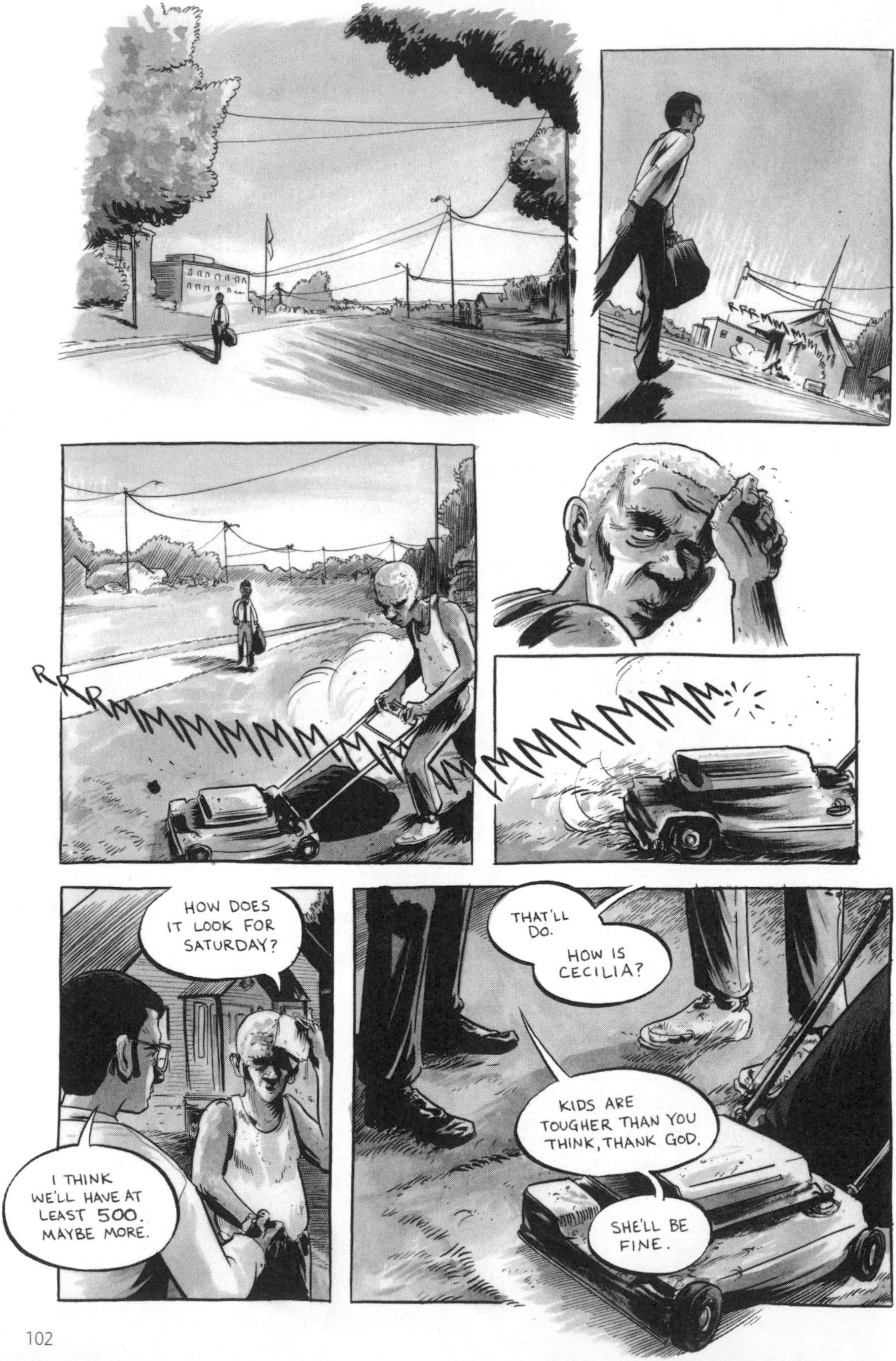
RRRMMMMMMMM
RRRMMMMMMMMMMMMMMMMMMMMMMMM
HOW DOES IT LOOK FOR SATURDAY?
I THINK WE'LL HAVE AT LEAST 500. MAYBE MORE.
THAT'LL DO.
HOW IS CECILIA?
KIDS ARE TOUGHER THAN YOU THINK, THANK GOD.
SHE'LL BE FINE.

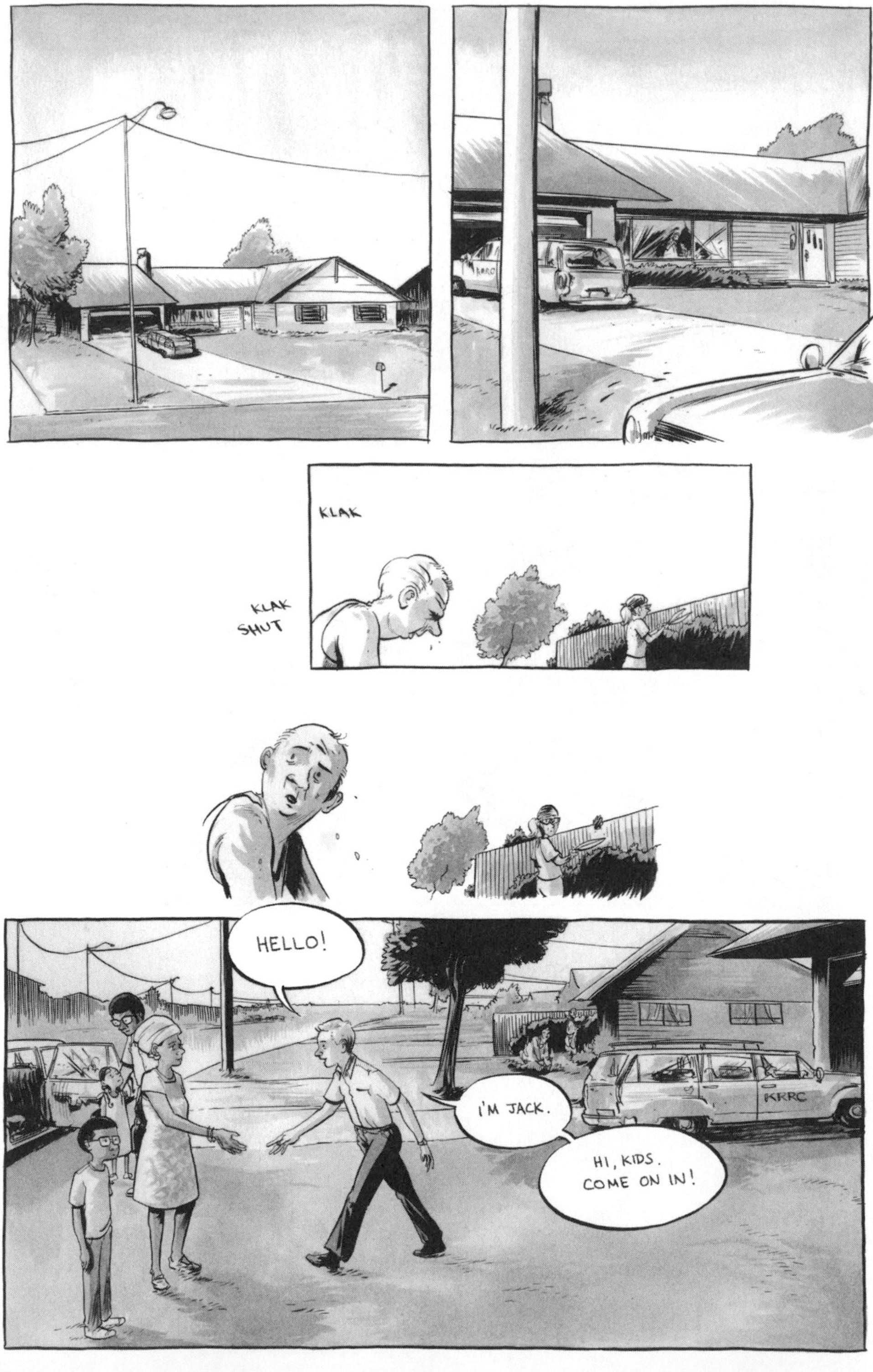
KLAK
KLAK
SHUT
HELLO!
I'M JACK.
HI, KIDS.
COME ON IN!

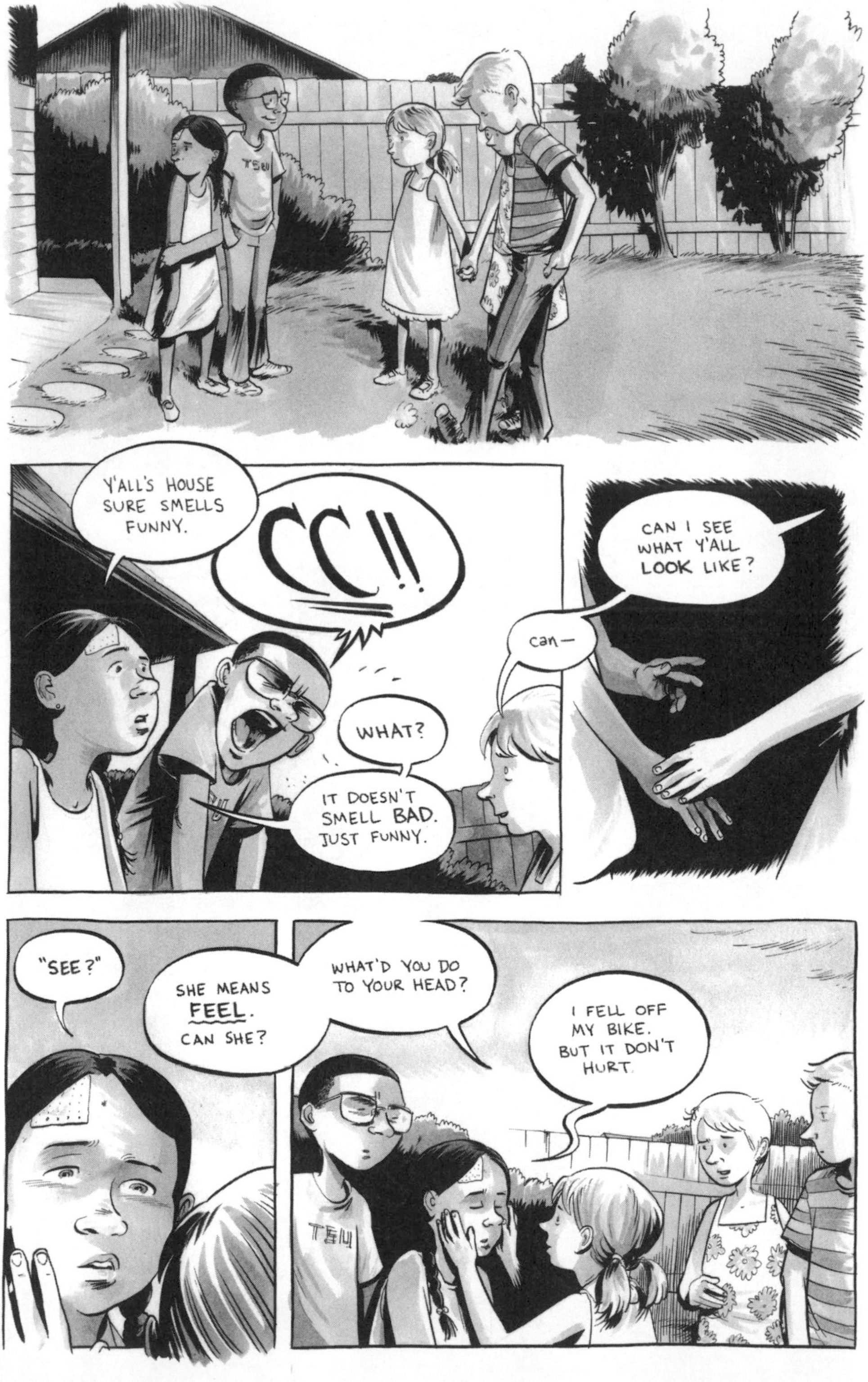
Y'ALL'S HOUSE SURE SMELLS FUNNY.
CC!!
WHAT?
IT DOESN'T SMELL BAD. JUST FUNNY.
CAN—
CAN I SEE WHAT Y'ALL LOOK LIKE?
"SEE?"
SHE MEANS FEEL. CAN SHE?
WHAT'D YOU DO TO YOUR HEAD?
I FELL OFF MY BIKE. BUT IT DON'T HURT.

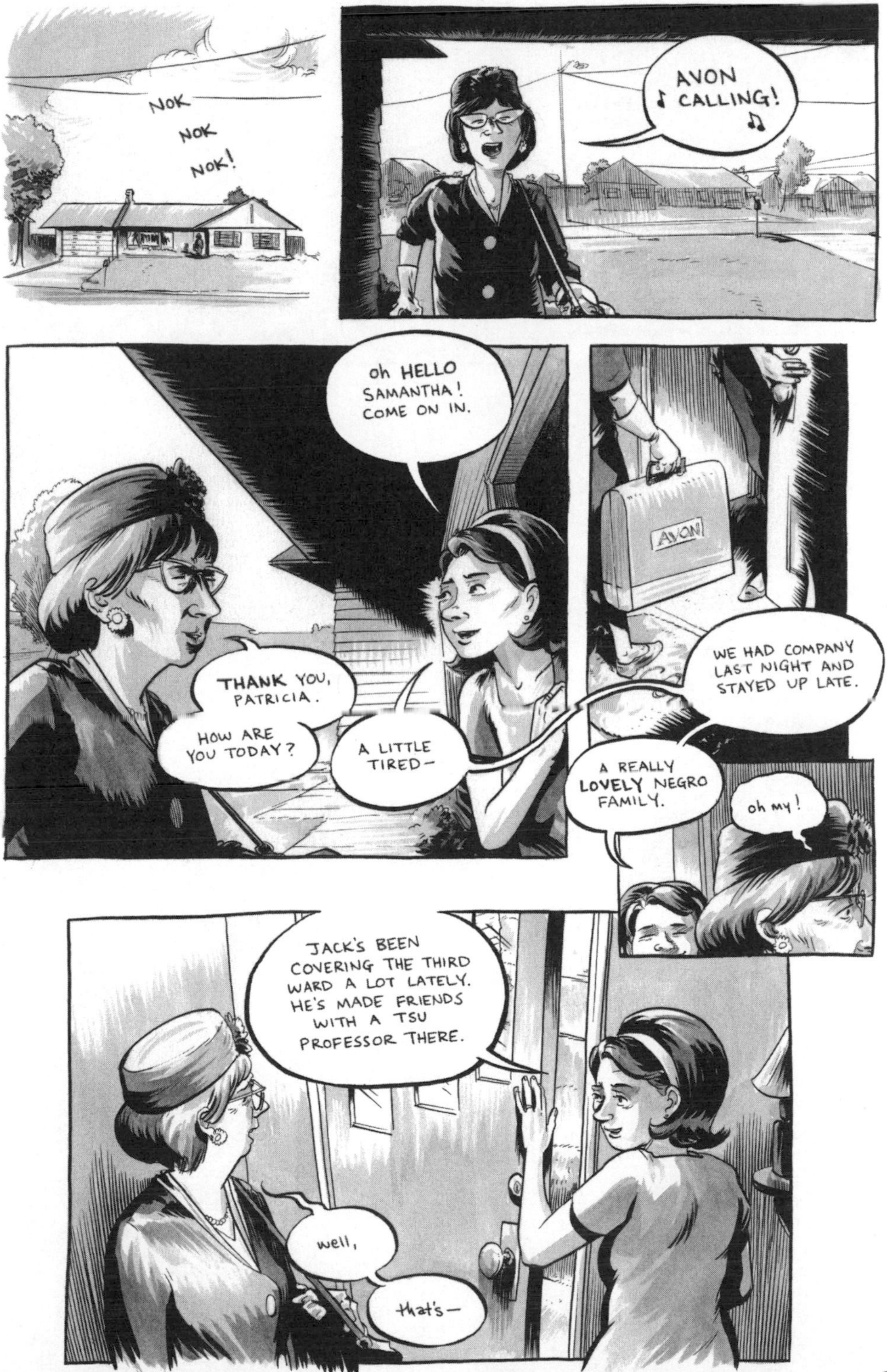
NOK
NOK
NOK!
AVON CALLING!
oh HELLO SAMANTHA! COME ON IN.
AVON
THANK YOU, PATRICIA.
HOW ARE YOU TODAY?
A LITTLE TIRED—
WE HAD COMPANY LAST NIGHT AND STAYED UP LATE.
A REALLY LOVELY NEGRO FAMILY.
oh my!
JACK'S BEEN COVERING THE THIRD WARD A LOT LATELY. HE'S MADE FRIENDS WITH A TSU PROFESSOR THERE.
well,
that's—

DING DONG!

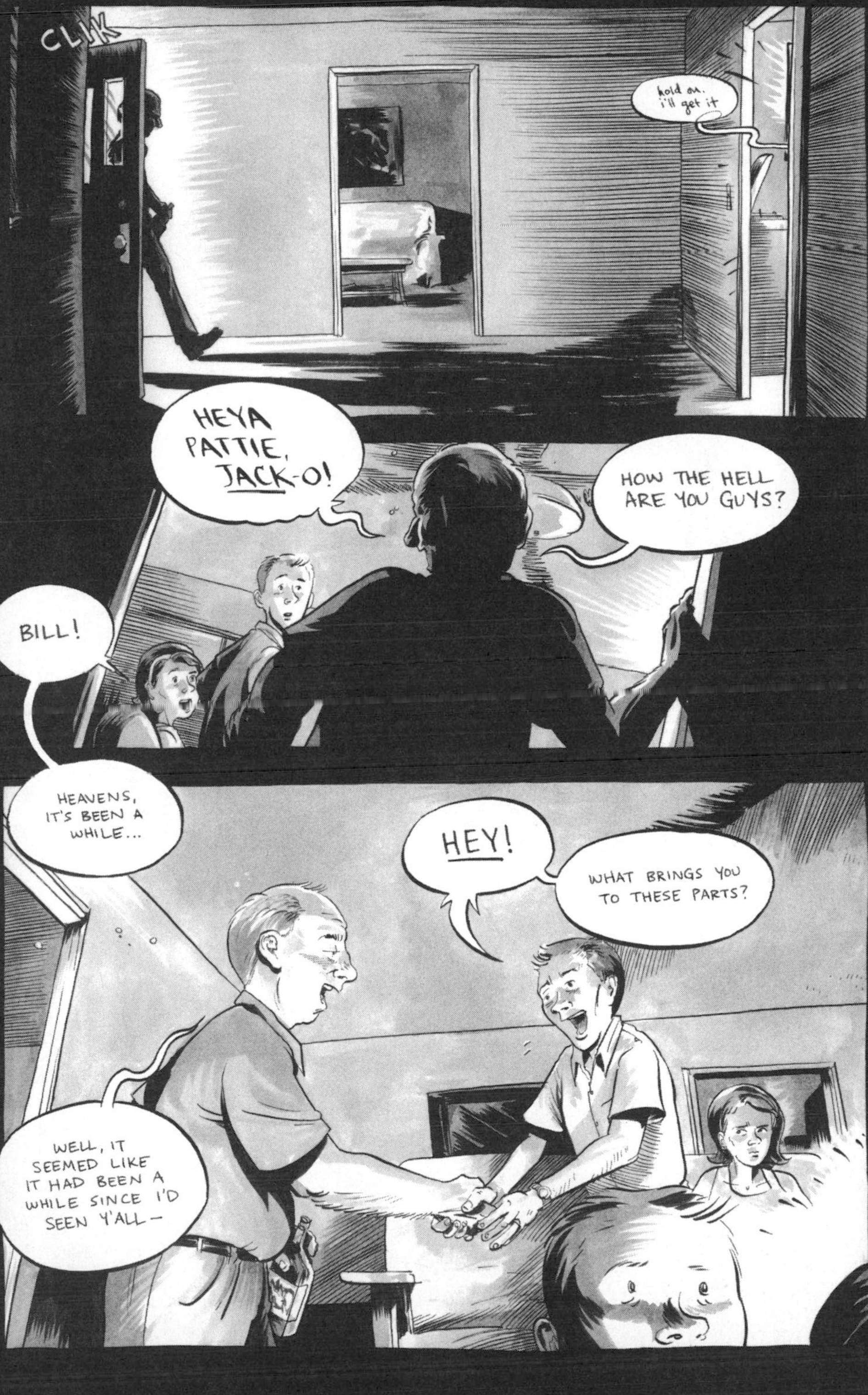
CLIK
hold on. i'll get it
HEYA PATTIE, JACK-O!
HOW THE HELL ARE YOU GUYS?
BILL!
HEAVENS, IT'S BEEN A WHILE...
HEY!
WHAT BRINGS YOU TO THESE PARTS?
WELL, IT SEEMED LIKE IT HAD BEEN A WHILE SINCE I'D SEEN Y'ALL—

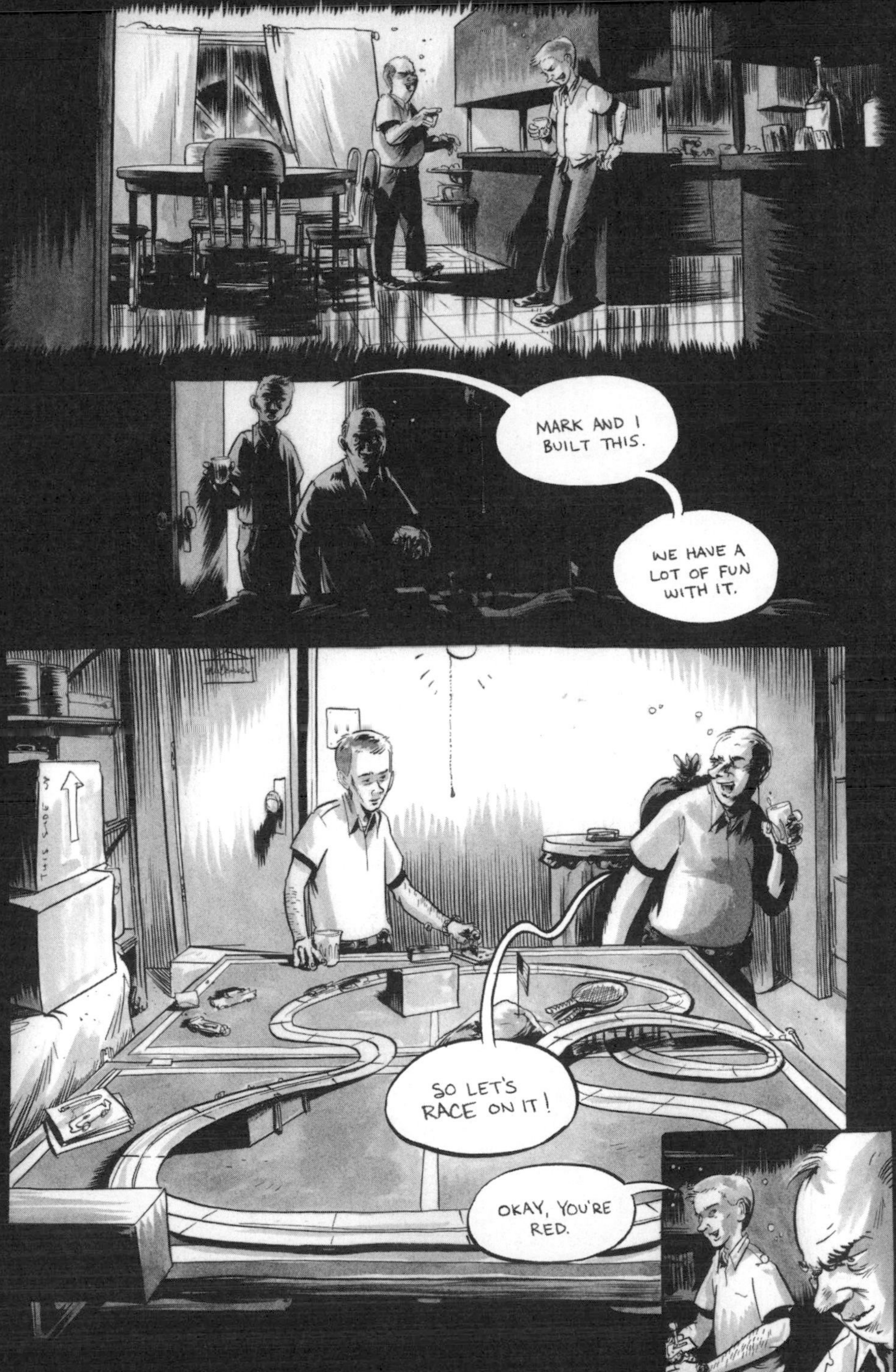
MARK AND I BUILT THIS.
WE HAVE A LOT OF FUN WITH IT.
THIS SIDE UP
SO LET'S RACE ON IT!
OKAY, YOU'RE RED.

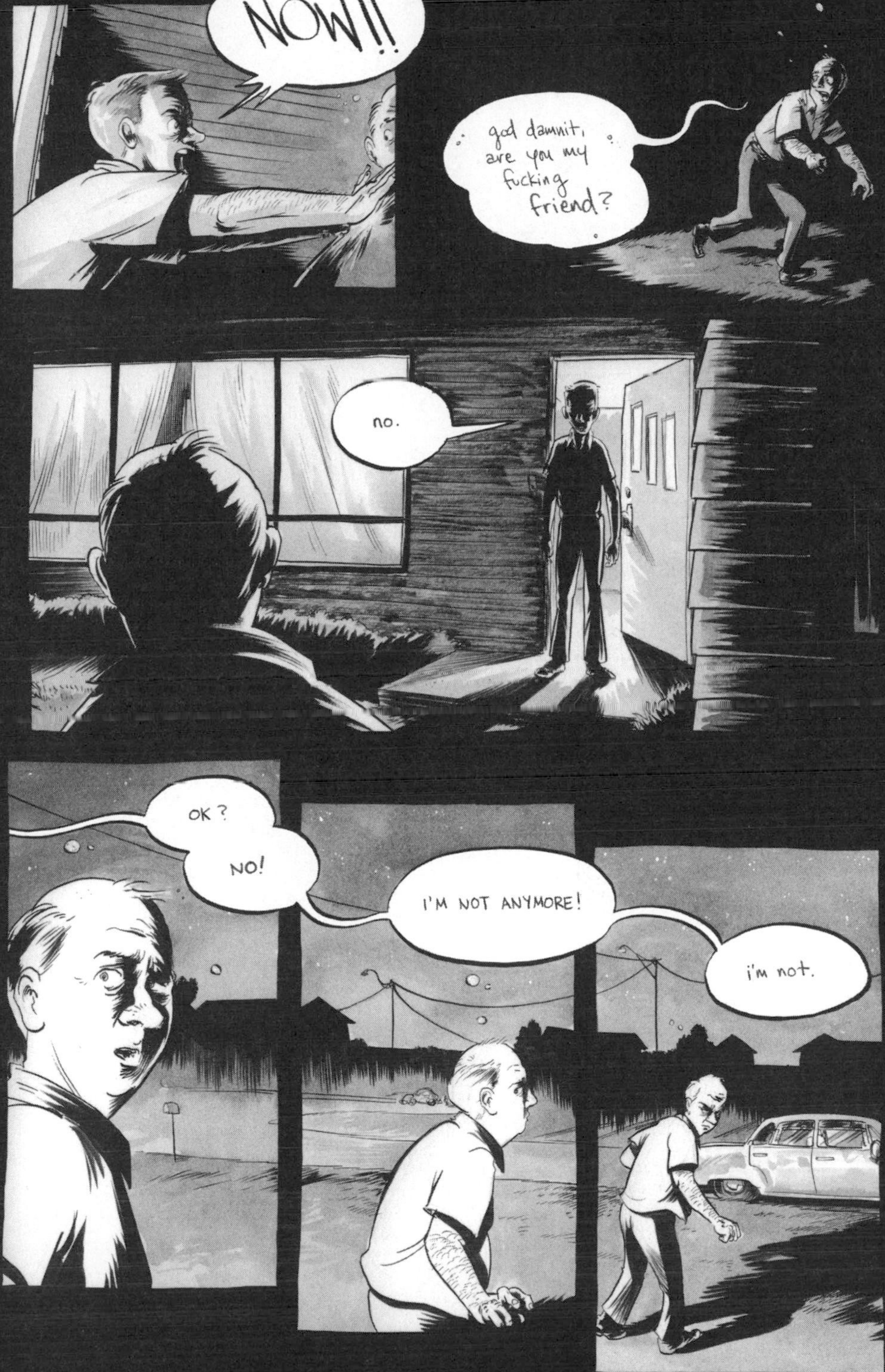
NOW!!
god damnit, are you my fucking friend?
no.
OK?
NO!
I'M NOT ANYMORE!
i'm not.

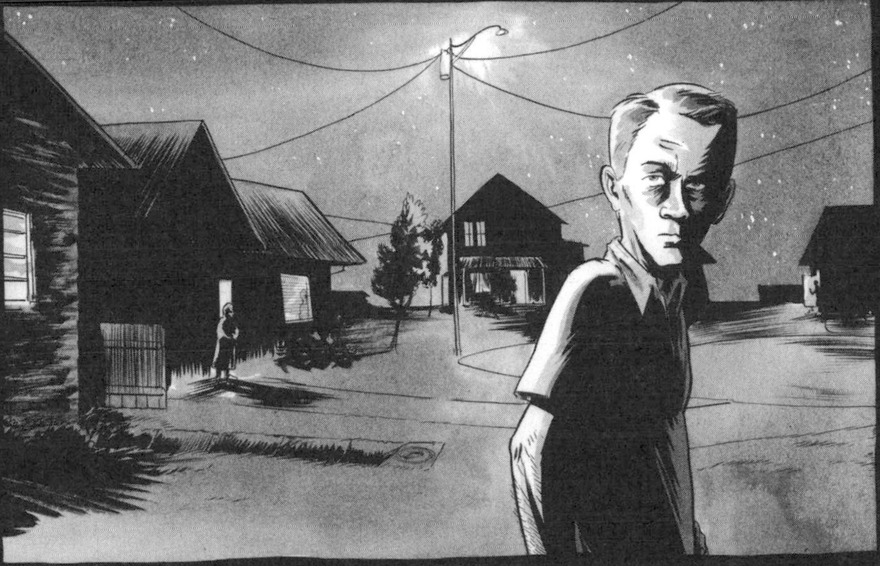
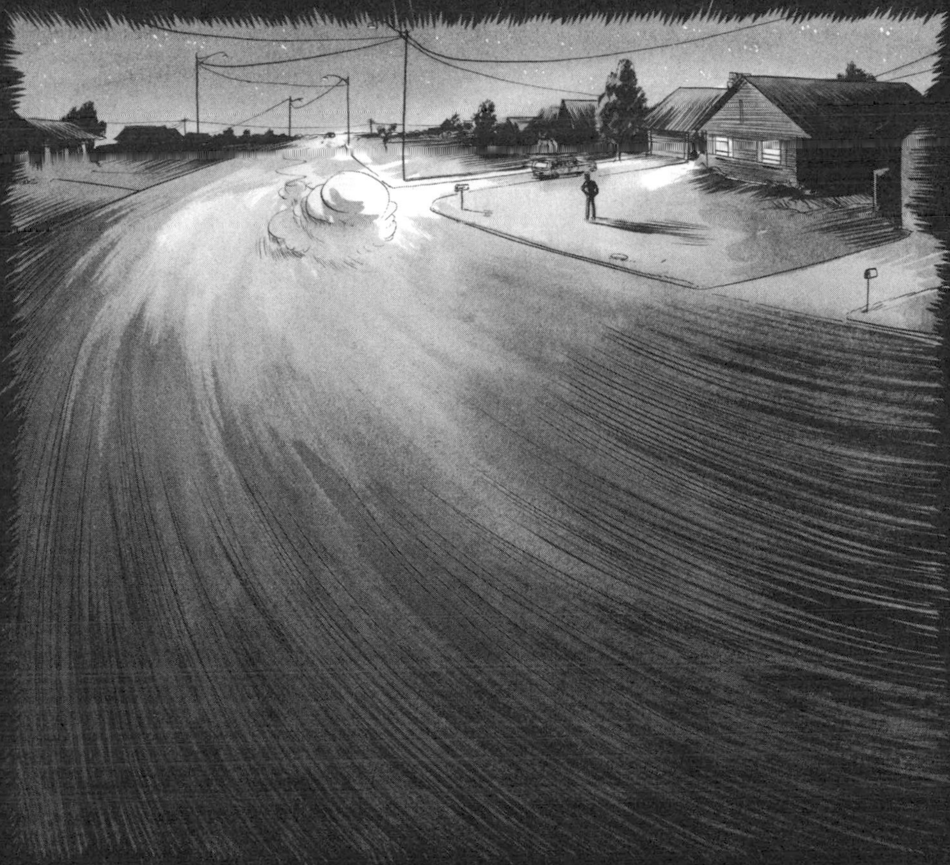

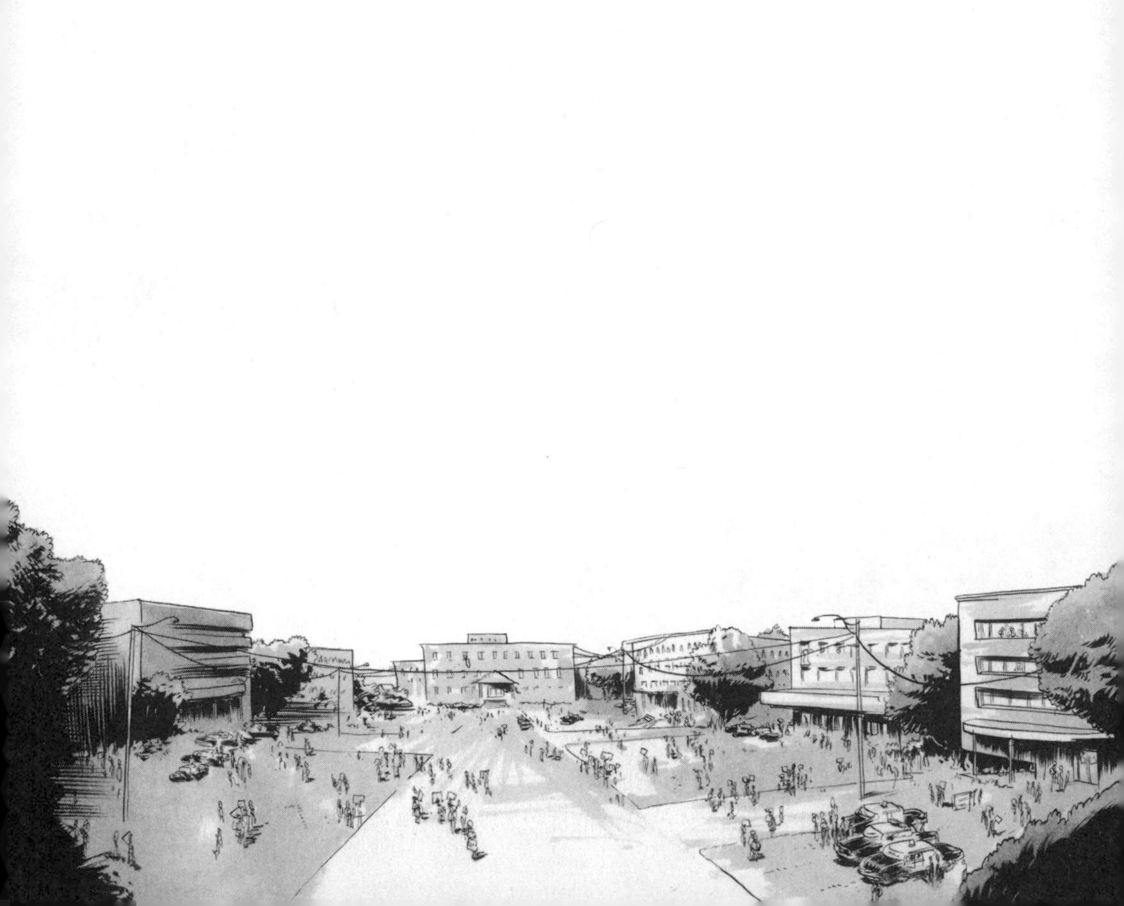

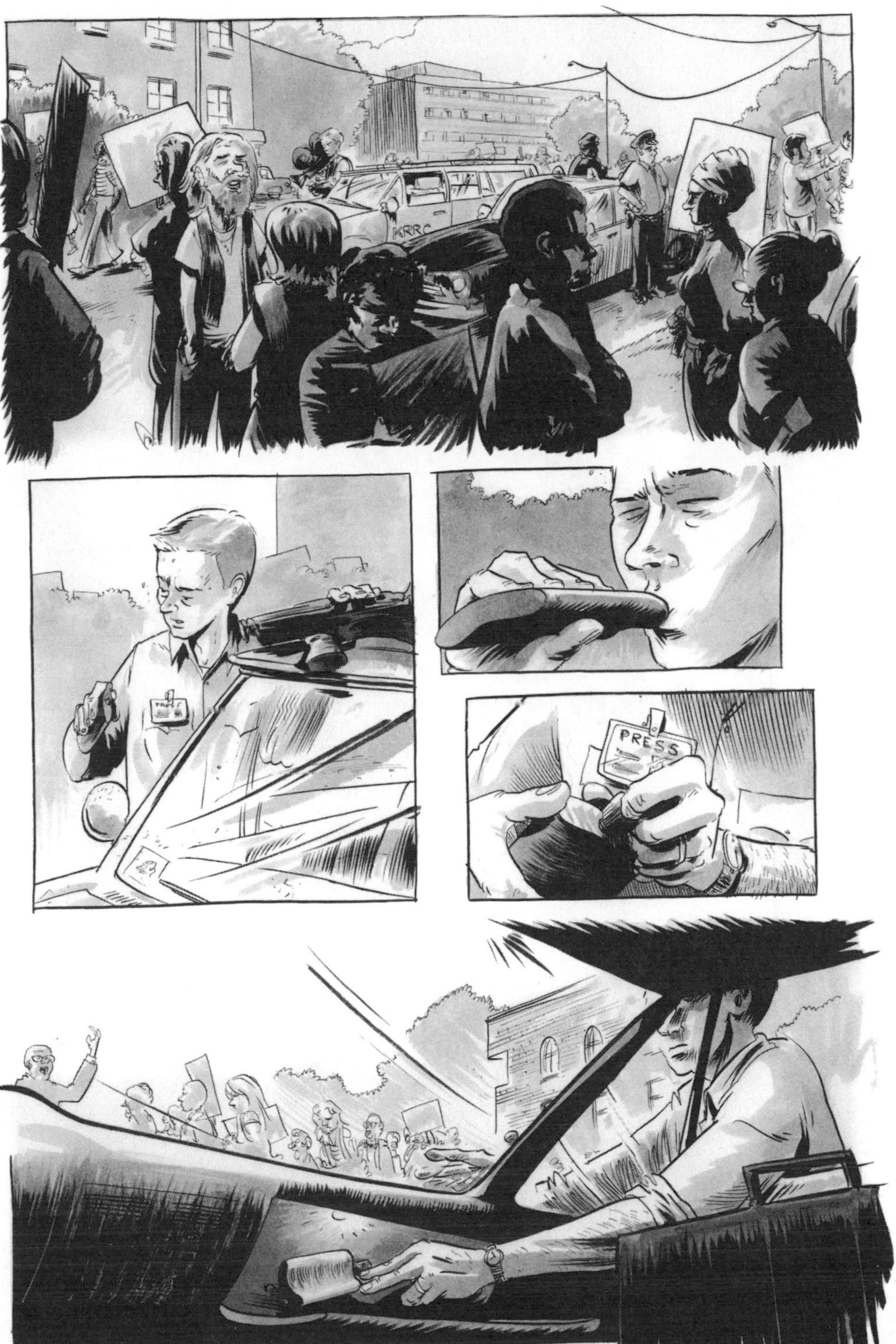
KRRC
PRESS

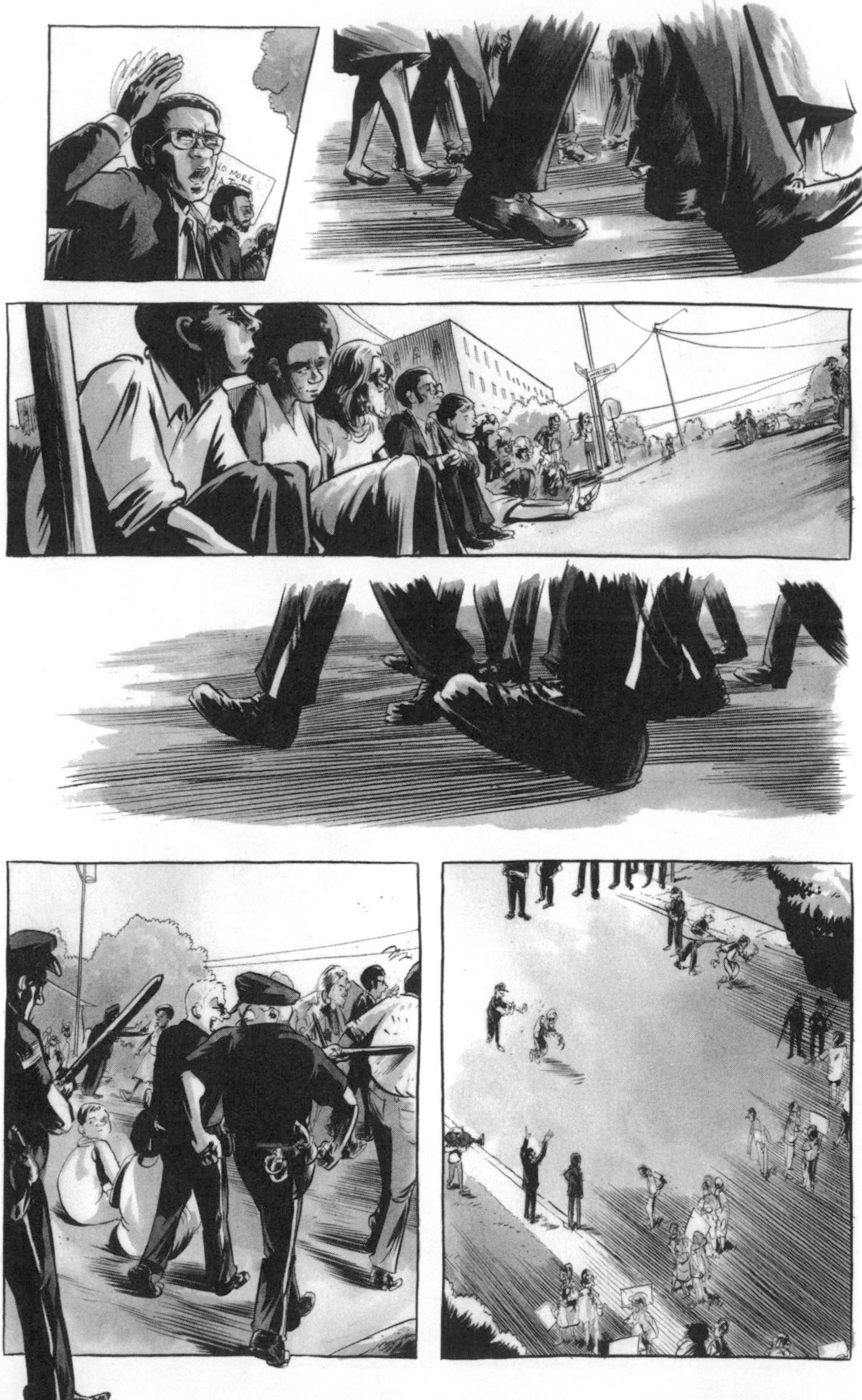
NO MORE

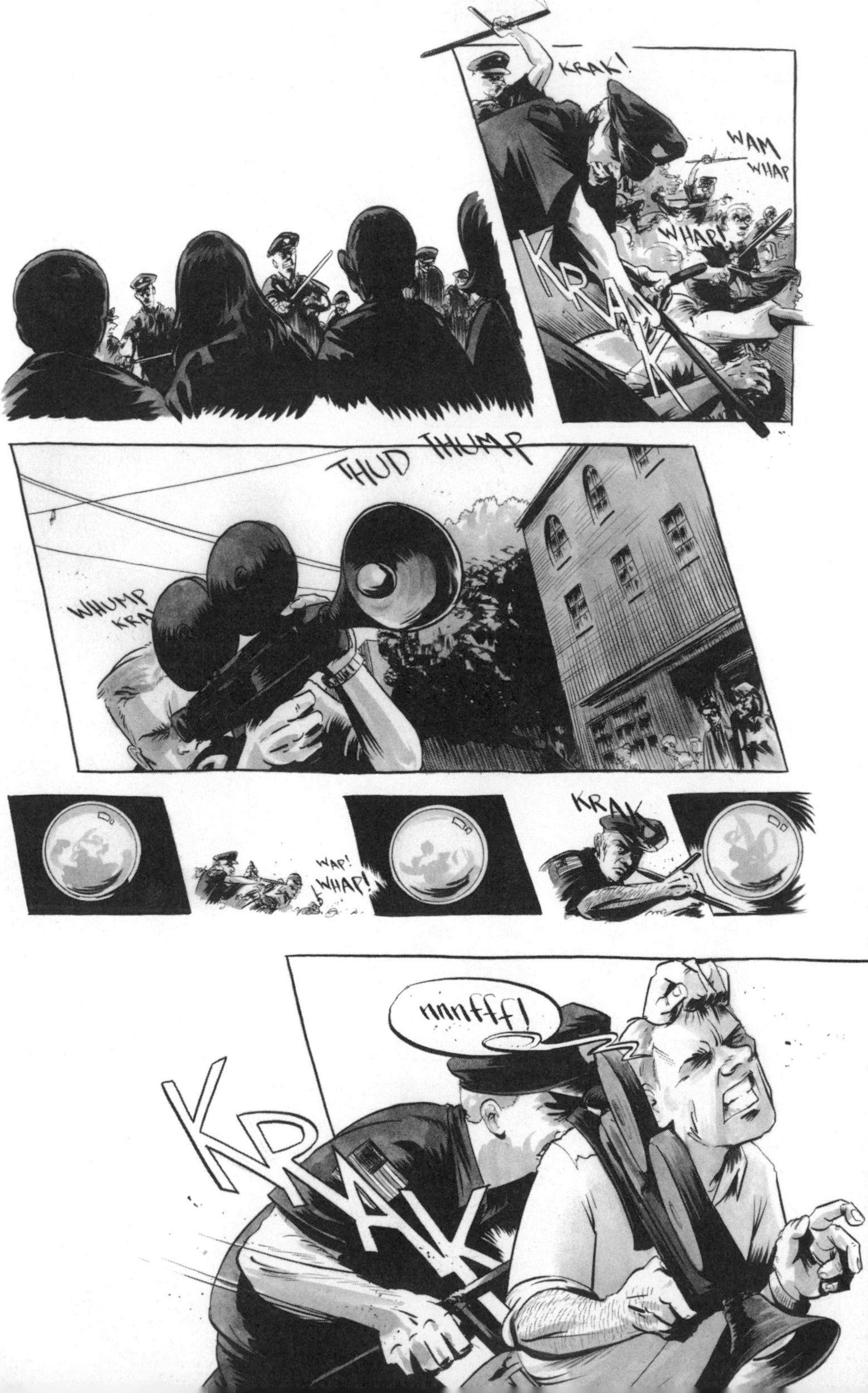
KRAK!
WAM
WHAP
WHAP!
KRAAK
THUD THUMP
WHUMP
KRAK
WAP!
WHAP!
KRAK
nnnfff!
KRAK

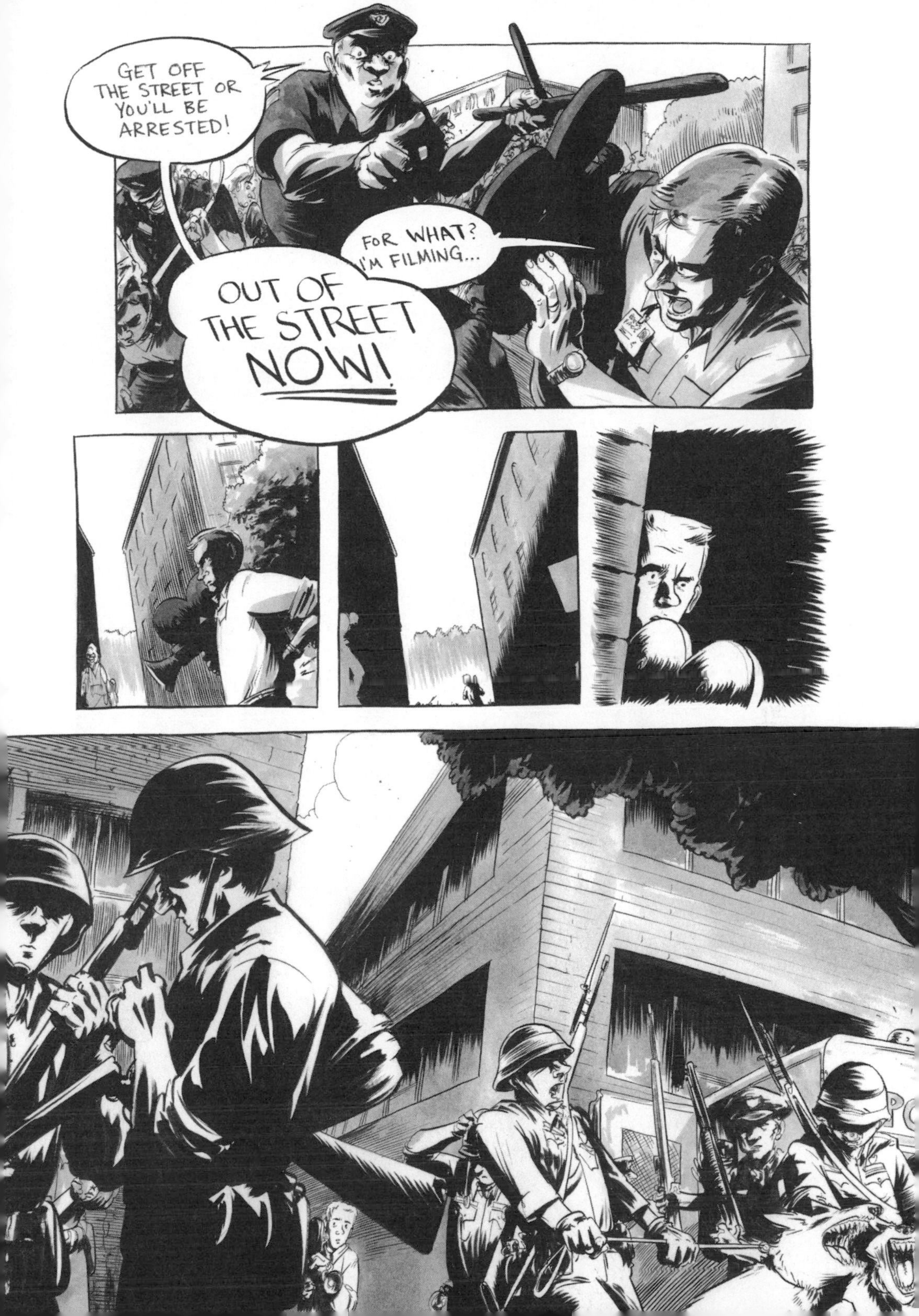
GET OFF THE STREET OR YOU'LL BE ARRESTED!
FOR WHAT? I'M FILMING...
OUT OF THE STREET NOW!

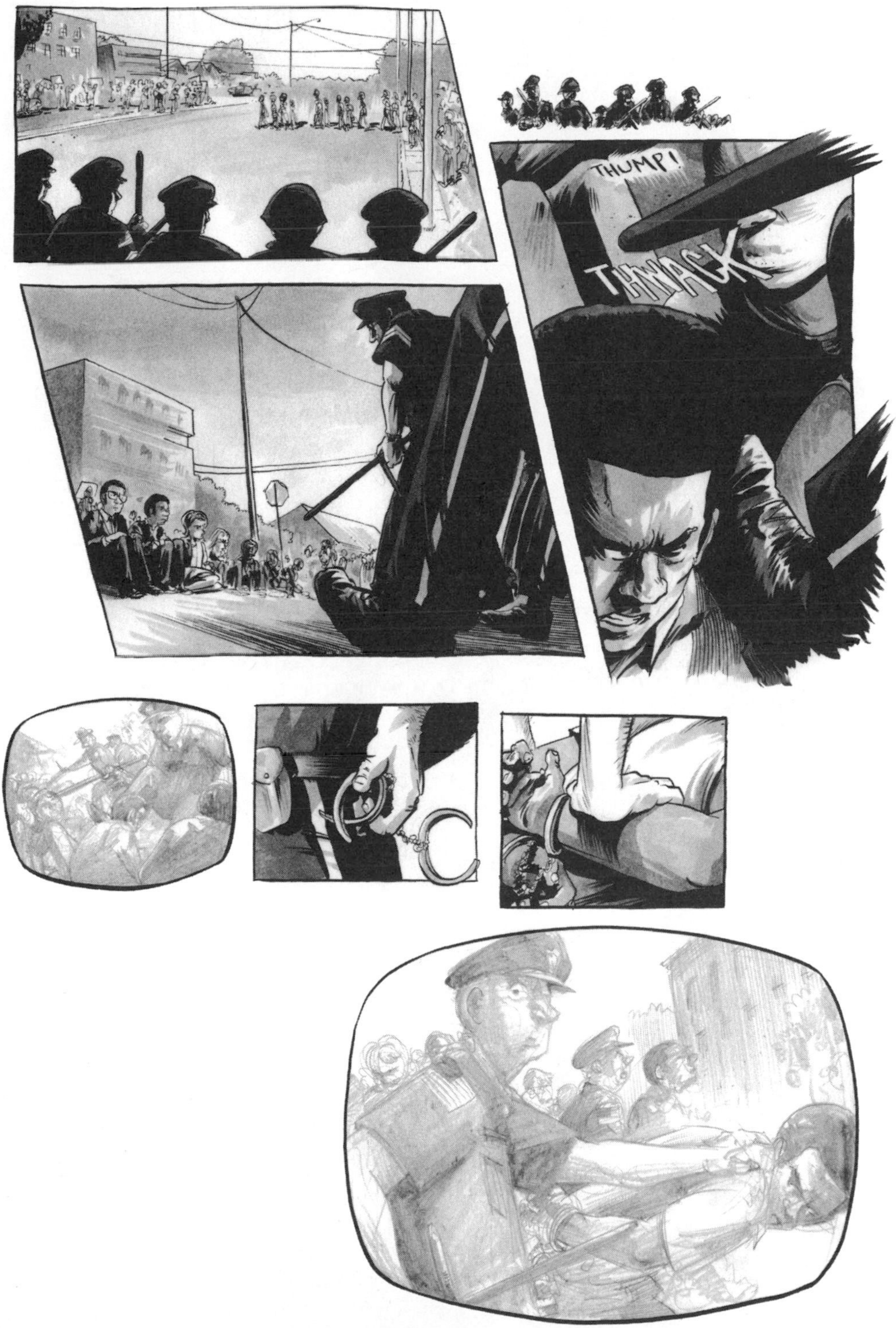
THUMP!
THWACK

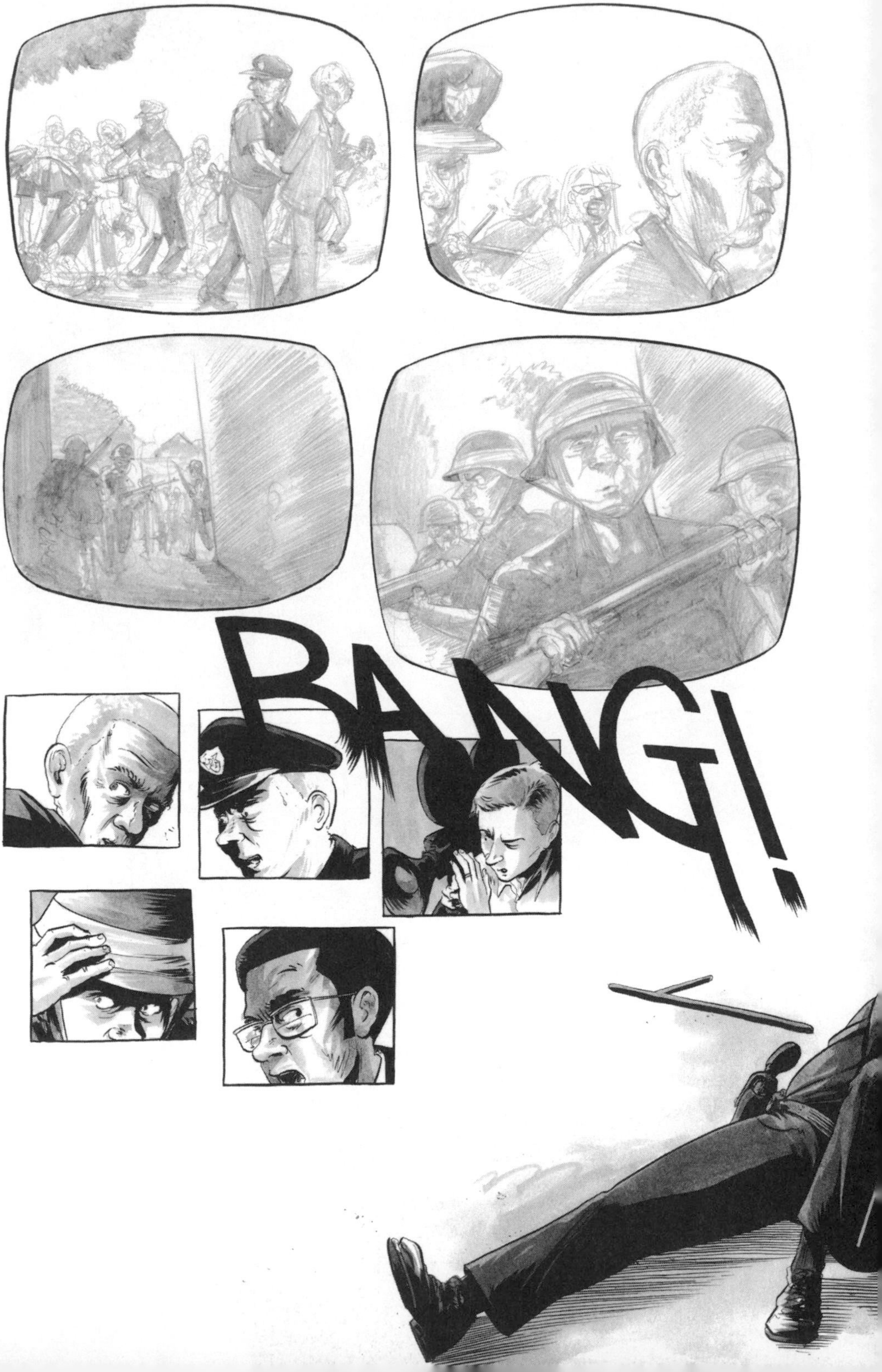
BANG!

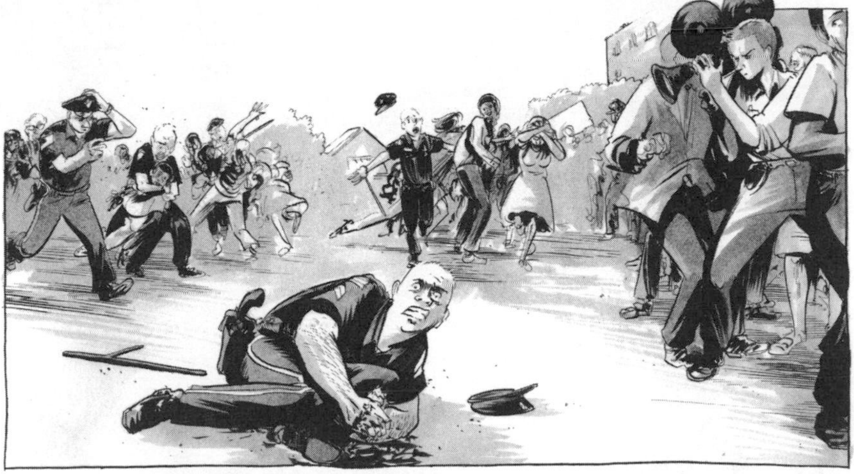

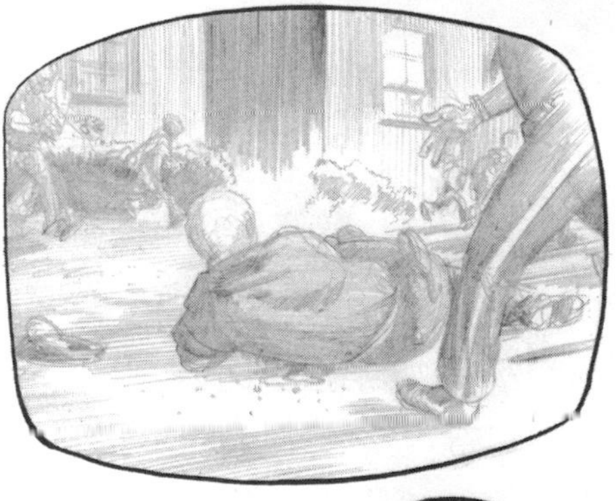

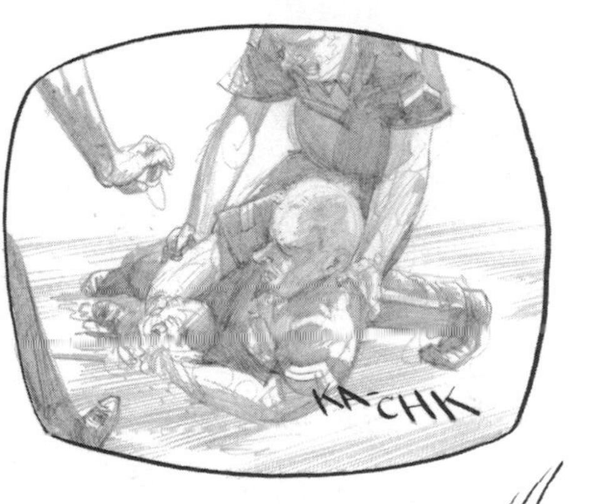
KA-CHK

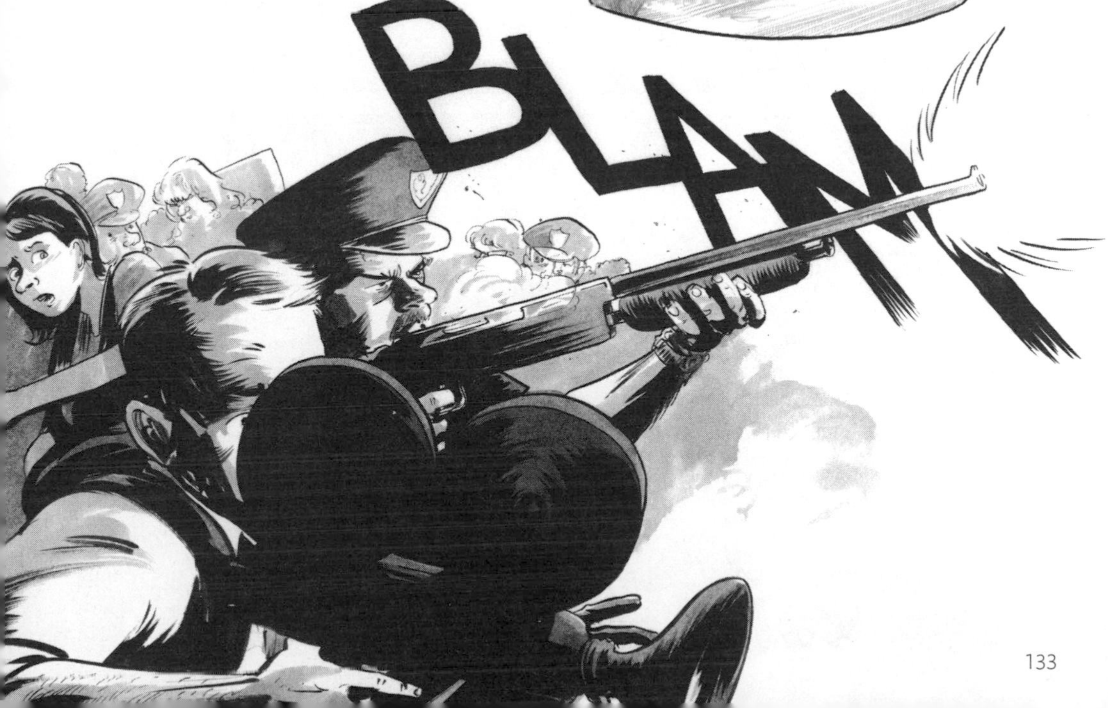
BLAM

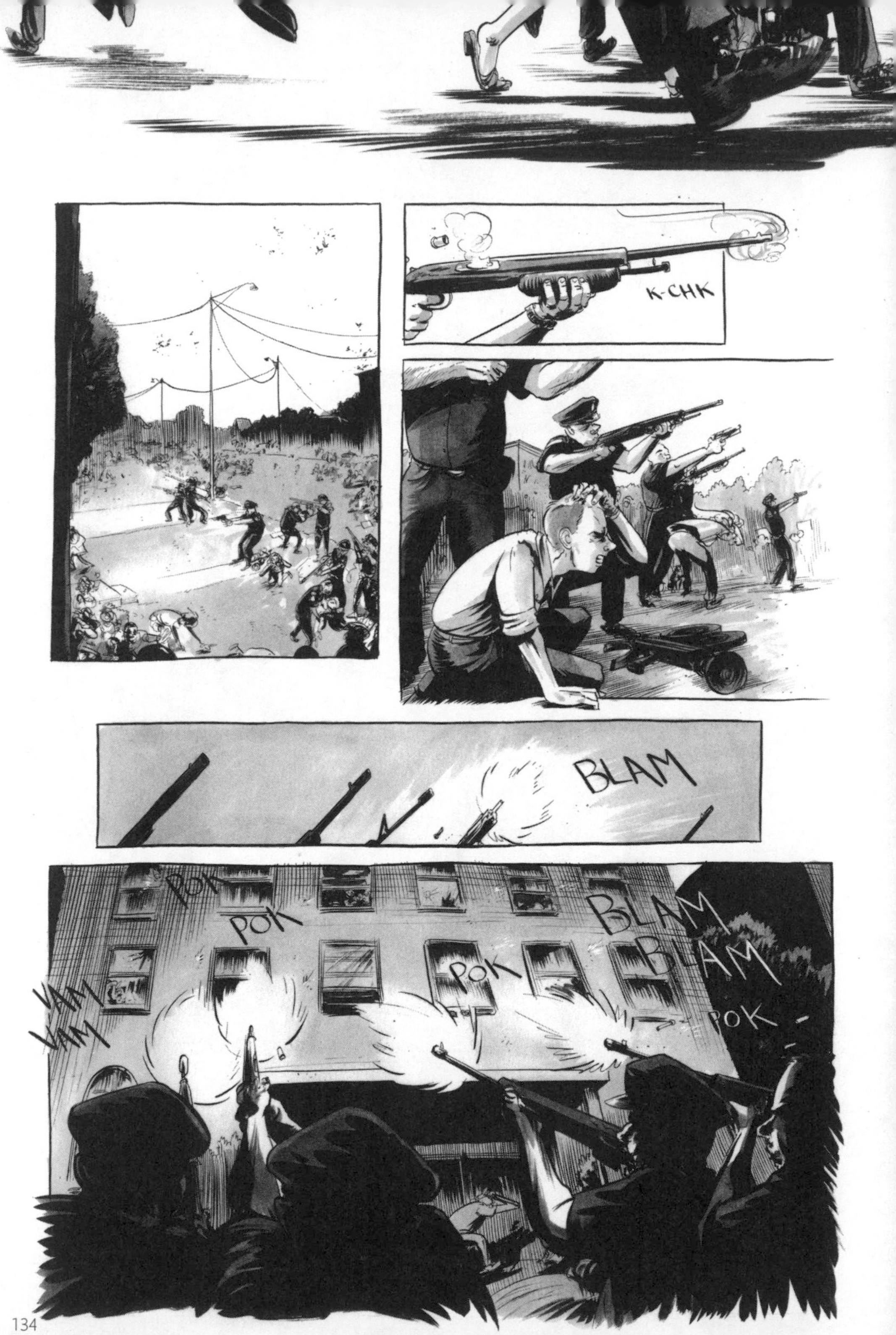
K-CHK
BLAM
POK
POK
VAM
VAM
POK
BLAM
BLAM
POK

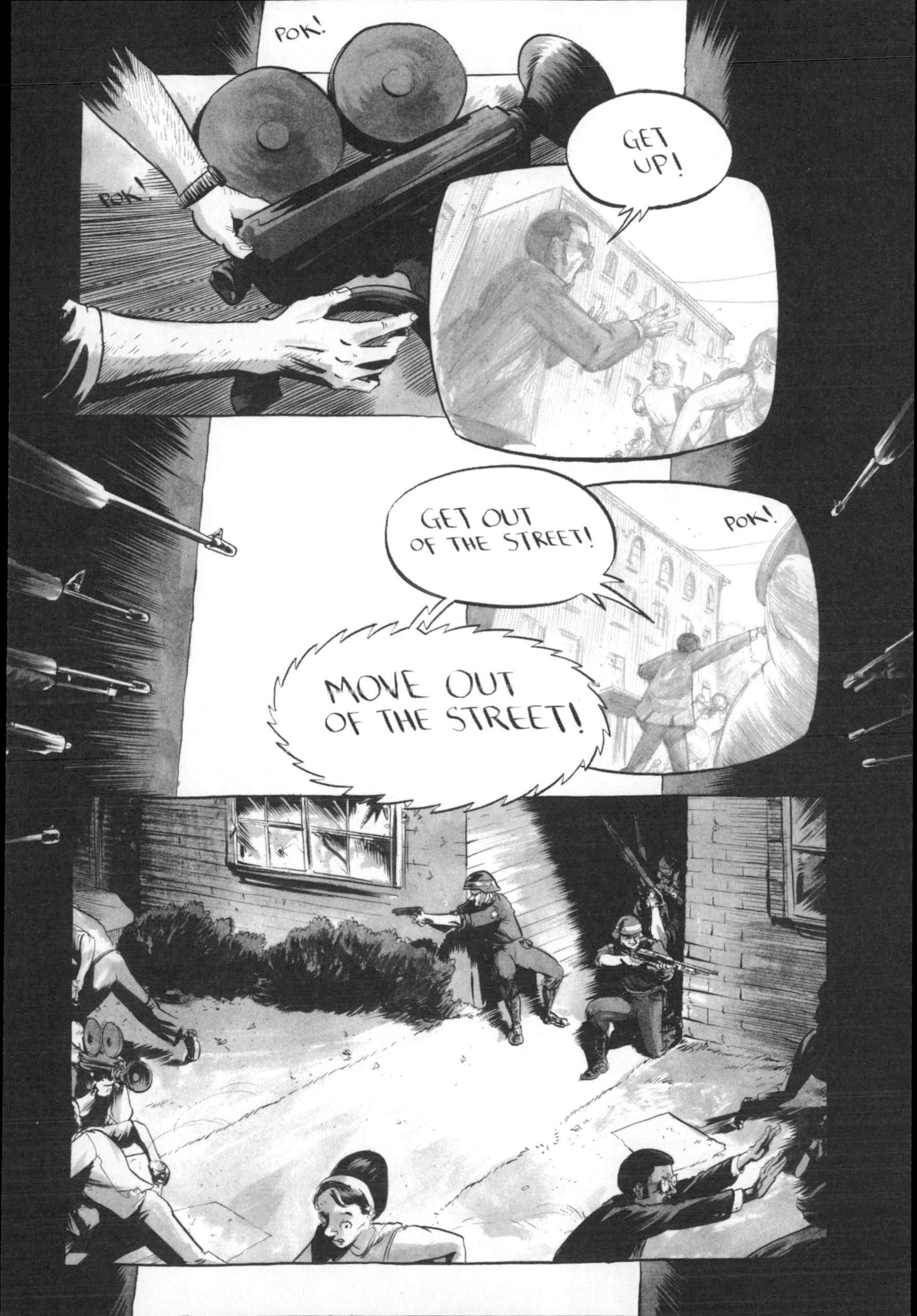
POK!
POK!
GET UP!
GET OUT OF THE STREET!
POK!
MOVE OUT OF THE STREET!

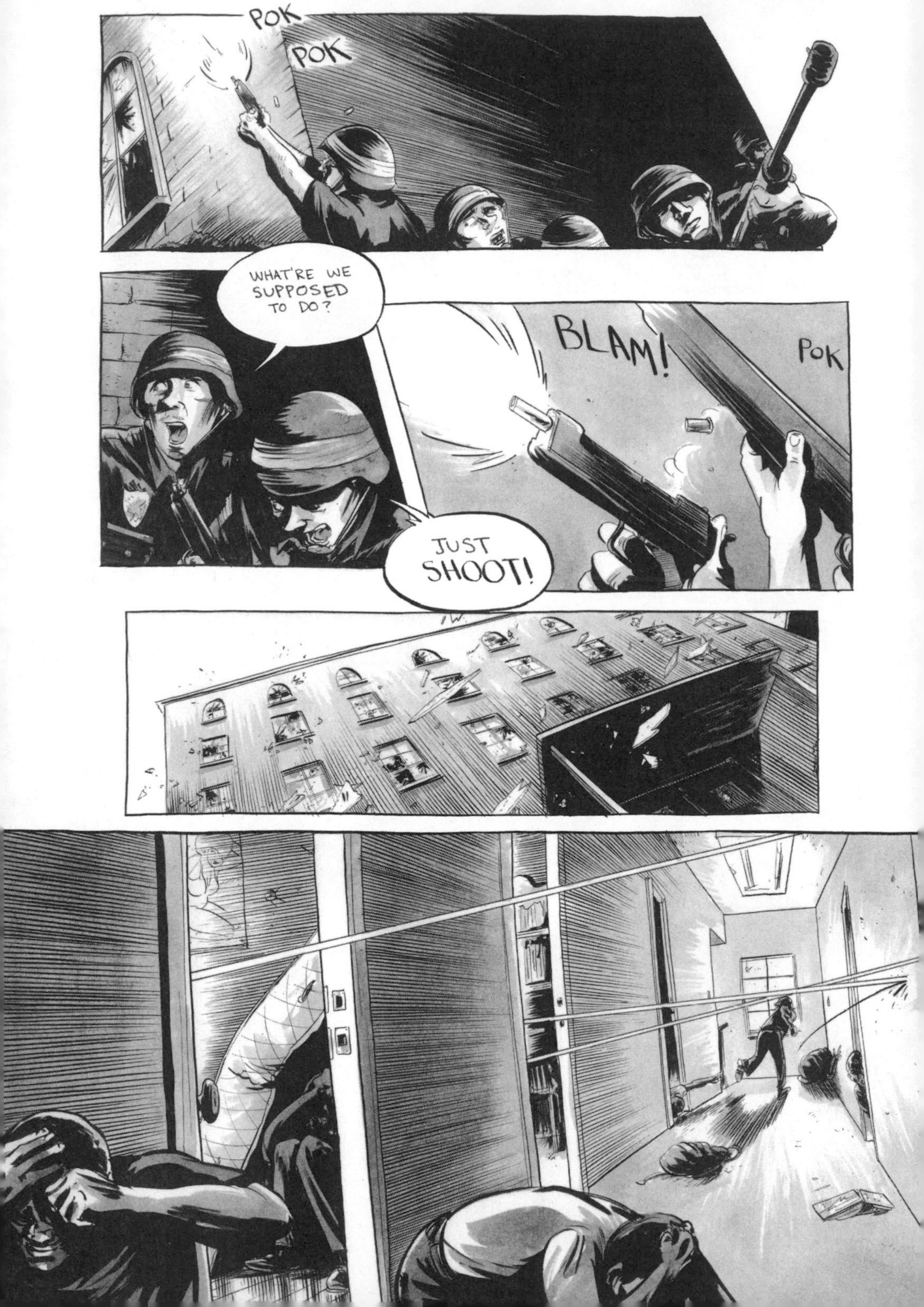
POK
POK
WHAT'RE WE SUPPOSED TO DO?
BLAM!
POK
JUST SHOOT!

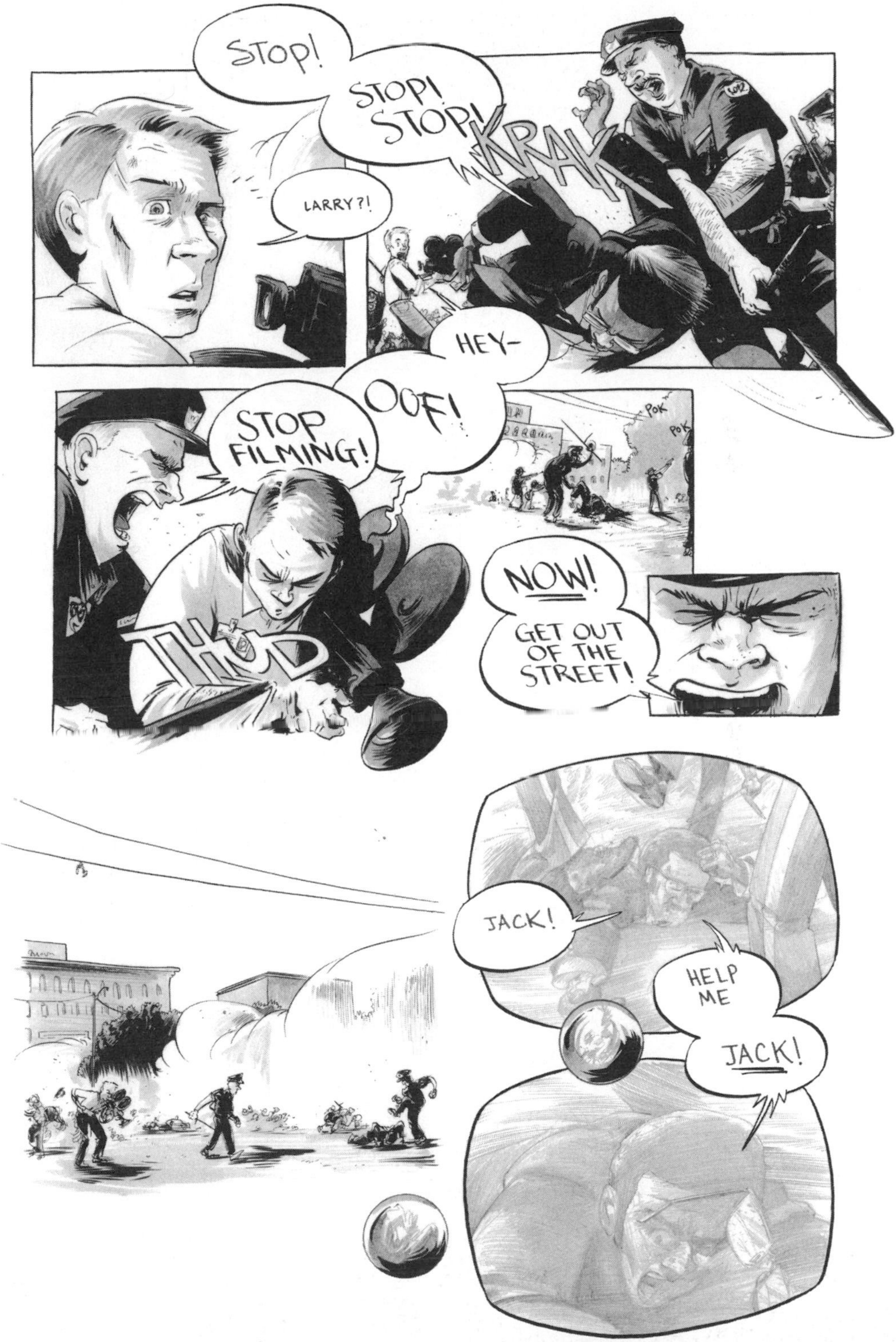
STOP!
STOP! STOP!
KRAK
LARRY?!
HEY-
STOP FILMING!
OOF!
THUD
POK
POK
NOW!
GET OUT OF THE STREET!
JACK!
HELP ME
JACK!

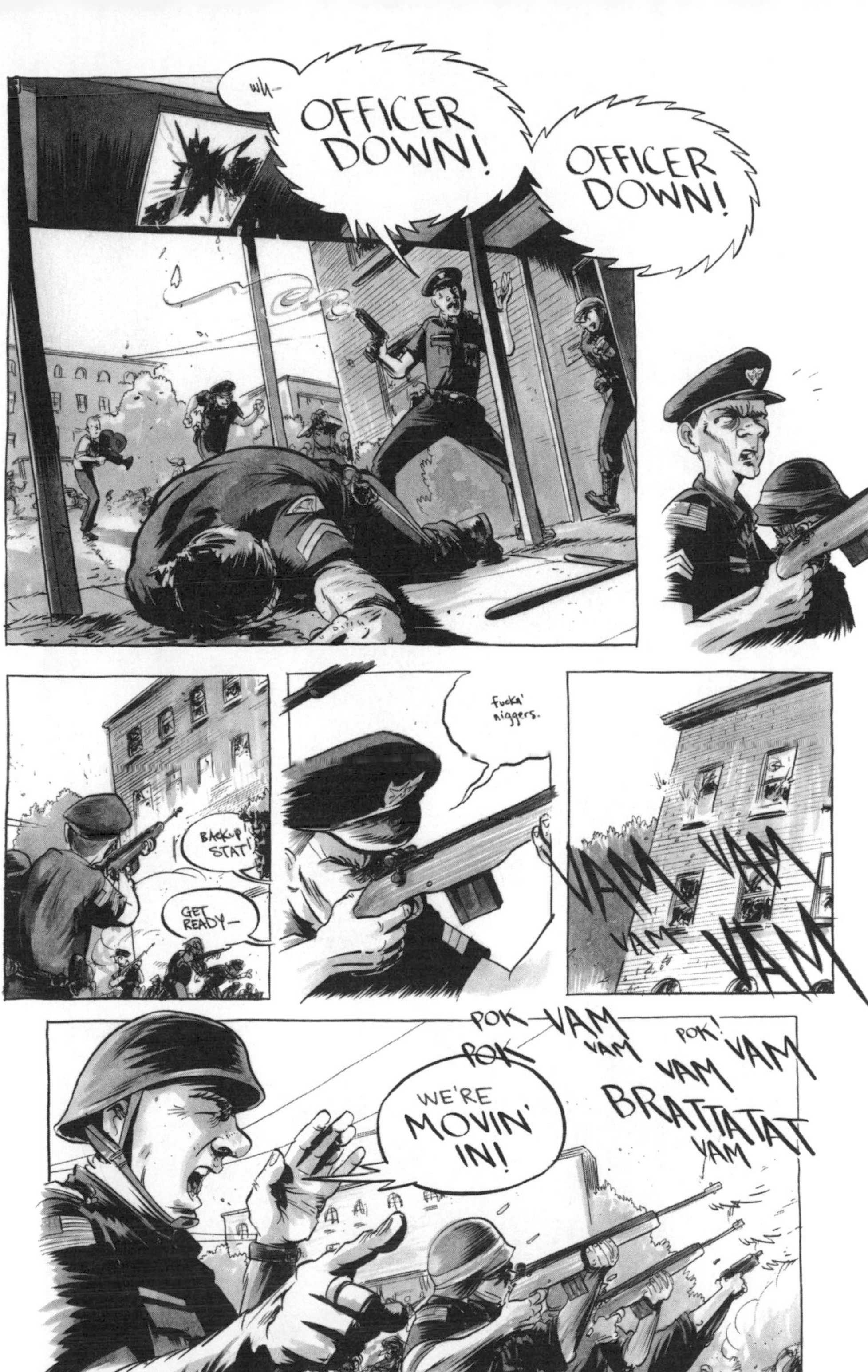

wu-
OFFICER DOWN!
OFFICER DOWN!
BACKUP STAT!
GET READY—
fucka' niggers.
VAM VAM
VAM VAM
POK POK VAM VAM
POK! VAM VAM
WE'RE MOVIN' IN!
BRATTATAT
VAM

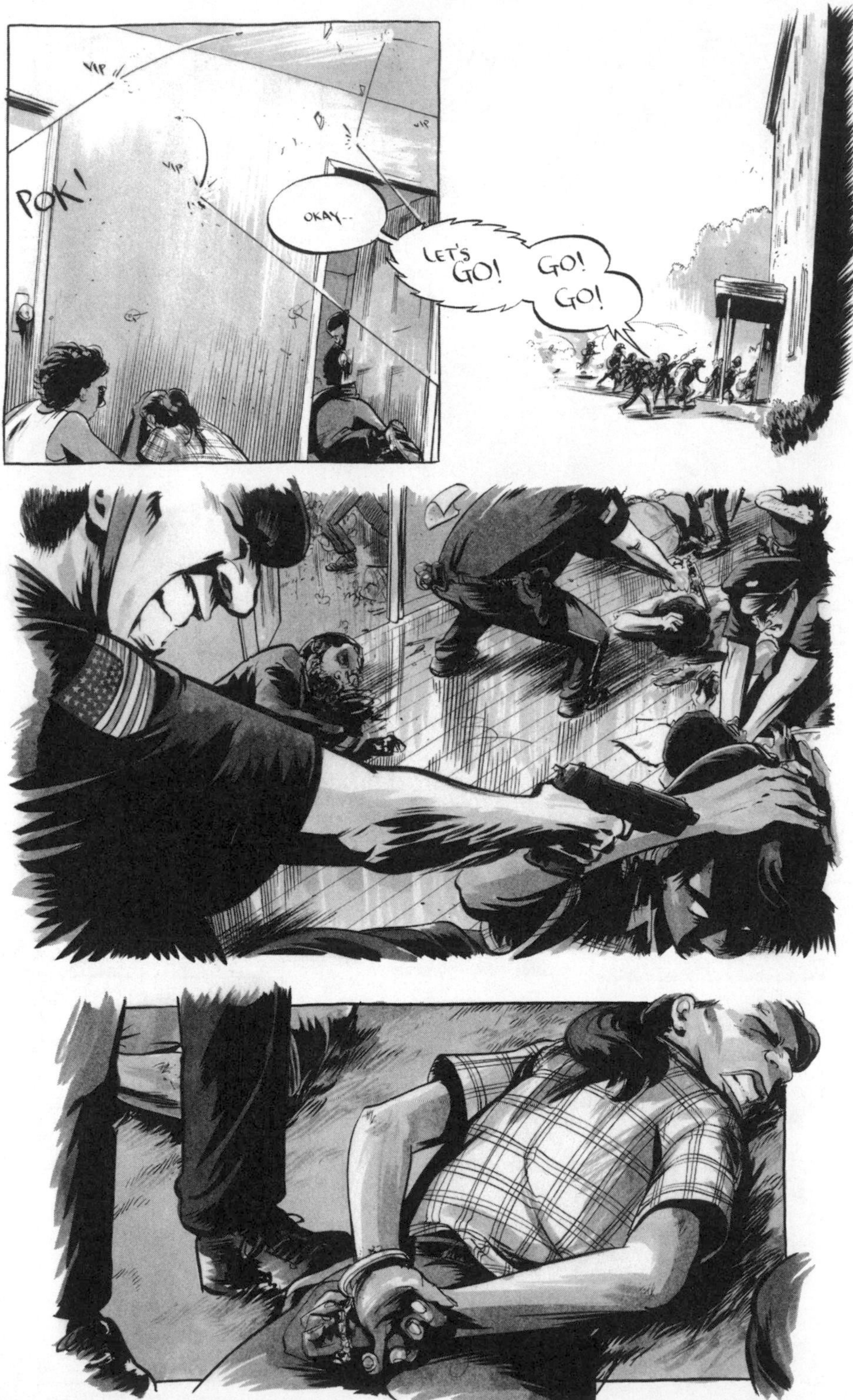
VIP
VIP
VIP
VIP
POK!
OKAY--
LET'S GO!
GO! GO!

142

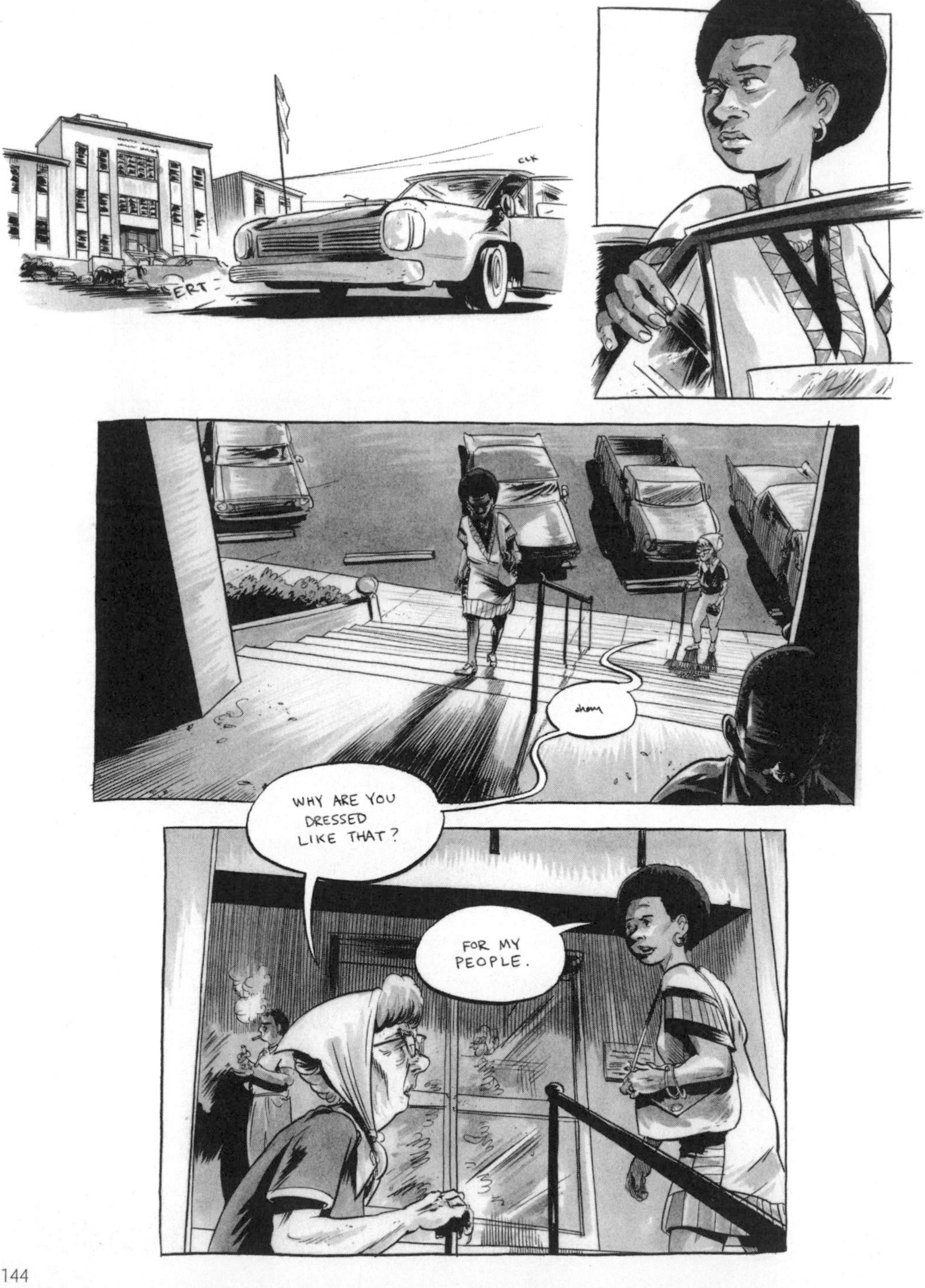
CLK
ERT
ahem
WHY ARE YOU DRESSED LIKE THAT?
FOR MY PEOPLE.

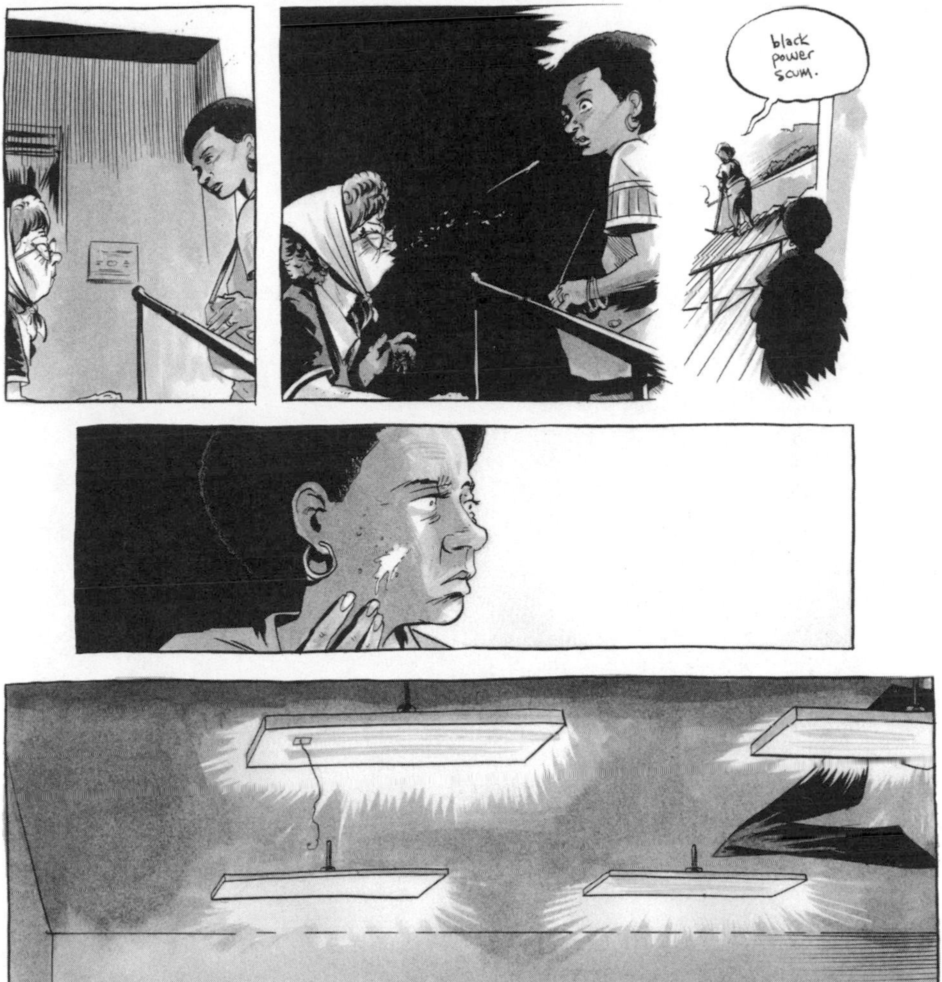
black power scum.
TEXAS

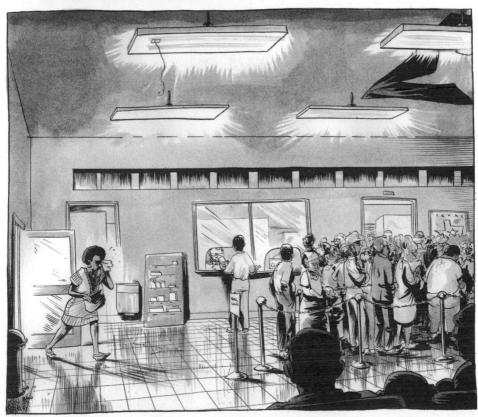

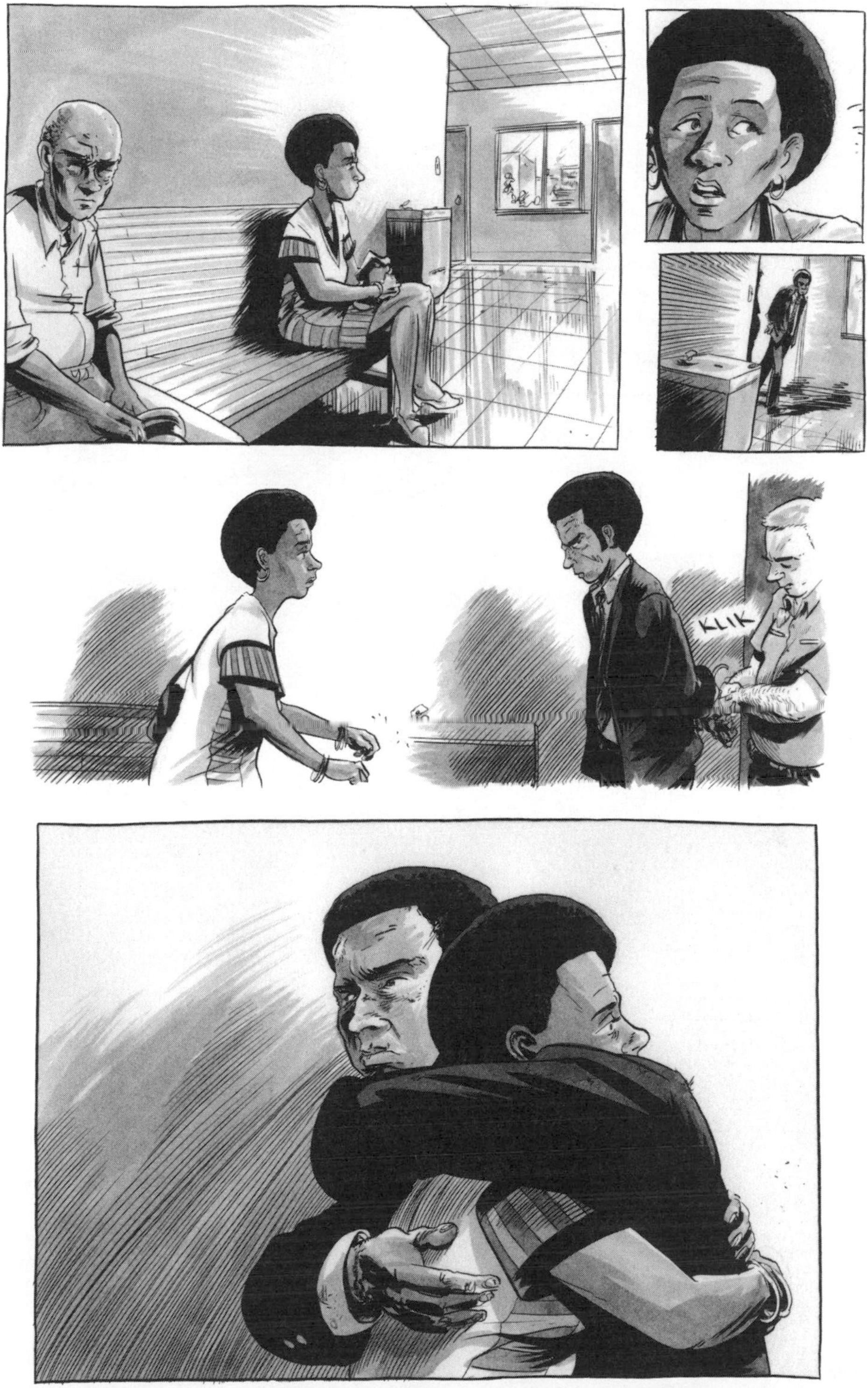
KLIK

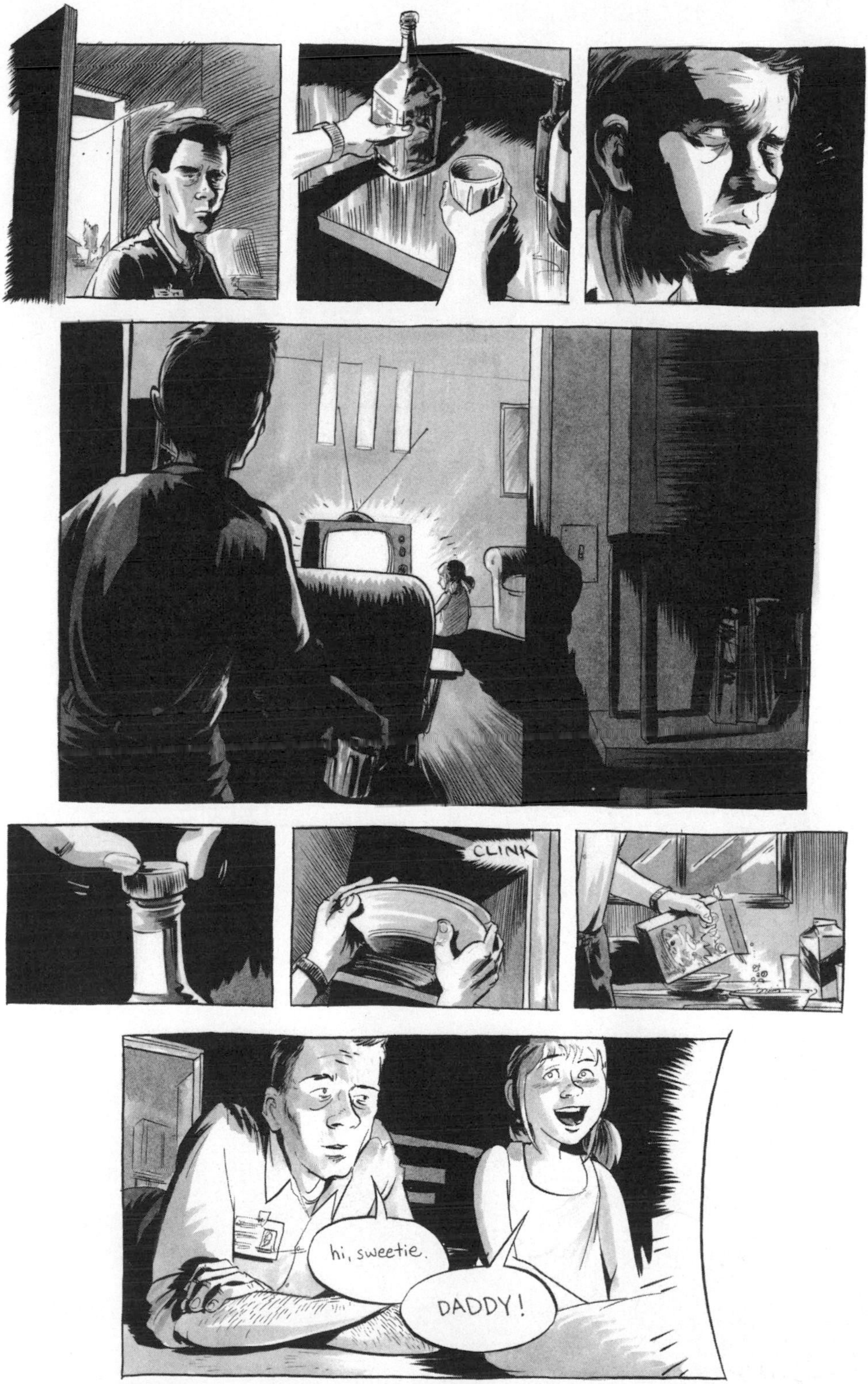
CLINK
hi, sweetie.
DADDY!

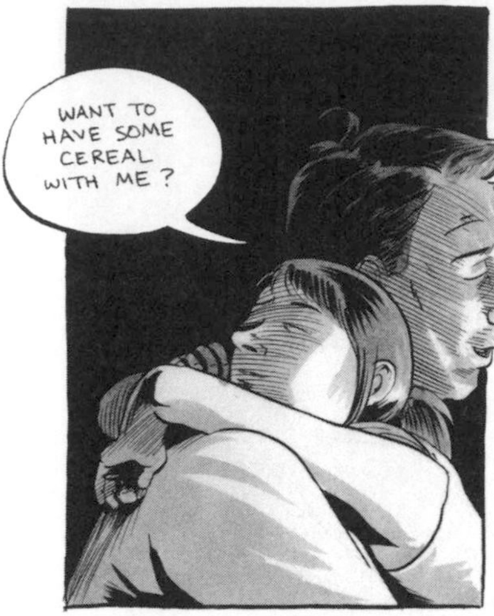
WANT TO HAVE SOME CEREAL WITH ME?
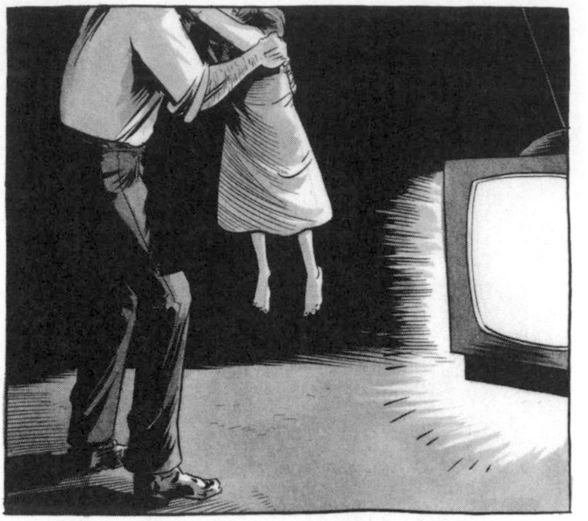
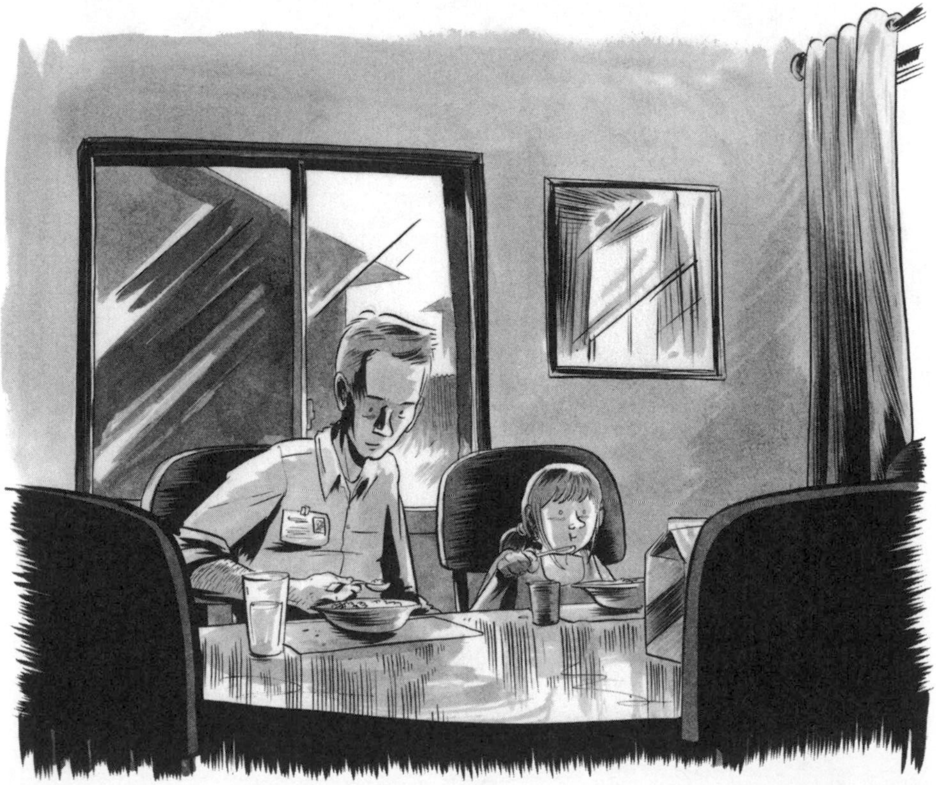

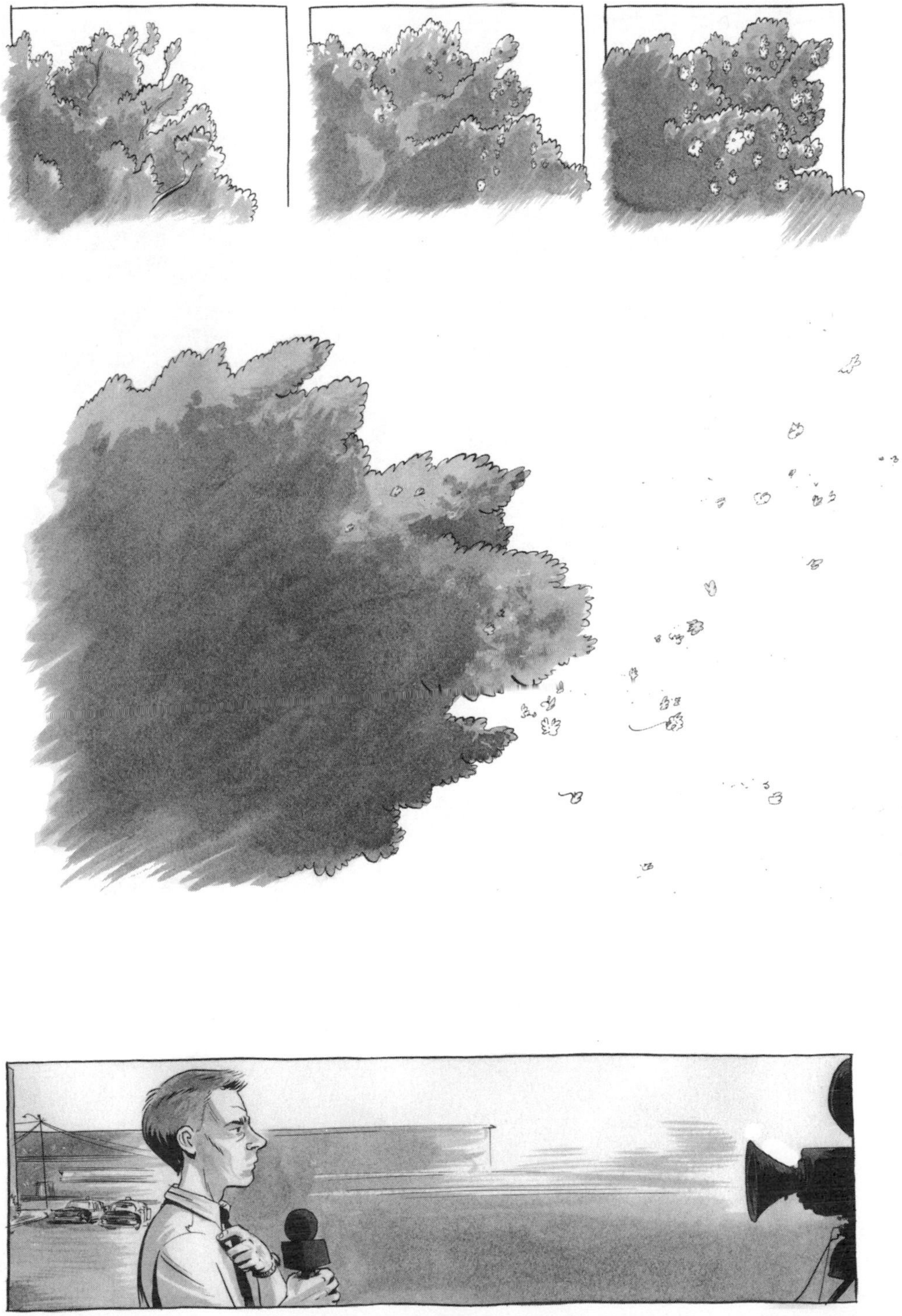

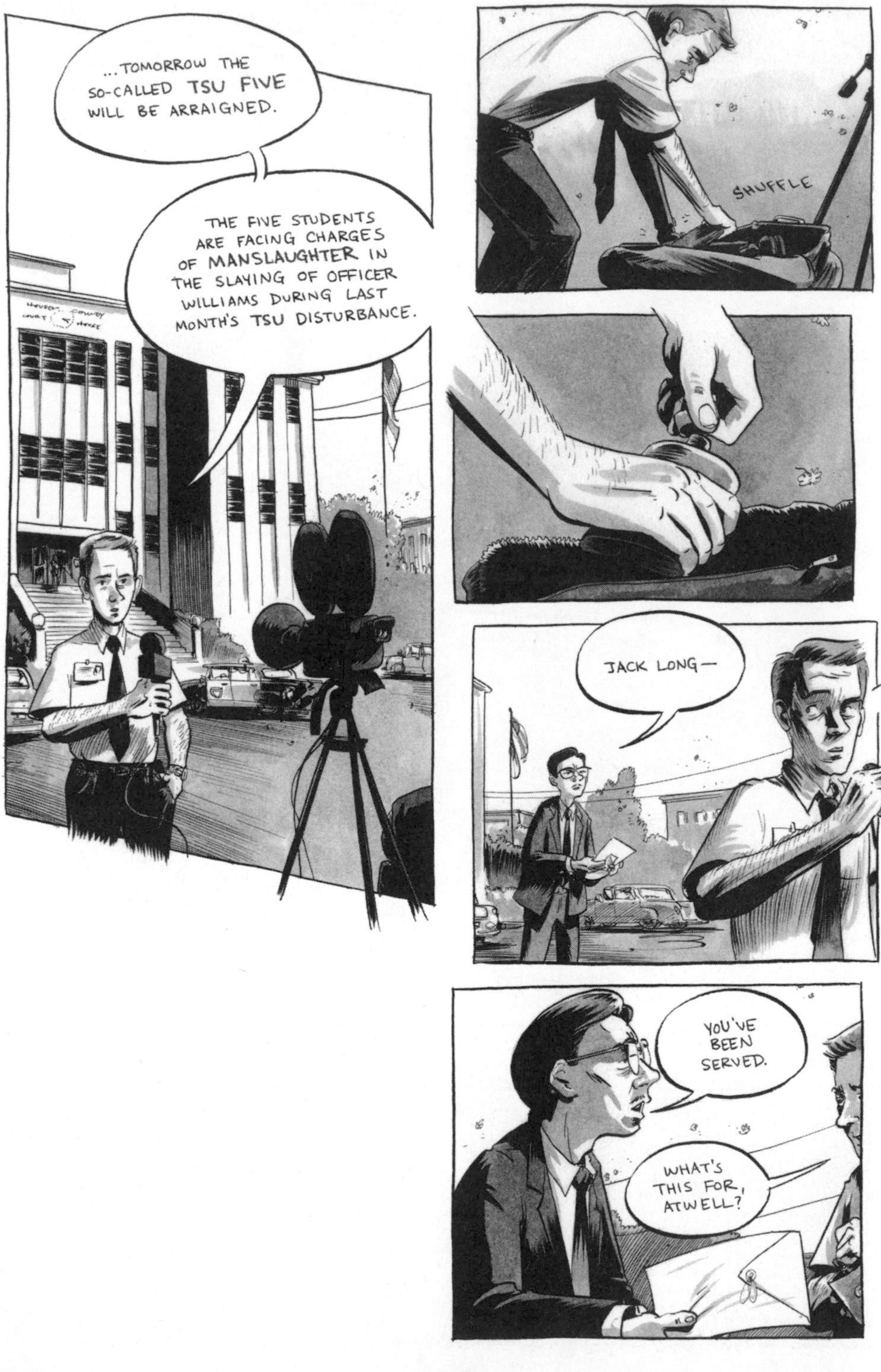
...TOMORROW THE SO-CALLED TSU FIVE WILL BE ARRAIGNED.
THE FIVE STUDENTS ARE FACING CHARGES OF MANSLAUGHTER IN THE SLAYING OF OFFICER WILLIAMS DURING LAST MONTH'S TSU DISTURBANCE.
SHUFFLE
JACK LONG—
YOU'VE BEEN SERVED.
WHAT'S THIS FOR, ATWELL?

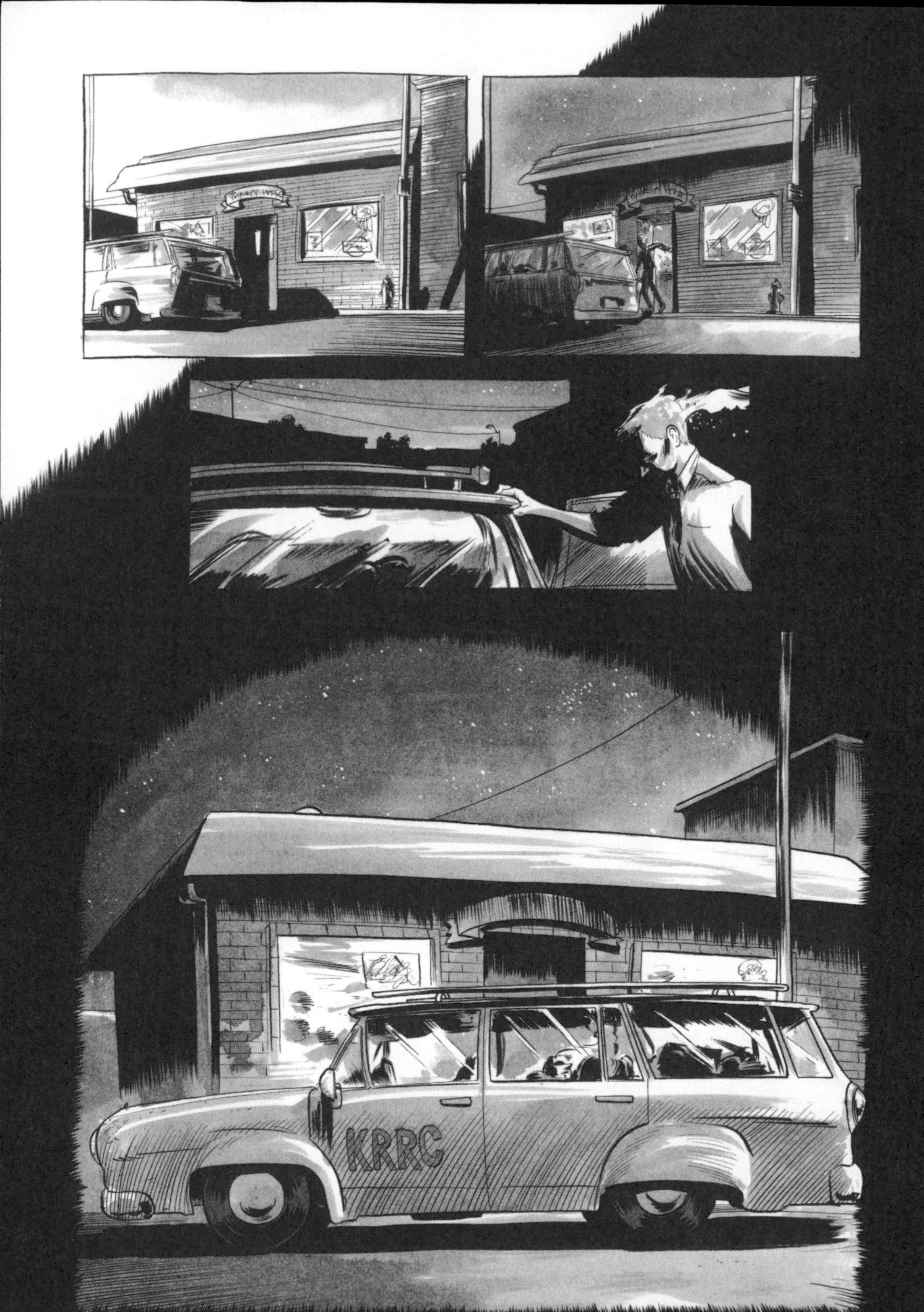
KRRC

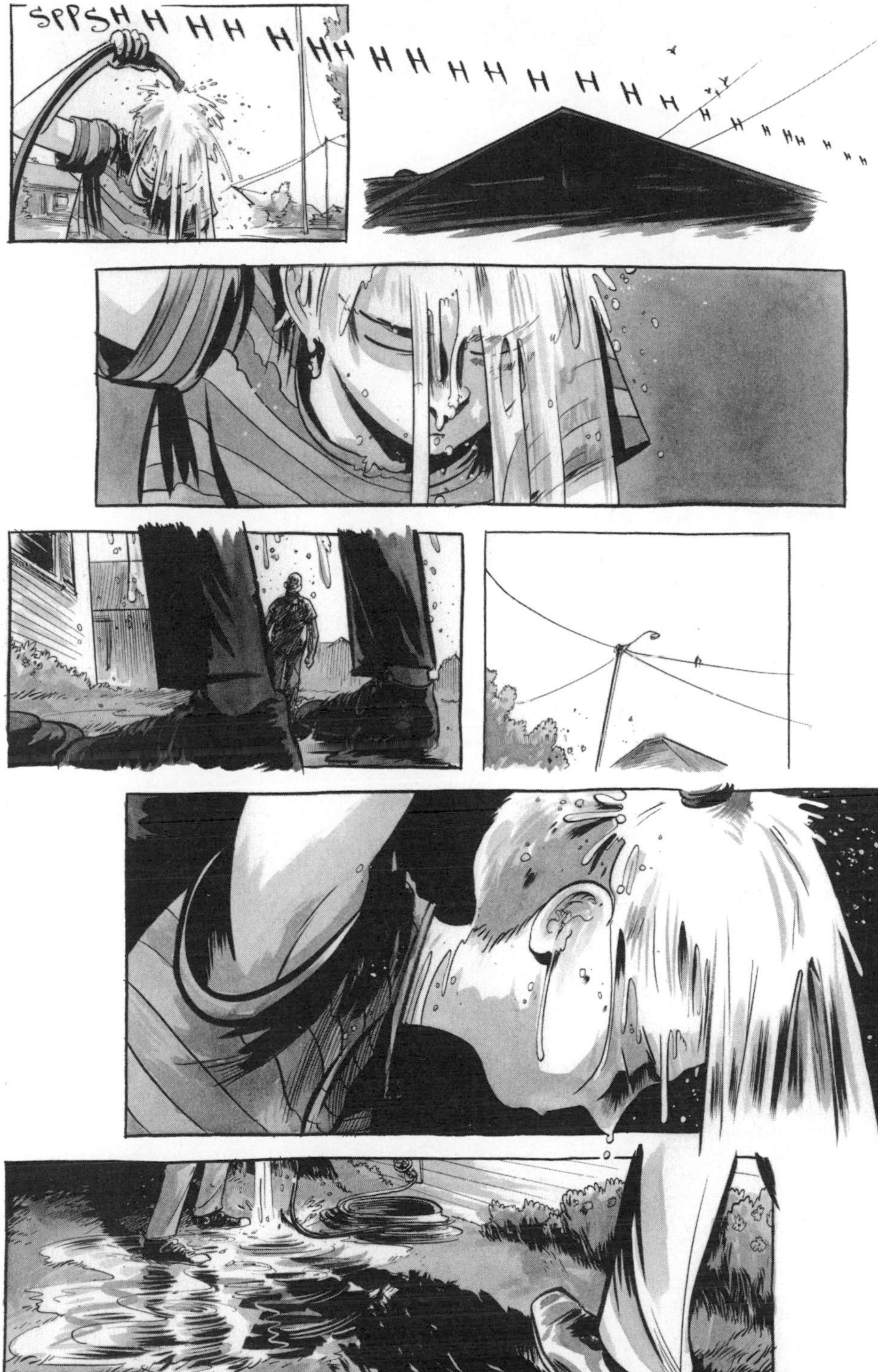
SPPSHHHHHHHHHHHHHHHHHHHHHH

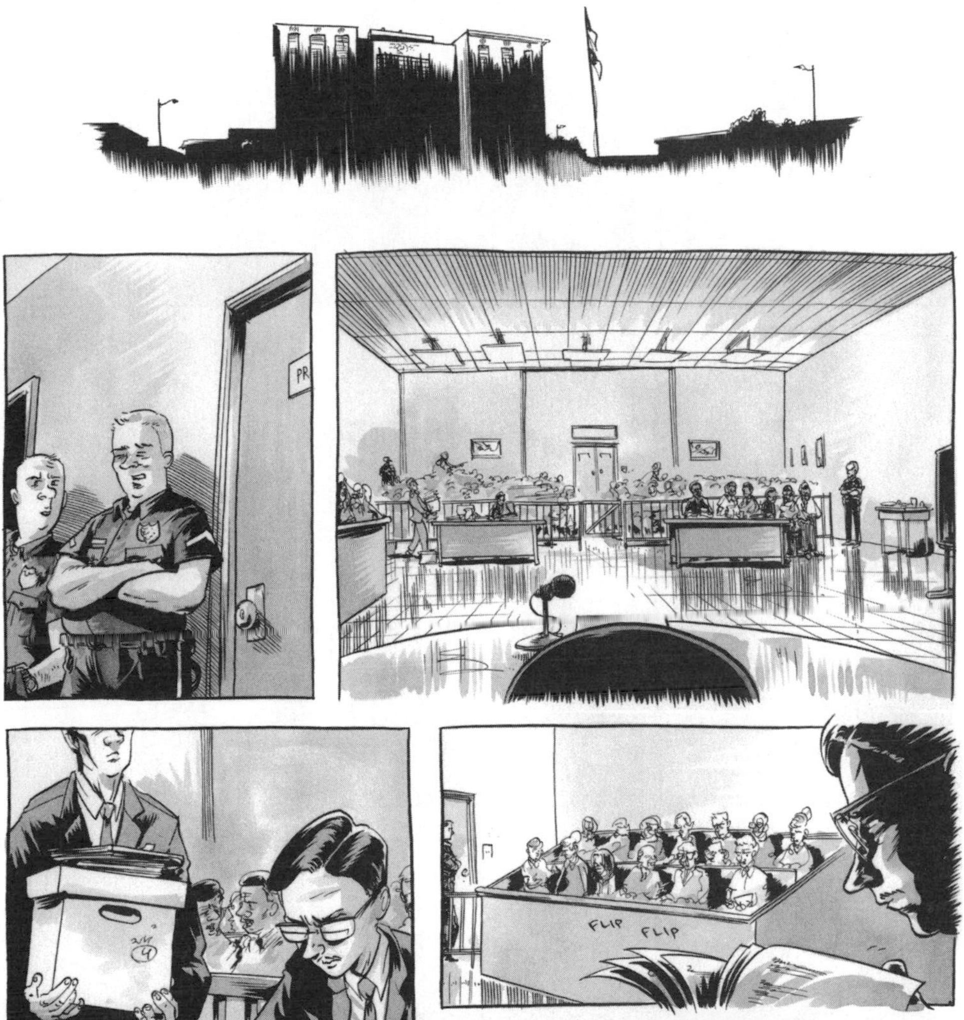
PR
SHUFFLE
FLIP FLIP

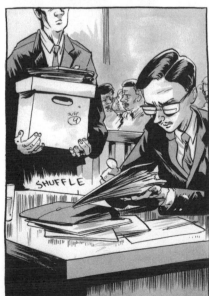

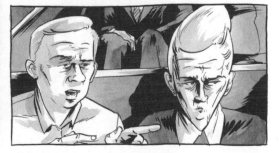

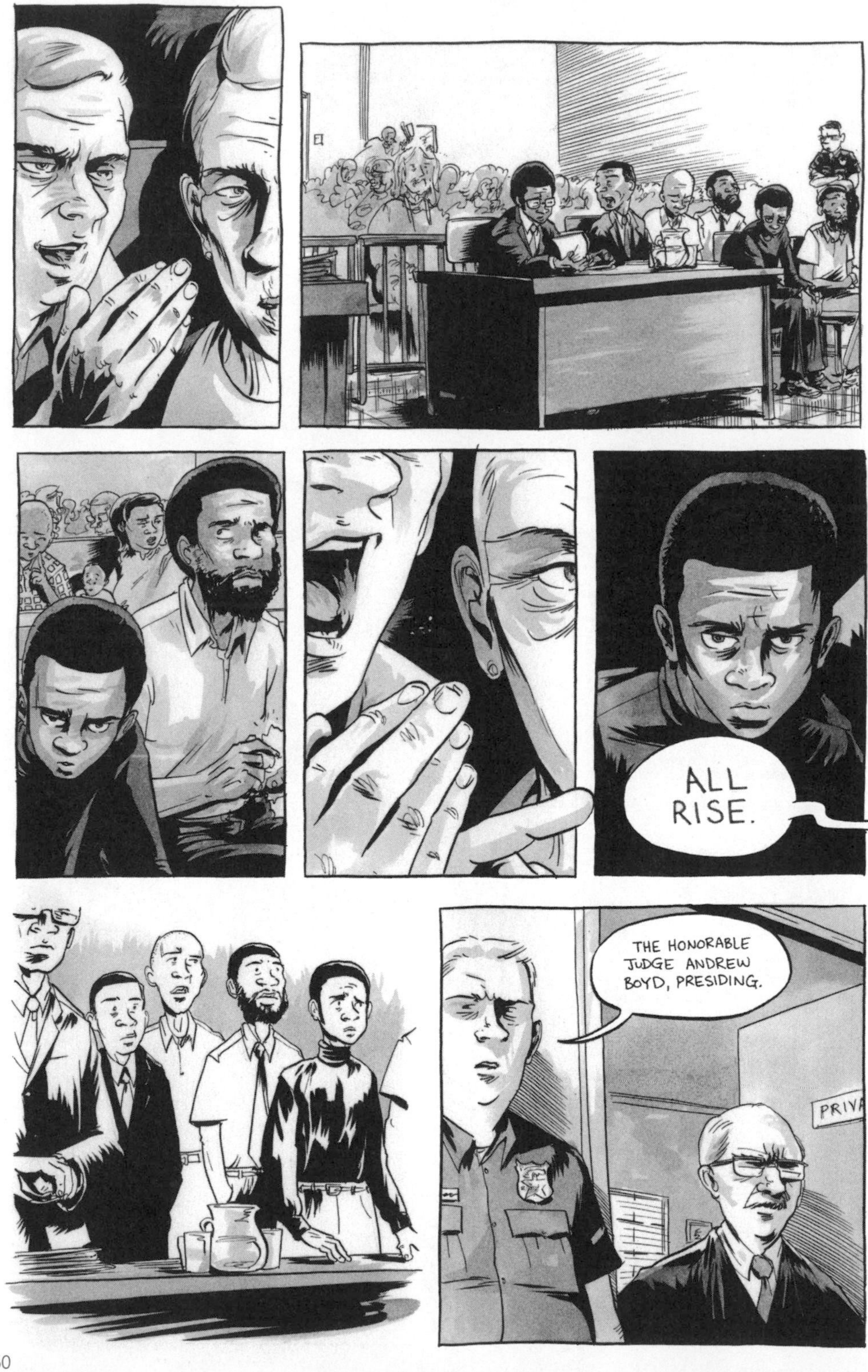
ALL RISE.
THE HONORABLE JUDGE ANDREW BOYD, PRESIDING.
PRIVA

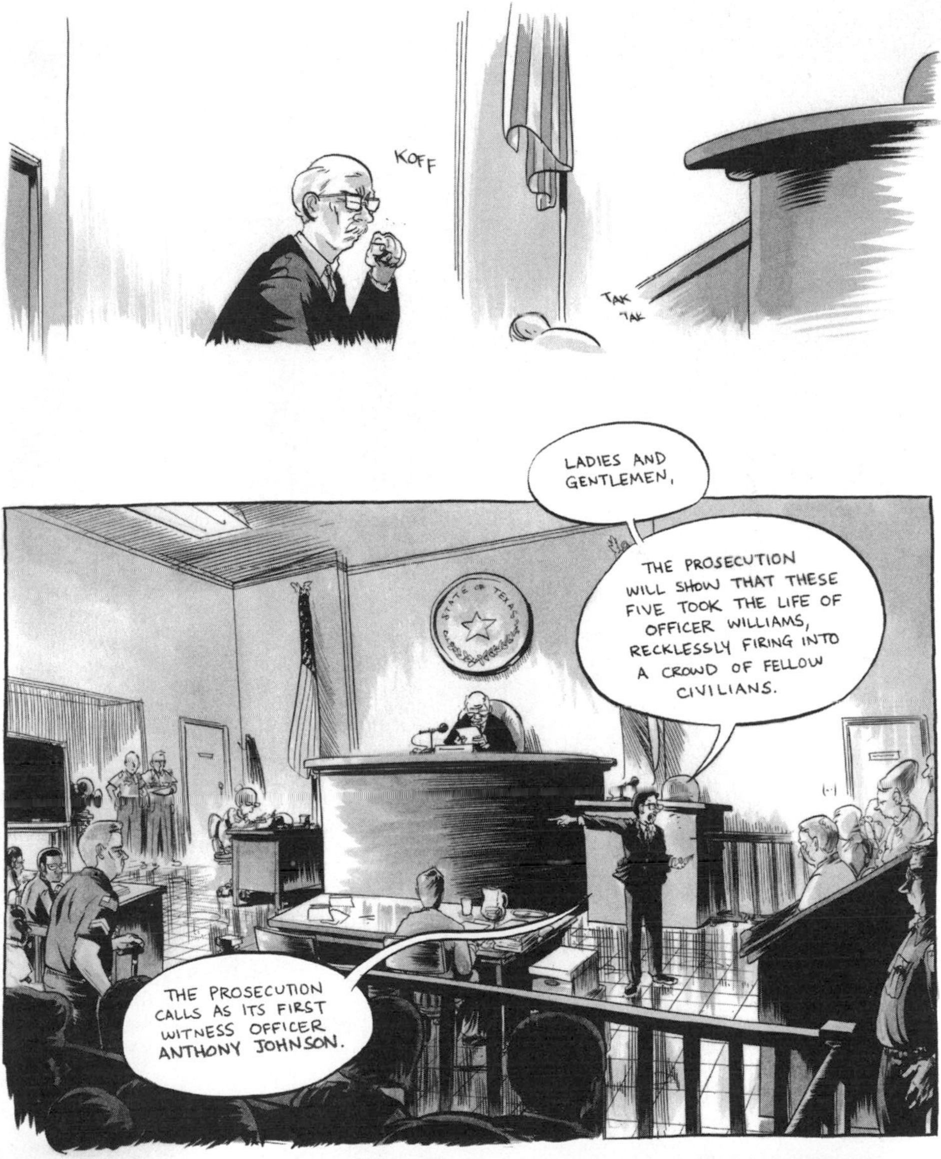
KOFF
TAK TAK
LADIES AND GENTLEMEN,
THE PROSECUTION WILL SHOW THAT THESE FIVE TOOK THE LIFE OF OFFICER WILLIAMS, RECKLESSLY FIRING INTO A CROWD OF FELLOW CIVILIANS.
THE PROSECUTION CALLS AS ITS FIRST WITNESS OFFICER ANTHONY JOHNSON.
CLUNK
PIK PIK
WHAT DID YOU SEE WHEN YOU FIRST ARRIVED, OFFICER JOHNSON?

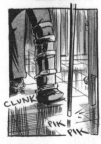

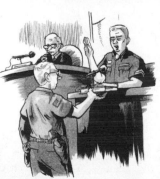

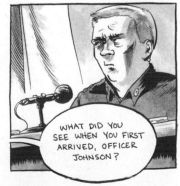

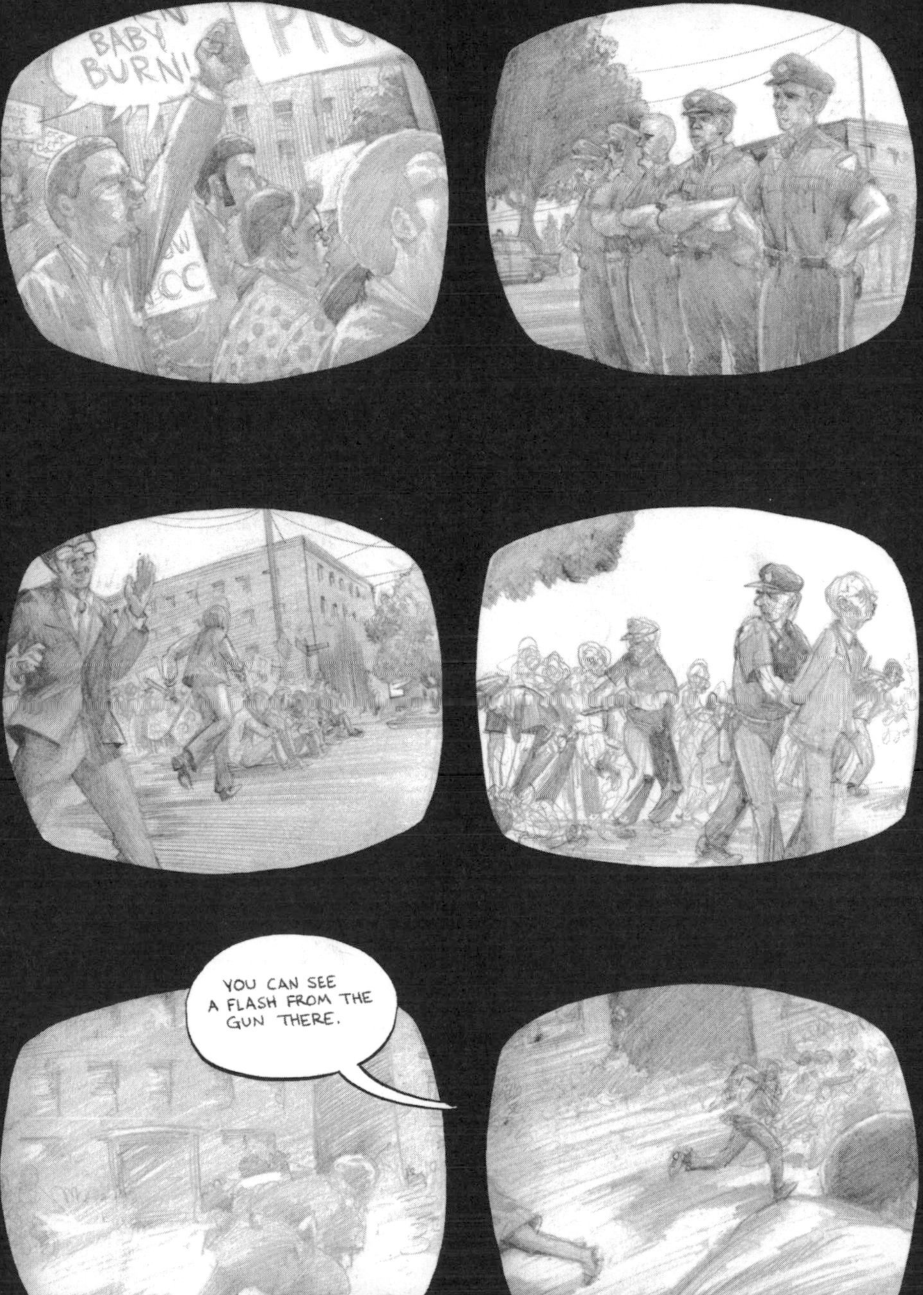
BABY BURN!
YOU CAN SEE A FLASH FROM THE GUN THERE.

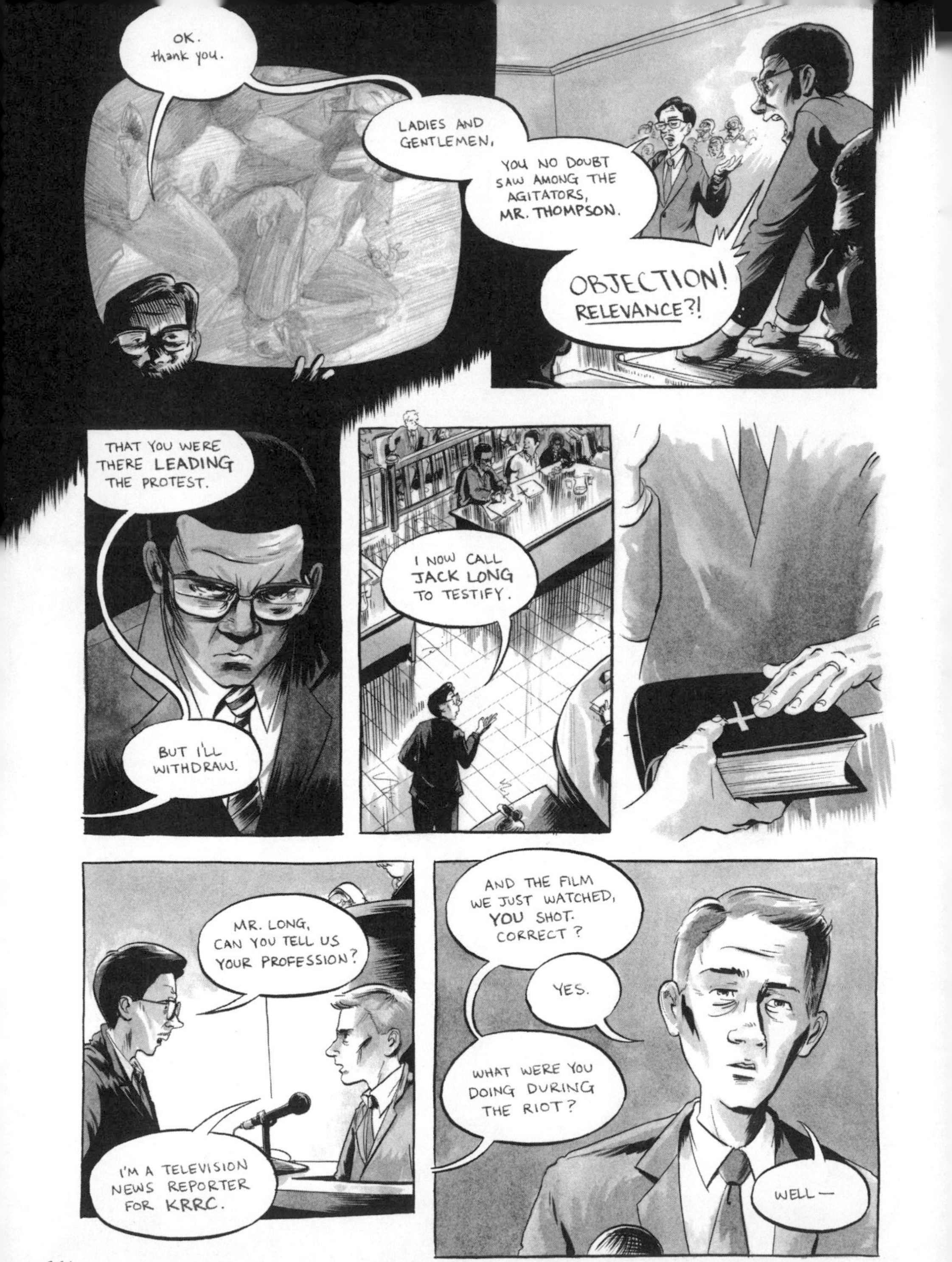
OK. thank you.
LADIES AND GENTLEMEN,
YOU NO DOUBT SAW AMONG THE AGITATORS, MR. THOMPSON.
OBJECTION! RELEVANCE?!
THAT YOU WERE THERE LEADING THE PROTEST.
BUT I'LL WITHDRAW.
I NOW CALL JACK LONG TO TESTIFY.
MR. LONG, CAN YOU TELL US YOUR PROFESSION?
I'M A TELEVISION NEWS REPORTER FOR KRRC.
AND THE FILM WE JUST WATCHED, YOU SHOT. CORRECT?
YES.
WHAT WERE YOU DOING DURING THE RIOT?
WELL—

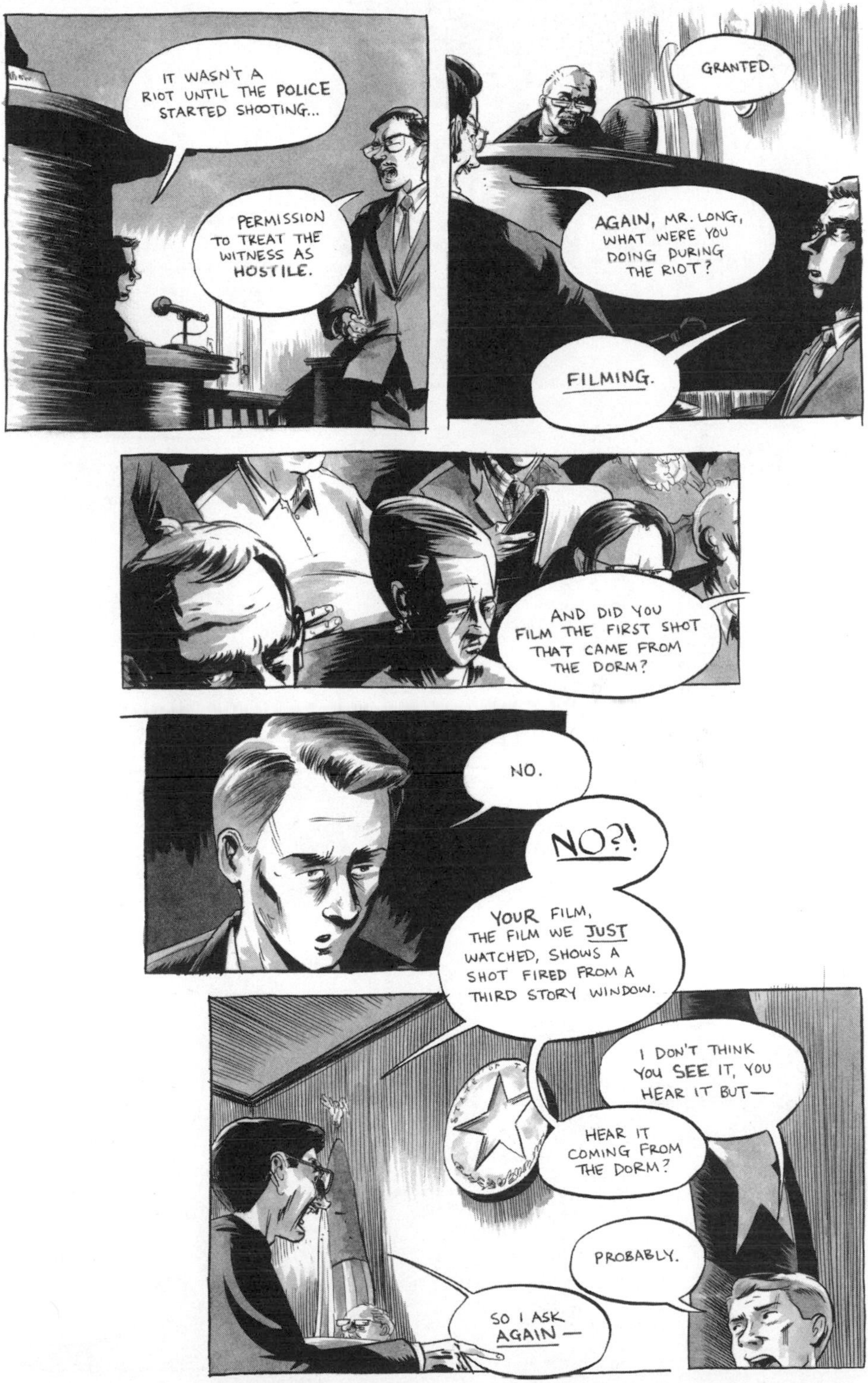
IT WASN'T A RIOT UNTIL THE POLICE STARTED SHOOTING...
PERMISSION TO TREAT THE WITNESS AS HOSTILE.
GRANTED.
AGAIN, MR. LONG, WHAT WERE YOU DOING DURING THE RIOT?
FILMING.
AND DID YOU FILM THE FIRST SHOT THAT CAME FROM THE DORM?
NO.
NO?!
YOUR FILM, THE FILM WE JUST WATCHED, SHOWS A SHOT FIRED FROM A THIRD STORY WINDOW.
I DON'T THINK YOU SEE IT, YOU HEAR IT BUT—
HEAR IT COMING FROM THE DORM?
PROBABLY.
SO I ASK AGAIN—

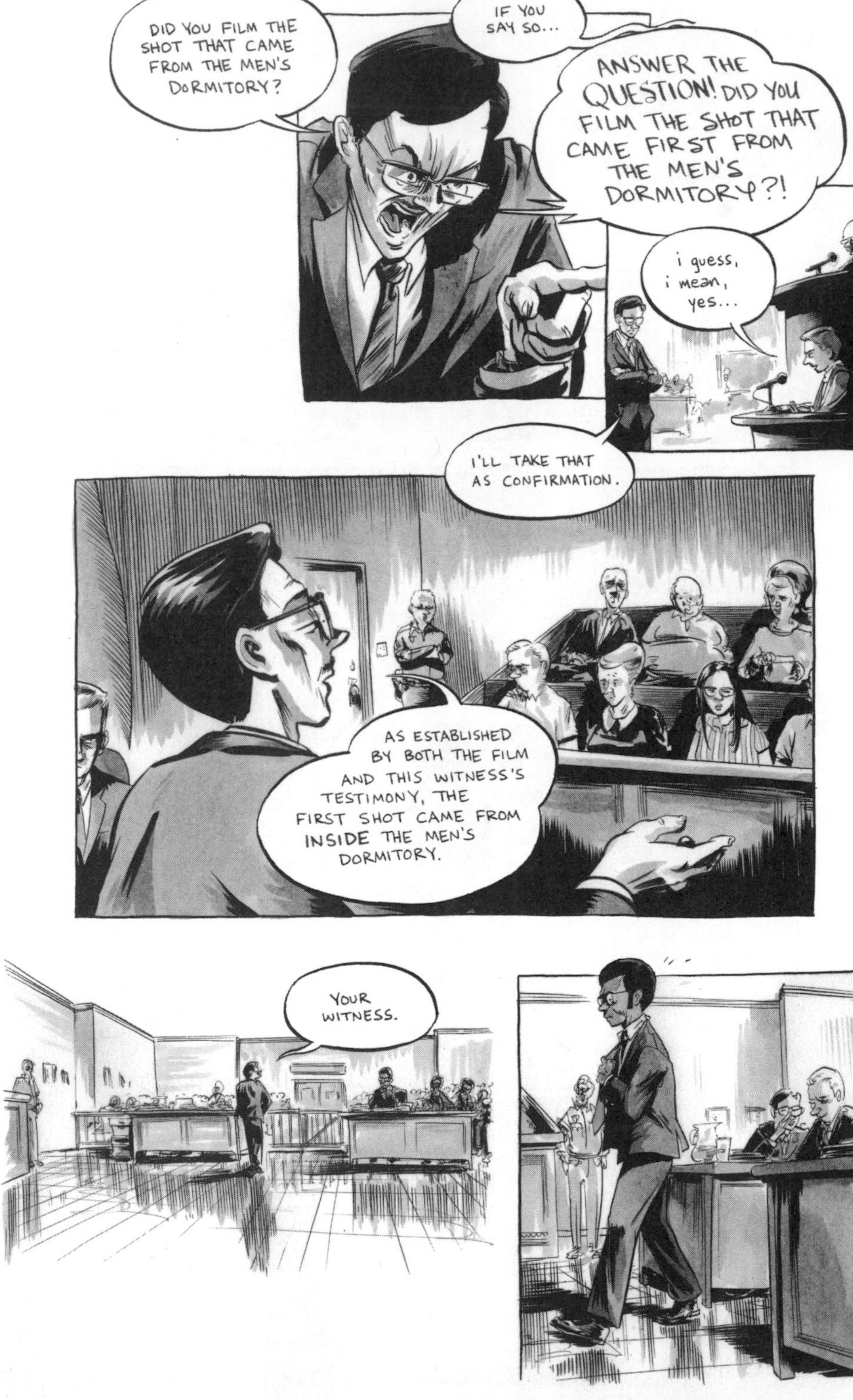
DID YOU FILM THE SHOT THAT CAME FROM THE MEN'S DORMITORY?
IF YOU SAY SO...
ANSWER THE QUESTION! DID YOU FILM THE SHOT THAT CAME FIRST FROM THE MEN'S DORMITORY?!
i guess, i mean, yes...
I'LL TAKE THAT AS CONFIRMATION.
AS ESTABLISHED BY BOTH THE FILM AND THIS WITNESS'S TESTIMONY, THE FIRST SHOT CAME FROM INSIDE THE MEN'S DORMITORY.
YOUR WITNESS.

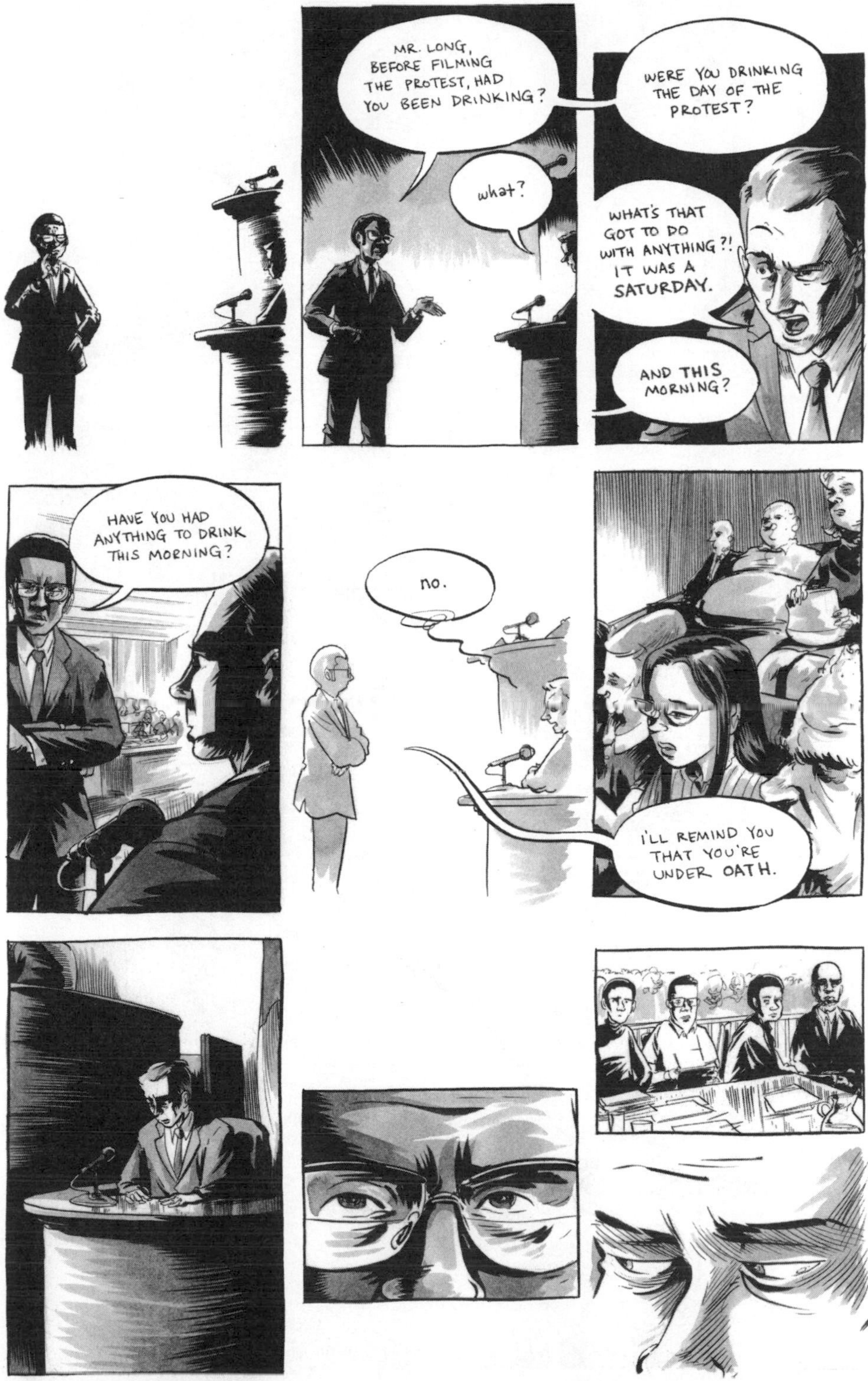
MR. LONG, BEFORE FILMING THE PROTEST, HAD YOU BEEN DRINKING?
WERE YOU DRINKING THE DAY OF THE PROTEST?
what?
WHAT'S THAT GOT TO DO WITH ANYTHING?! IT WAS A SATURDAY.
AND THIS MORNING?
HAVE YOU HAD ANYTHING TO DRINK THIS MORNING?
no.
I'LL REMIND YOU THAT YOU'RE UNDER OATH.

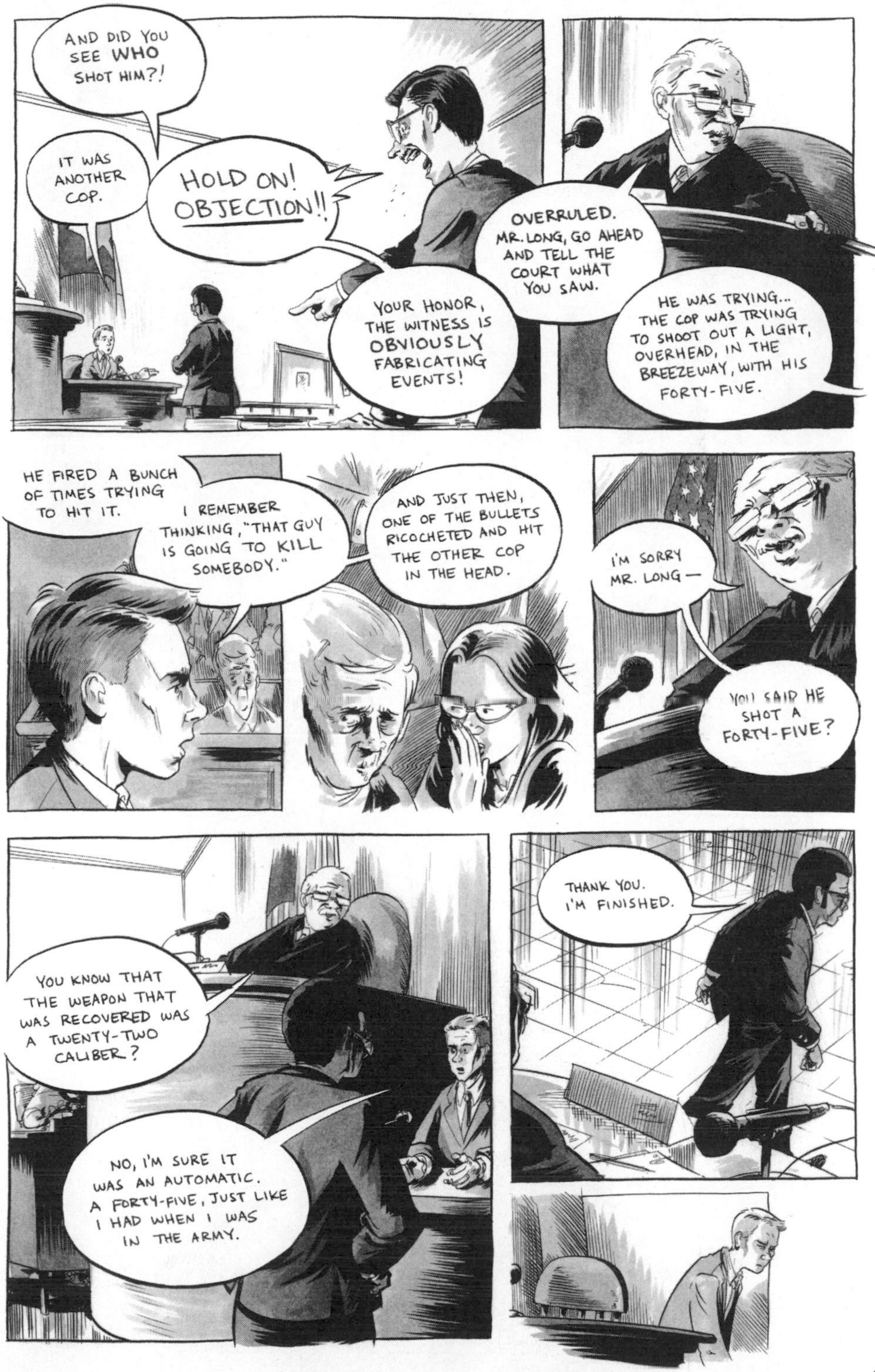
AND DID YOU SEE WHO SHOT HIM?!
IT WAS ANOTHER COP.
HOLD ON! OBJECTION!!
YOUR HONOR, THE WITNESS IS OBVIOUSLY FABRICATING EVENTS!
OVERRULED. MR. LONG, GO AHEAD AND TELL THE COURT WHAT YOU SAW.
HE WAS TRYING... THE COP WAS TRYING TO SHOOT OUT A LIGHT, OVERHEAD, IN THE BREEZEWAY, WITH HIS FORTY-FIVE.
HE FIRED A BUNCH OF TIMES TRYING TO HIT IT.
I REMEMBER THINKING, "THAT GUY IS GOING TO KILL SOMEBODY."
AND JUST THEN, ONE OF THE BULLETS RICOCHETED AND HIT THE OTHER COP IN THE HEAD.
I'M SORRY MR. LONG—
YOU SAID HE SHOT A FORTY-FIVE?
YOU KNOW THAT THE WEAPON THAT WAS RECOVERED WAS A TWENTY-TWO CALIBER?
NO, I'M SURE IT WAS AN AUTOMATIC. A FORTY-FIVE, JUST LIKE I HAD WHEN I WAS IN THE ARMY.
THANK YOU. I'M FINISHED.

WELL, THAT WAS A DRAMATIC TURN. HMM.

MOST SURPRISING...

THIS REMINDS ME OF THE LITTLE BOY LOOKING AT THE BLACKSMITH AS HE HAMMERED A RED-HOT HORSESHOE INTO THE PROPER SHAPE.

AFTER MINUTES OF HAMMERING, THE BLACKSMITH TOOK THE HORSESHOE, SPLASHED IT INTO A TUB OF WATER, AND THREW IT STEAMING ONTO A SAWDUST PILE.

"NO SIR. IT JUST DON'T TAKE ME LONG TO LOOK AT A HORSESHOE."

"WHAT'S THE MATTER, SON? IS THAT SHOE TOO HOT TO HANDLE?"

HA HA
CHUCKLE

IT'S NOT GOING TO TAKE YOU GOOD FOLKS LONG TO LOOK AT THE STORY THE DEFENSE WANTS YOU TO BELIEVE AND DROP **IT** TOO.

JACK LONG WAS PROBABLY DRUNK WHEN THE RIOT STARTED. HE'S AN UNRELIABLE WITNESS. HIS FILM IS THE **ONLY** THING WORTH PAYING ATTENTION TO.

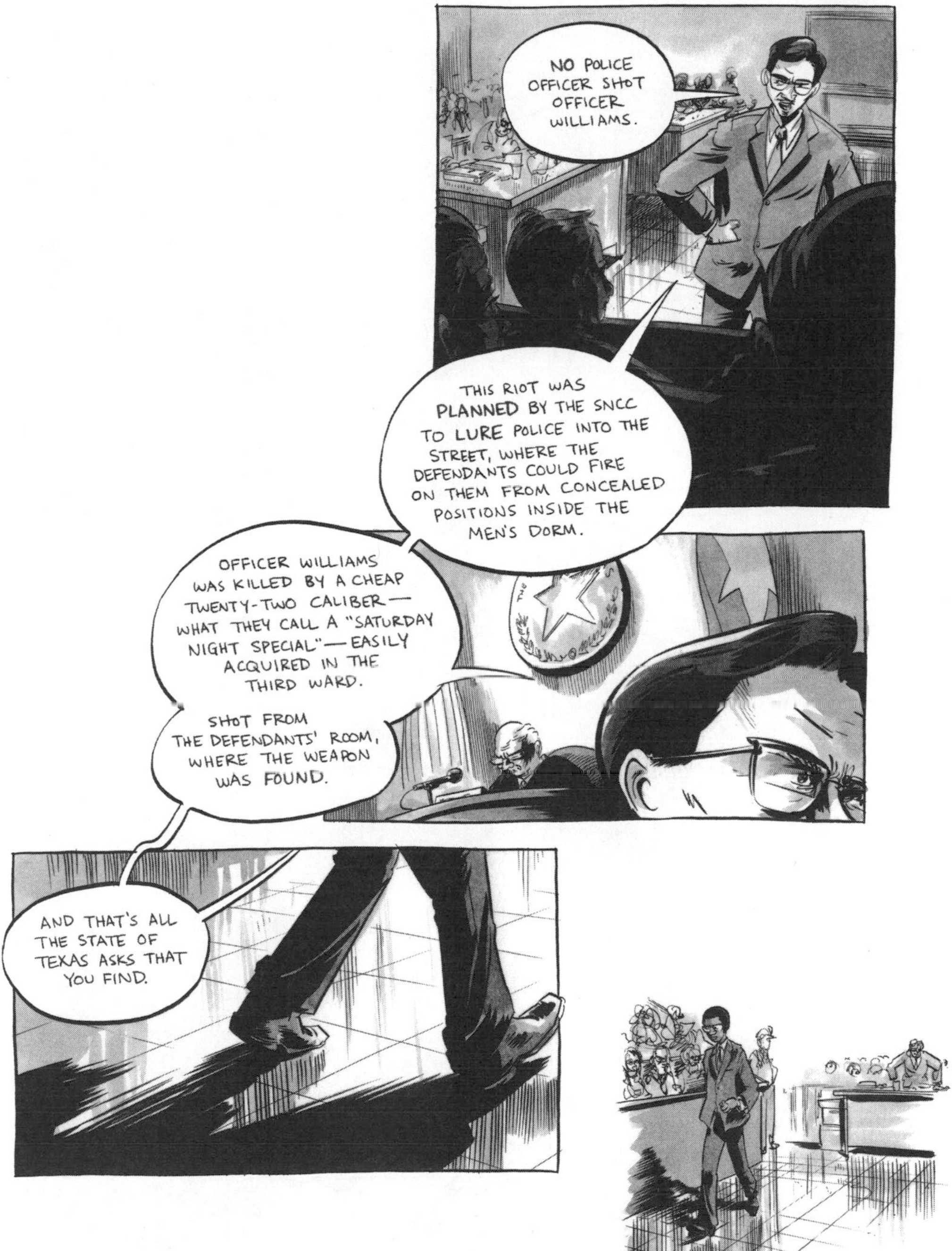
NO POLICE OFFICER SHOT OFFICER WILLIAMS.
THIS RIOT WAS PLANNED BY THE SNCC TO LURE POLICE INTO THE STREET, WHERE THE DEFENDANTS COULD FIRE ON THEM FROM CONCEALED POSITIONS INSIDE THE MEN'S DORM.
OFFICER WILLIAMS WAS KILLED BY A CHEAP TWENTY-TWO CALIBER— WHAT THEY CALL A "SATURDAY NIGHT SPECIAL"— EASILY ACQUIRED IN THE THIRD WARD.
SHOT FROM THE DEFENDANTS' ROOM, WHERE THE WEAPON WAS FOUND.
AND THAT'S ALL THE STATE OF TEXAS ASKS THAT YOU FIND.

THESE STUDENTS DID **NOT** KILL OFFICER WILLIAMS.

WE HAVE AN EYEWITNESS WHO SAYS THEY DIDN'T. AND THEIR PROTEST— **OUR PROTEST**— WAS NOT SOME FAR-FETCHED PLAN TO AMBUSH POLICE.

WE PROTESTED BECAUSE WE ARE DETERMINED TO BE MEN—

AND NOT LIVE LIKE WE ARE **FORCED** TO LIVE.

WHEN THESE STUDENTS SAT DOWN ON WHEELER AVENUE, THEY WERE IN REALITY **STANDING UP** FOR WHAT IS BEST IN THE AMERICAN DREAM.

that's right!

OFFICER WILLIAMS WAS SHOT BY A FELLOW POLICE OFFICER, **NOT** BY THE DEFENDANTS.

ABUSED AND PERSECUTED AS THESE STUDENTS HAVE BEEN, THEY **ARE** INNOCENT.

AND AS SUCH, THEY MUST BE <u>SET FREE</u>!

SET THEM FREE!

SET THEM FREE!

SET THEM FREE!

BAM

BAM BAM

SETTLE DOWN!

SETTLE DOWN NOW!!

c'mon, set them free...

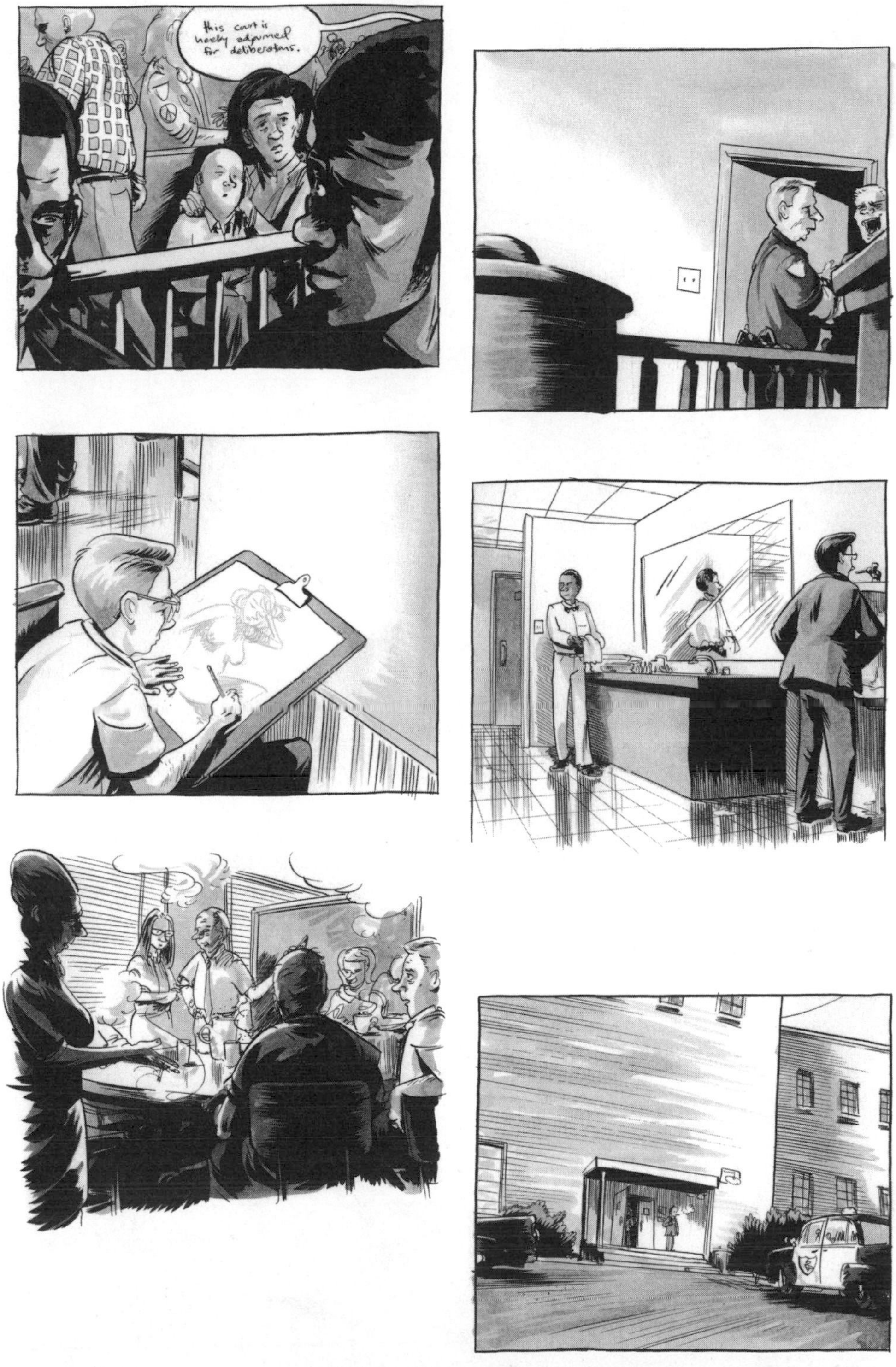
this court is hereby adjourned for deliberations.

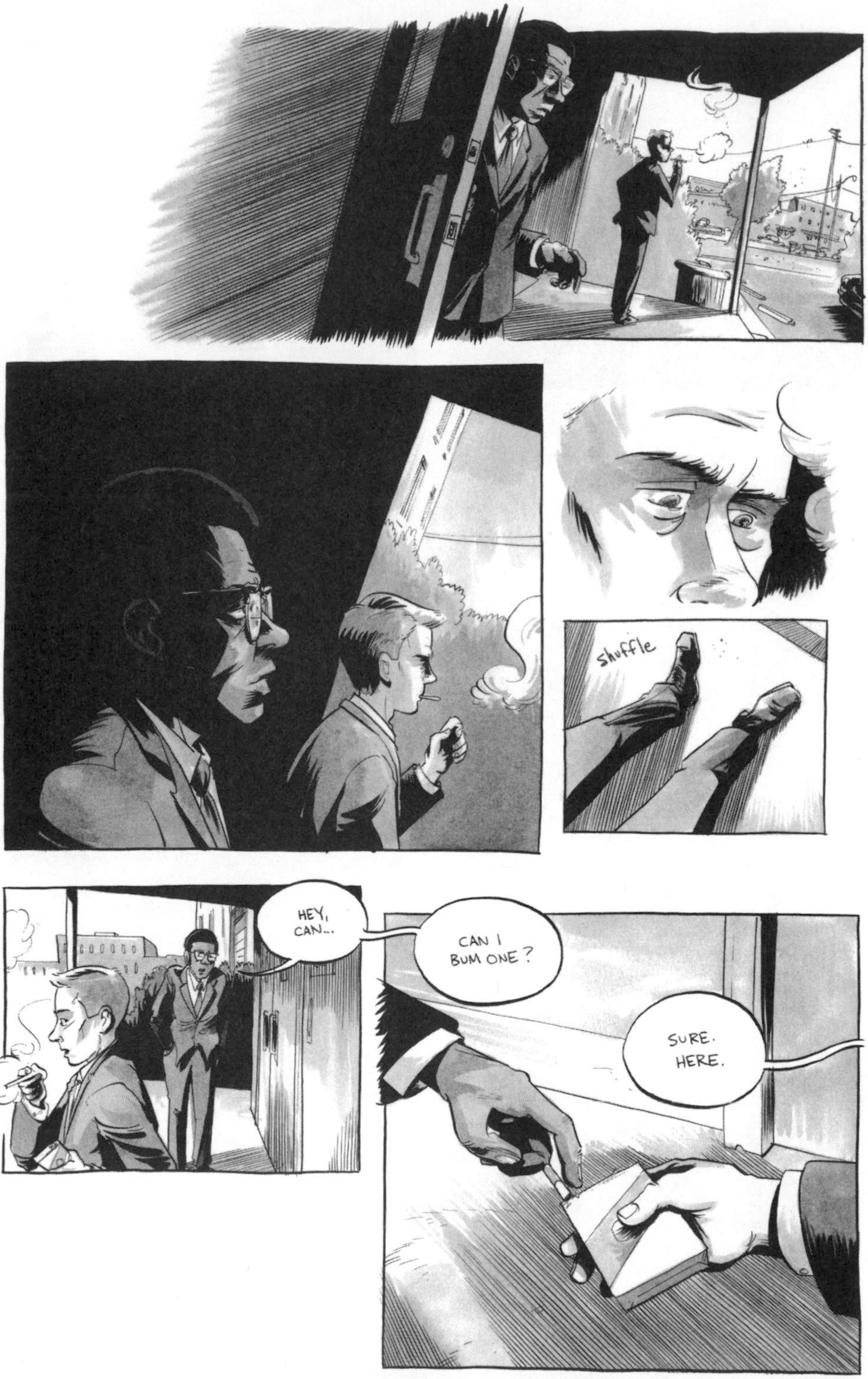
shuffle
HEY, CAN...
CAN I BUM ONE?
SURE. HERE.

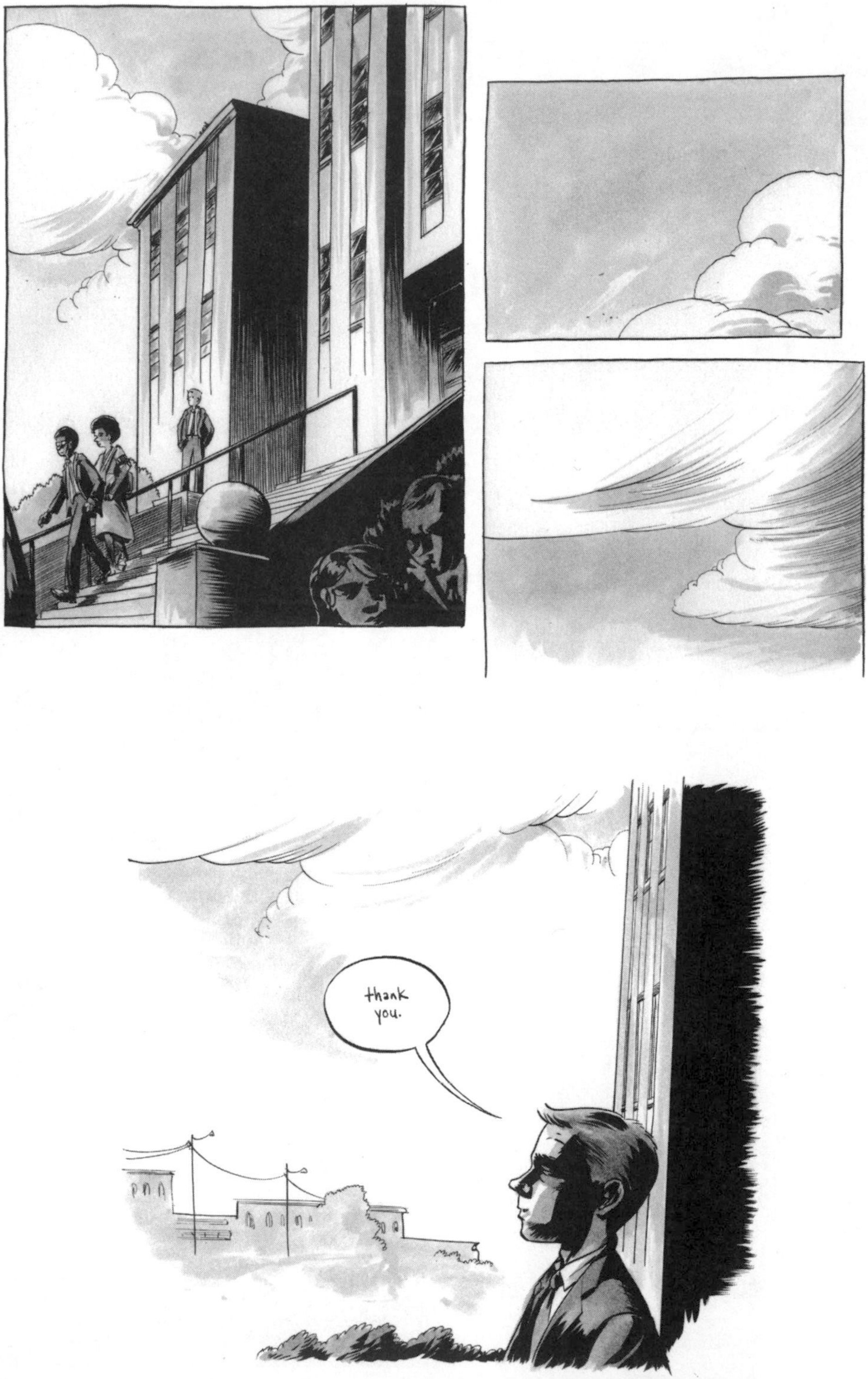
thank you.

J...

CLIK
CLIK

U...

TIK
CLIK

L... T-TK

I... E!

TAK

LOOK,
MR. DAWSON!

OH,
GOOD,
JULIE!

WHY DON'T
YOU GO SHOW
MISS RADISH?

All by
myself?

SURE.
YOU CAN
DO IT.

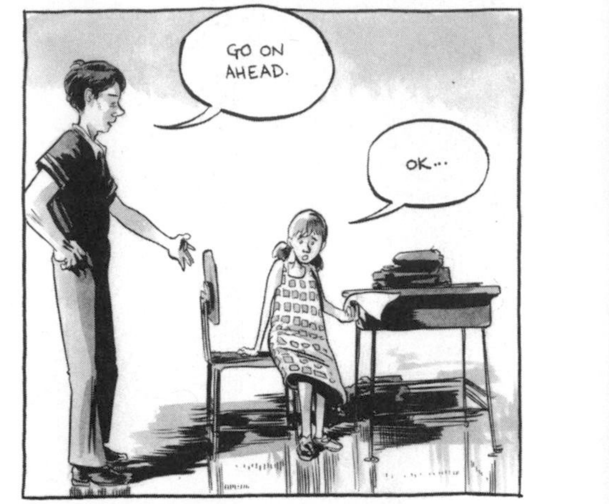
GO ON AHEAD.
OK...

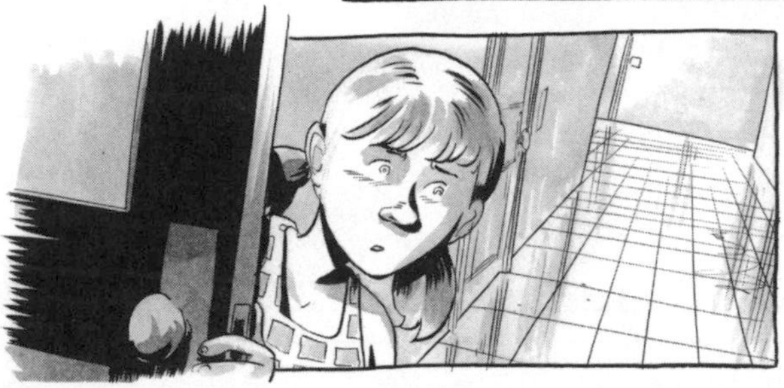

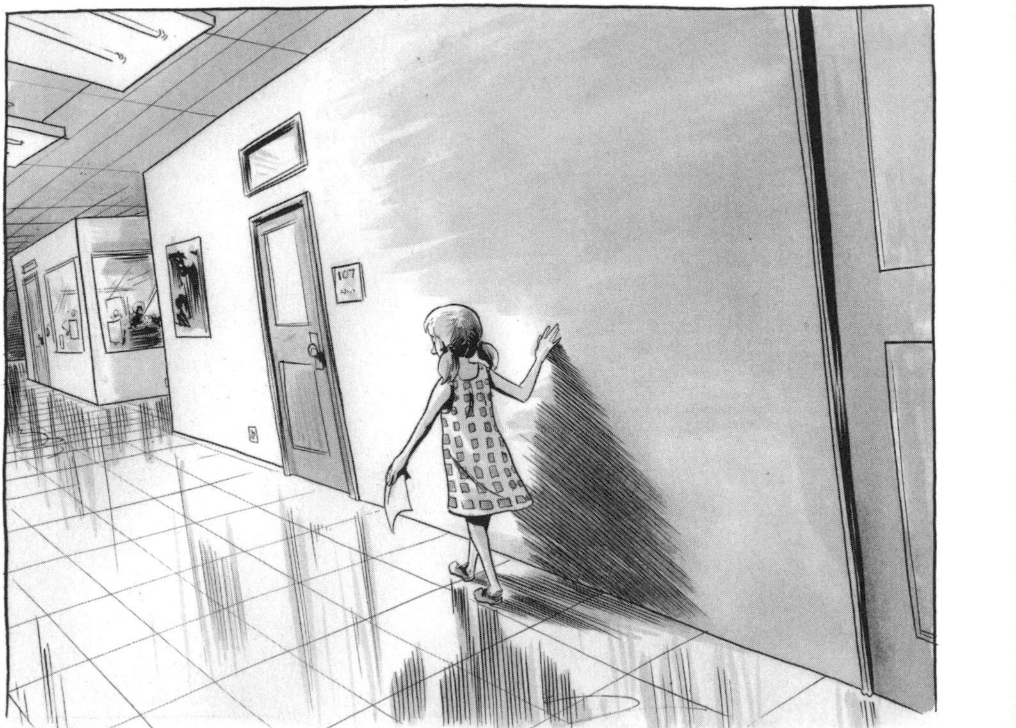
107

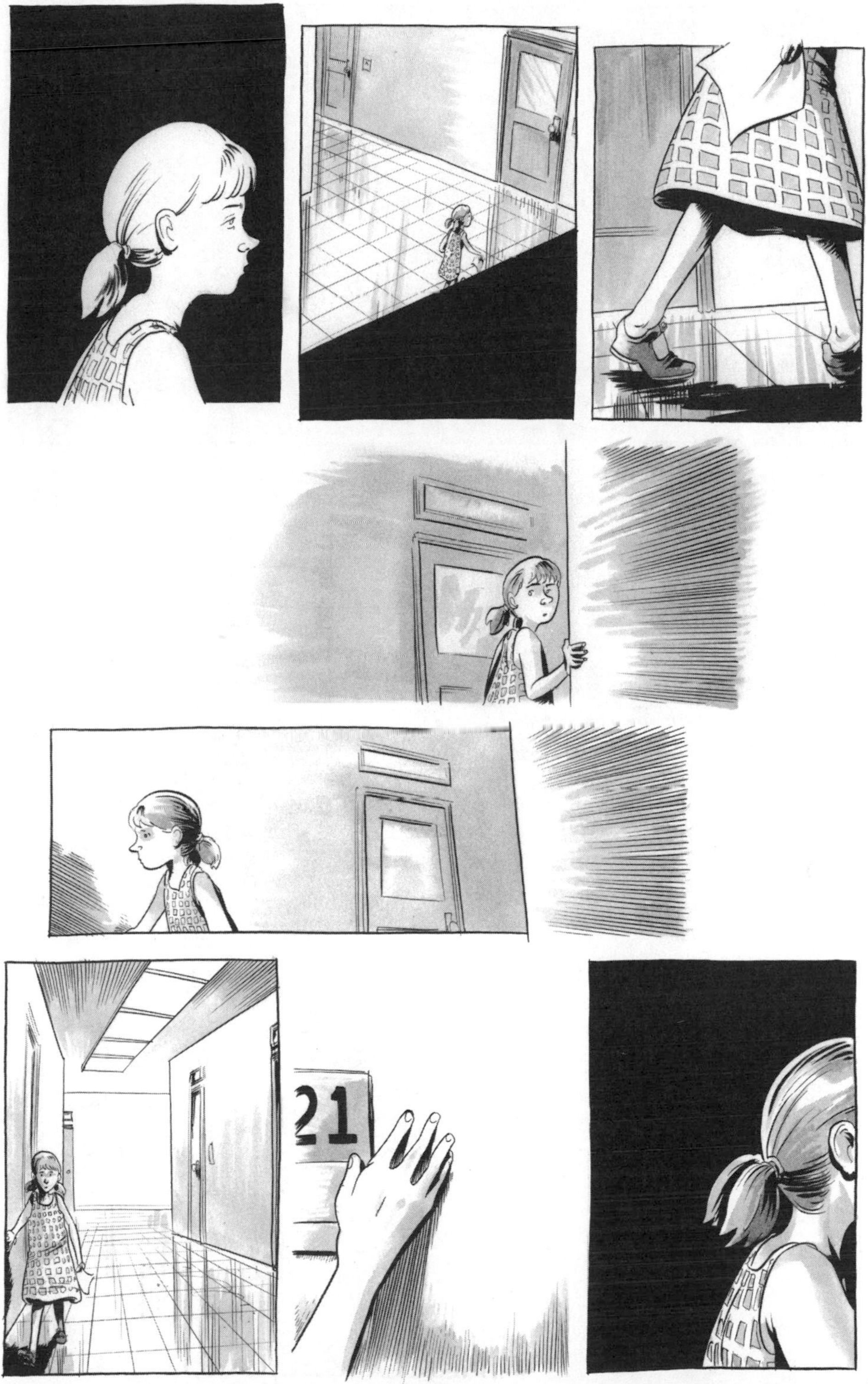
21

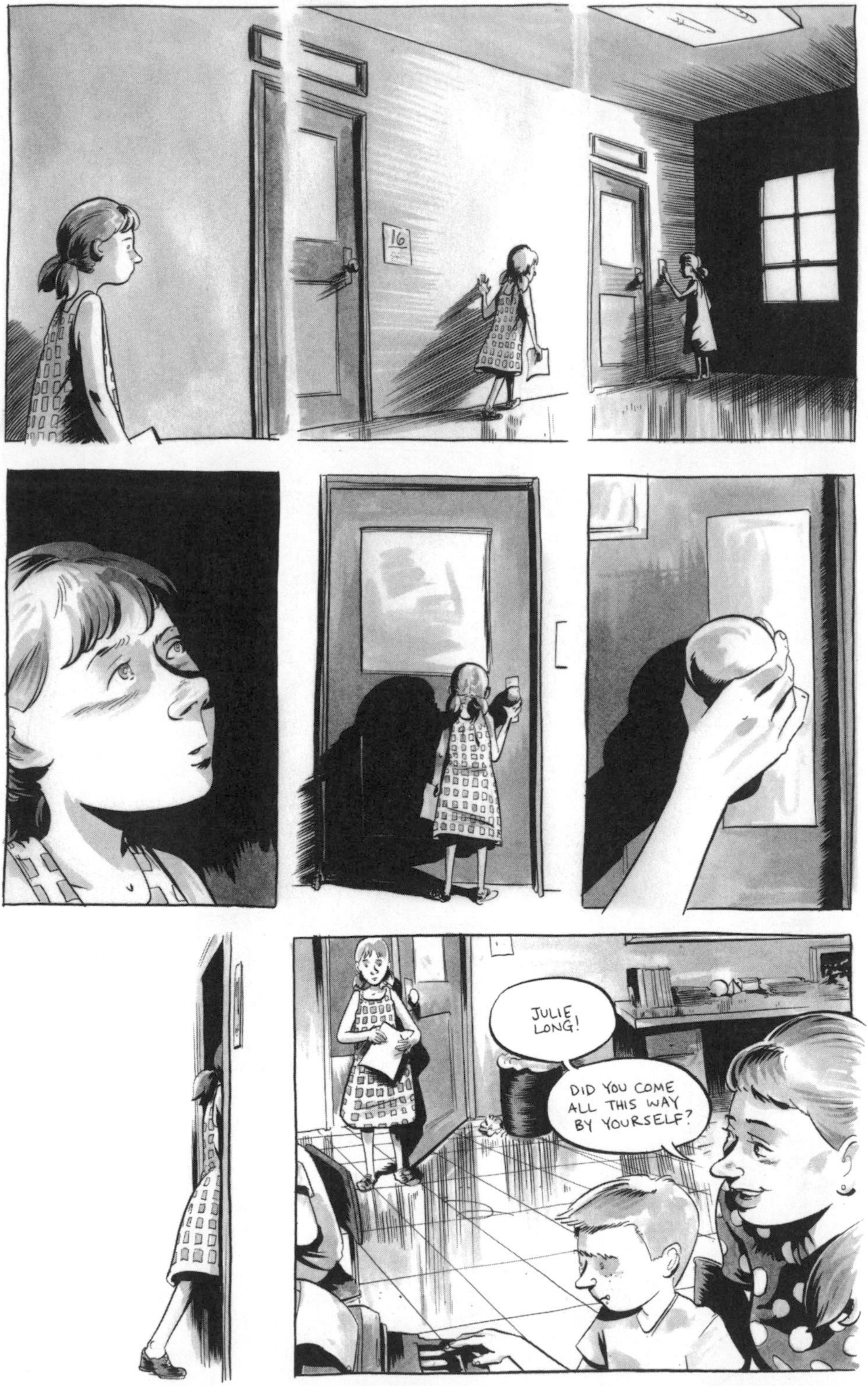
16
JULIE LONG!
DID YOU COME ALL THIS WAY BY YOURSELF?

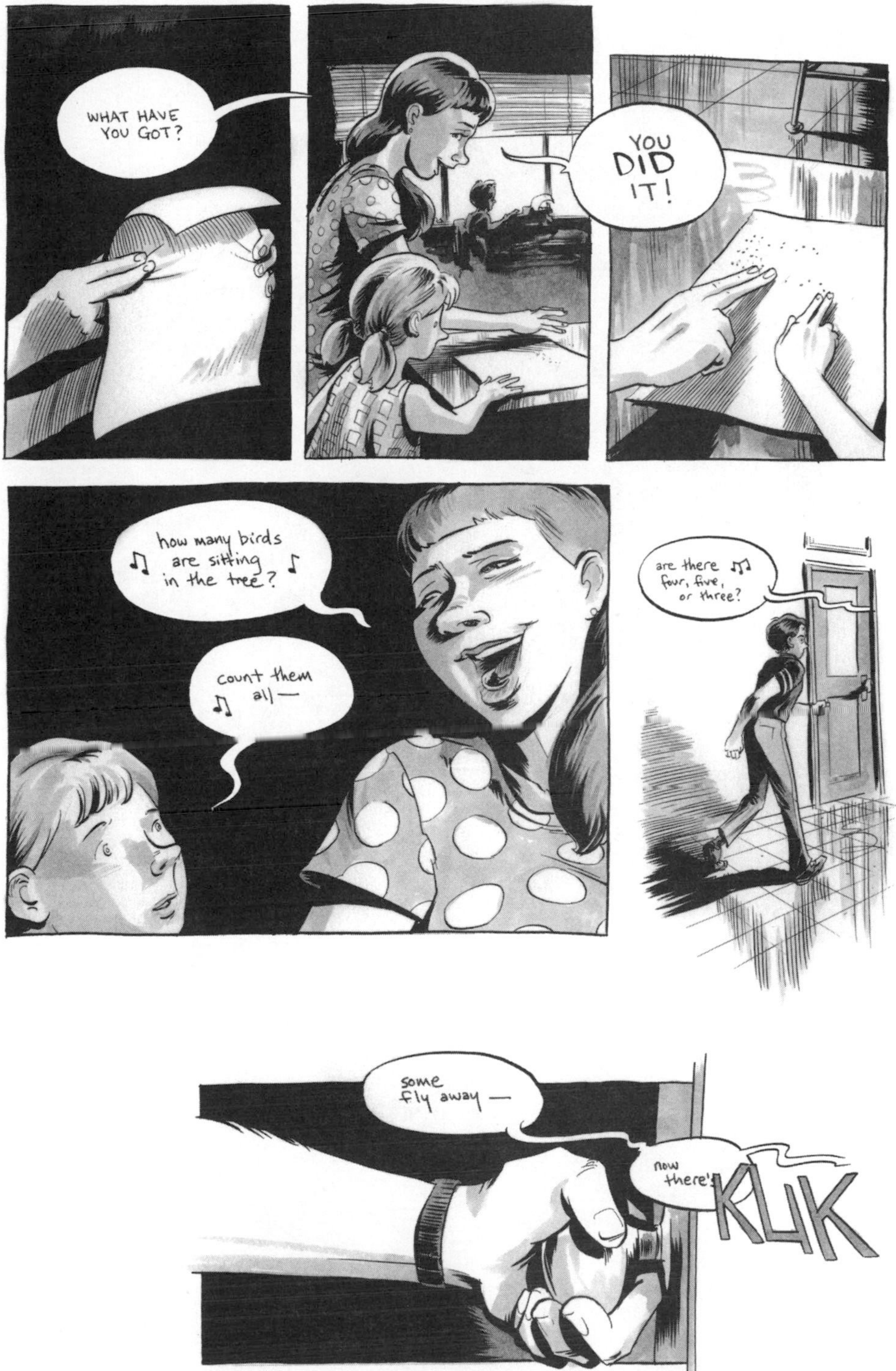
WHAT HAVE YOU GOT?
YOU DID IT!
how many birds ♫ are sitting in the tree? ♪
count them ♫ all—
are there ♫ four, five, or three?
some fly away—
now there's
KLIK

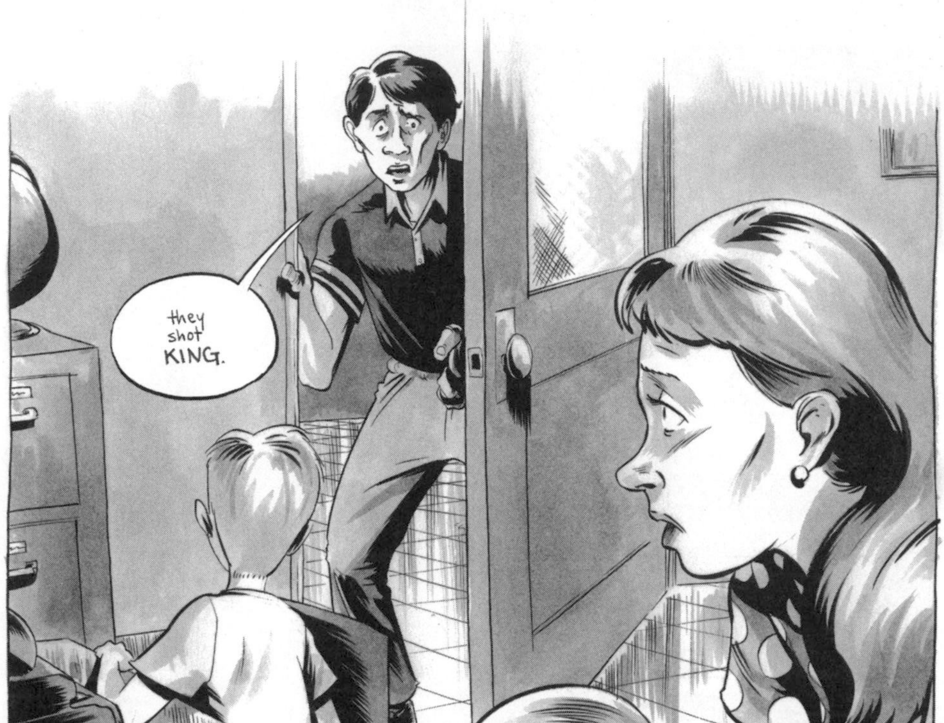
they shot KING.

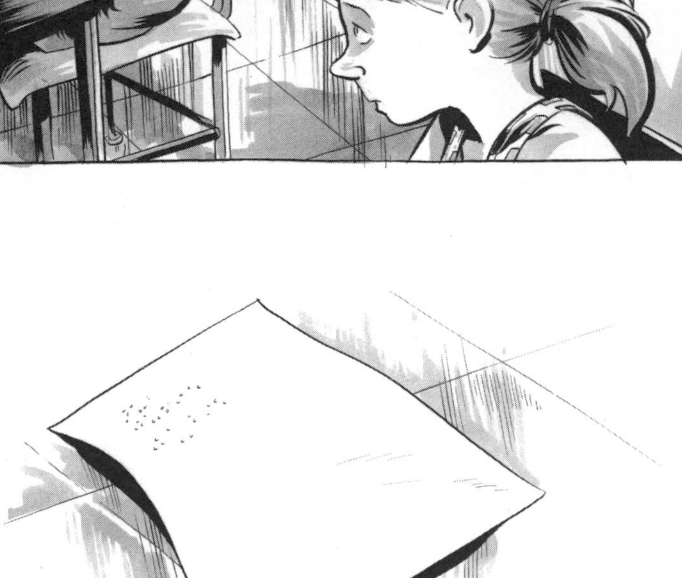

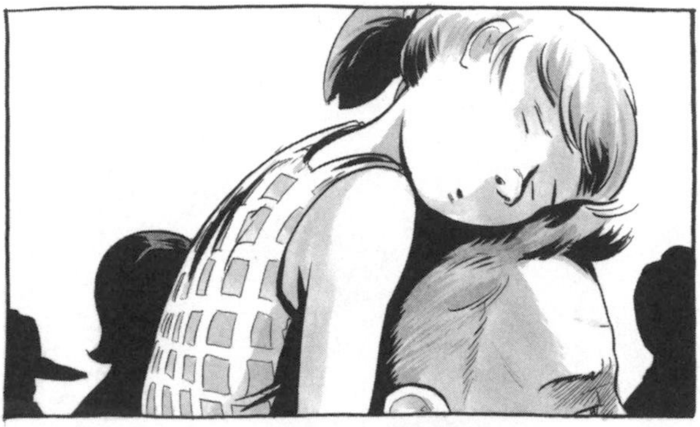

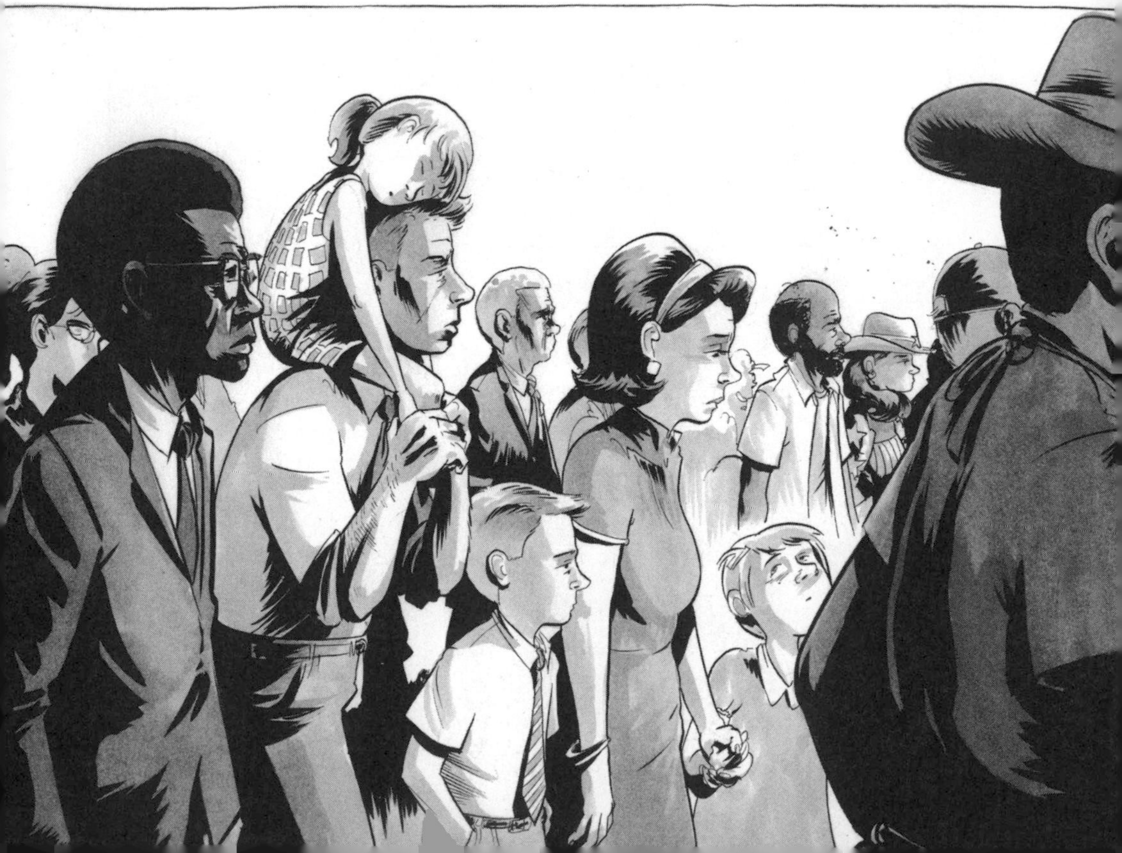

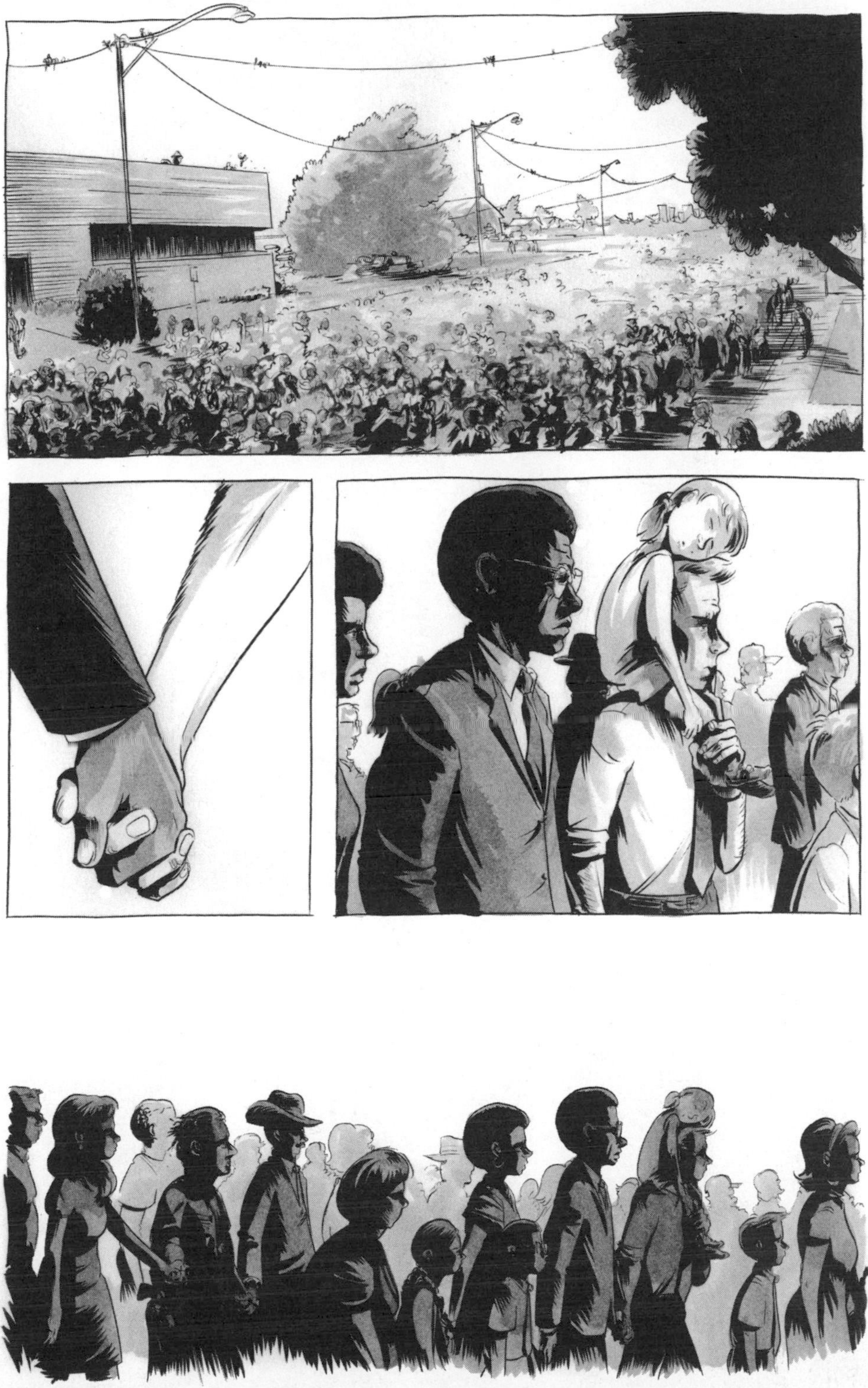

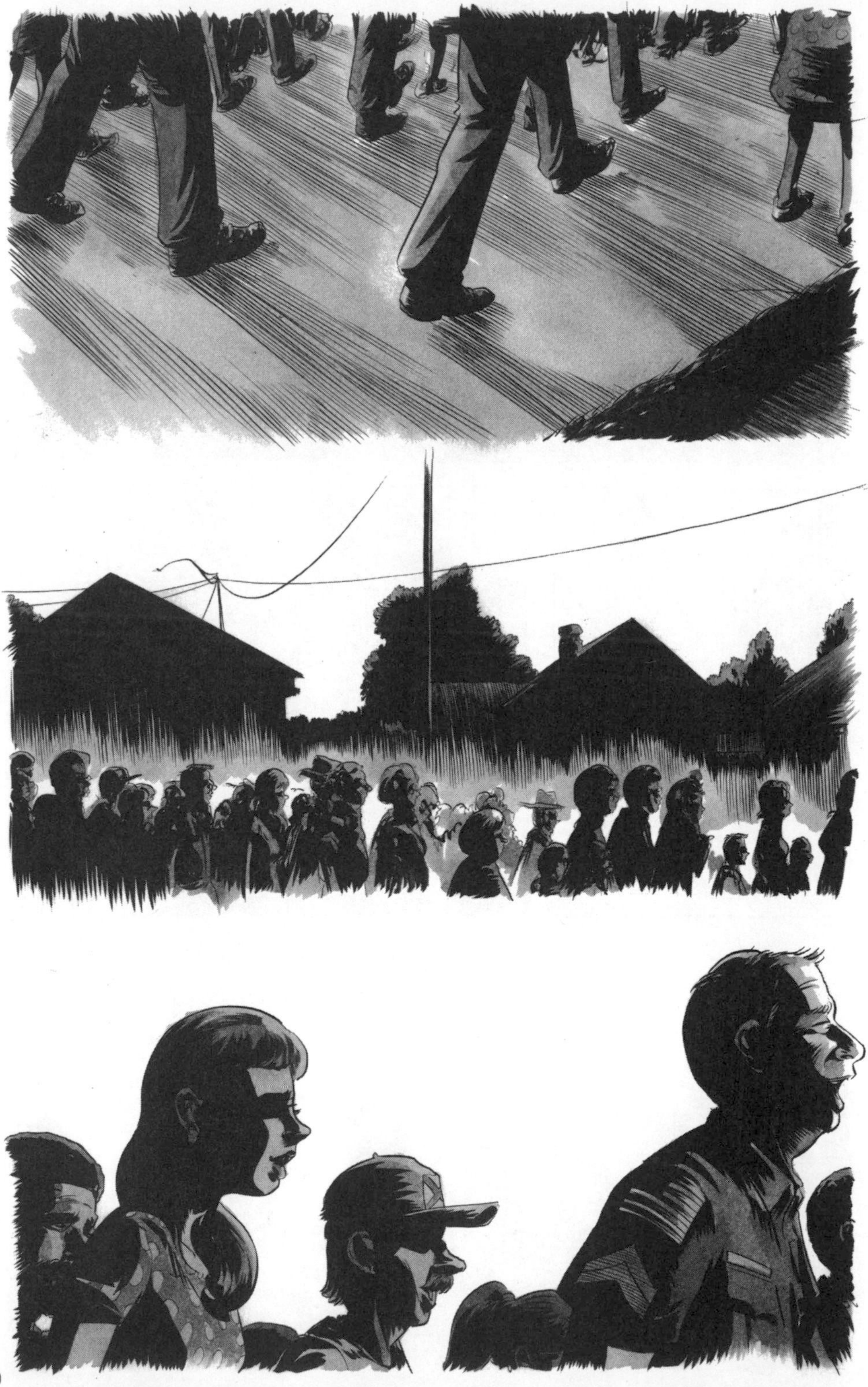

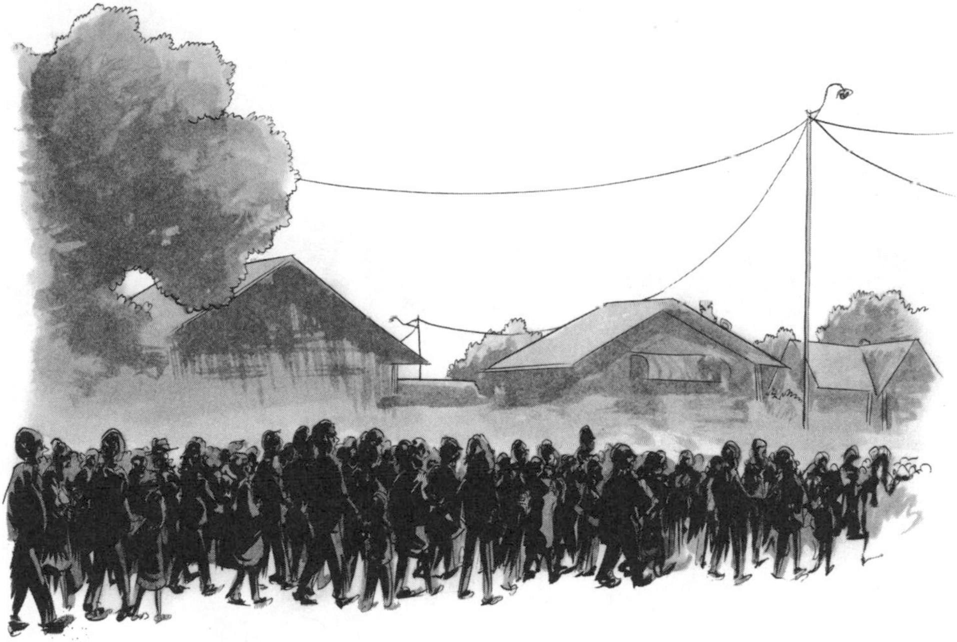

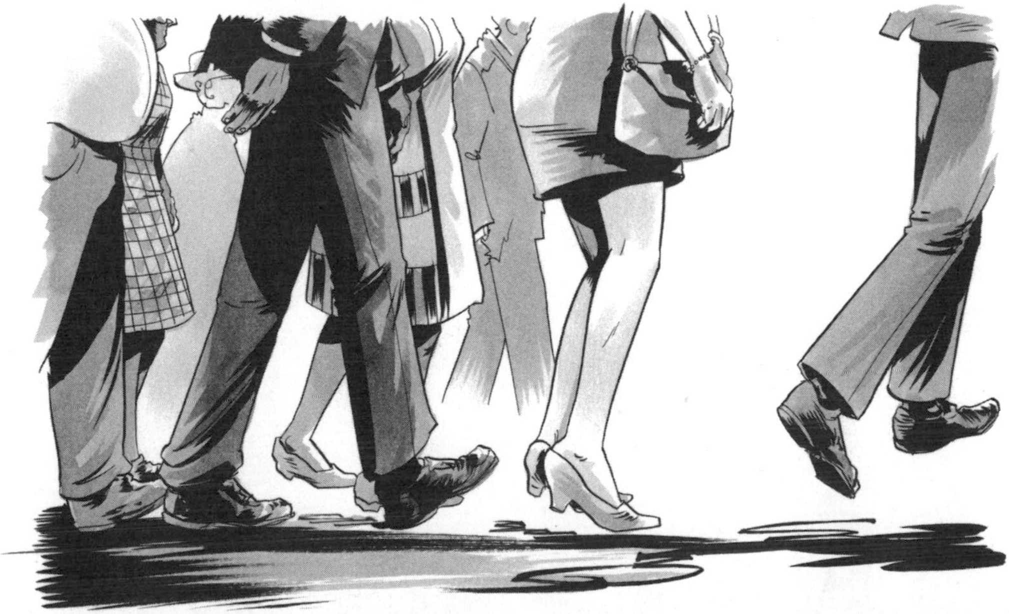

"IN THE END,
WE WILL REMEMBER NOT
THE WORDS OF OUR ENEMIES...

...BUT THE SILENCE OF OUR FRIENDS."

–Dr. Martin Luther King, Jr.

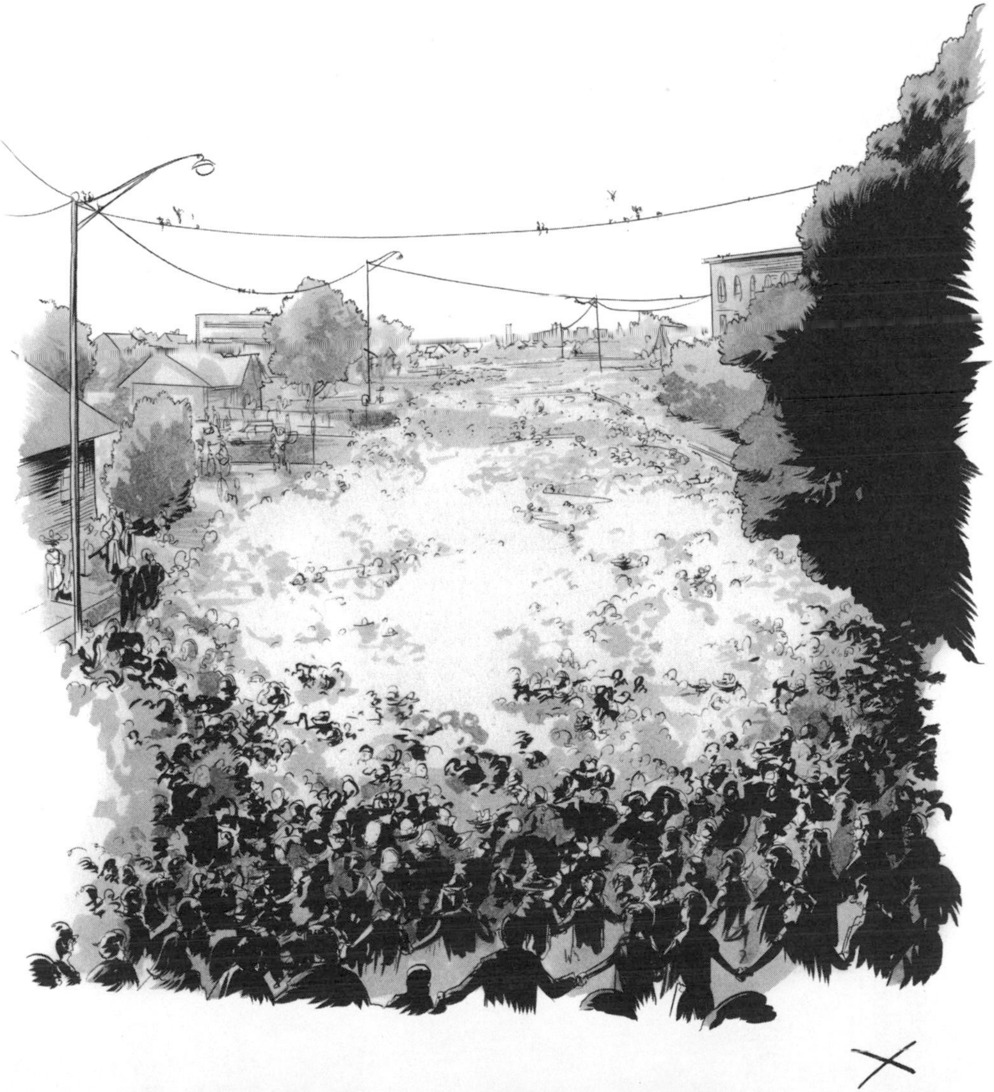

AUTHOR'S NOTE

The past is a foreign country. They do things differently there.

—L.P. Hartley

In 1966 my father moved our family from San Antonio to Houston to take a job there as a local television reporter. Television reporting back then was more like newspaper reporting—hard work, long hours, and decidedly little glamour. In the years before live broadcasts or even videotape, TV reporters were one-man bands, investigating, filming, interviewing, and then racing back to the station to develop and edit their film while writing and recording the voice-over. The film was often still wet from the lab as it was thrown up on the reel minutes before broadcast.

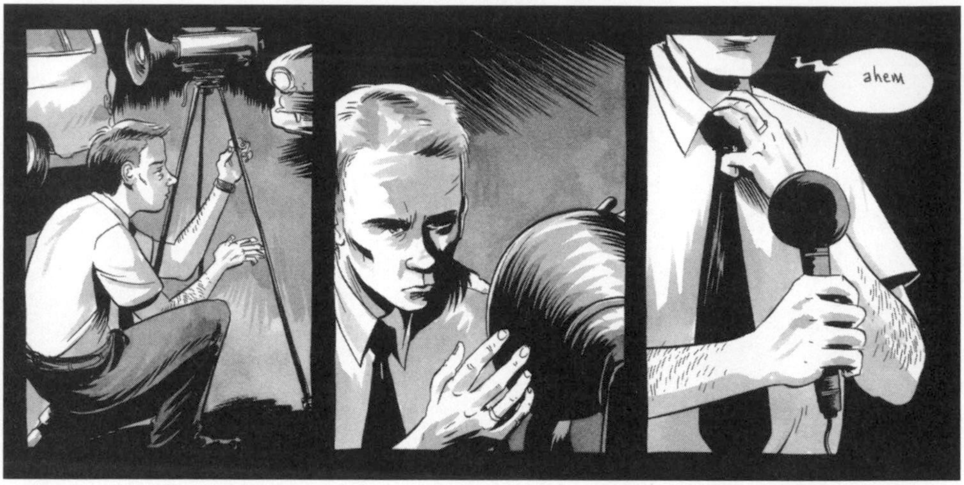
ahem

For a reporter, race was *the* issue in the late sixties. It was exciting, dangerous, and the local news outlets competed with each other to cover it. My father had covered the barrio in San Antonio and joined KPRC to cover Houston's equivalent in the Third and Fifth Wards, but things were different in Houston. Civil rights protests were moving on to university campuses, and the clashes were becoming violent. And in 1967 the crucible of racial tension in Houston was Wheeler Avenue.

Wheeler was a downtown street that ran through the heart of Texas Southern University, a historically African American college. Today the TSU section of the street is a beautiful red brick pedestrian way shaded by live oaks. But in the late 1960s, at the height of the civil rights struggle in Houston, racist whites would cruise down Wheeler in cars, hurling obscenities at students, and often doing violence. TSU was at one end of the street. At the other was Wheeler Avenue Baptist Church, Houston's "Ebenezer" and the spiritual seat of Houston's Third Ward. It was said you could go from terror to joy in a city block on Wheeler. It was on Wheeler that my father met Larry Thomas.

Larry was the editor of *The Voice of Hope*, an antipoverty weekly put out by the Human Organizational Political and Economic (HOPE) Development—the most grass roots level group of the Fifth Ward. Larry was also an activist, organizing for the right of the Student Nonviolent Coordinating Committee (SNCC) to meet on the TSU campus. After the riots at Fisk University in April of 1967, the SNCC and in particular its chairman, Stokely Carmichael, were increasingly portrayed in the media as outside agitators bringing violence to any school that allowed them on campus. On Wheeler, Larry protected my father from an angry crowd of students who had just been denied the right to meet as SNCC on the TSU campus, and the two struck up a friendship that soon included their families.

Crossing the color line in Houston was literally an act of courage in 1967. There was the real possibility of violence, especially in our neighborhood, Sharpstown, where the Ku Klux Klan left fliers advertising rallies rubber-banded to our front doorknob. When the Thomas family first visited our home, it was as if aliens had landed in our front yard. The entire block came out to gawk, and we weren't much better ourselves. I had never met a black person before. And I don't think they had ever played with white kids. I recall our fascination simply with the texture of each other's hair.

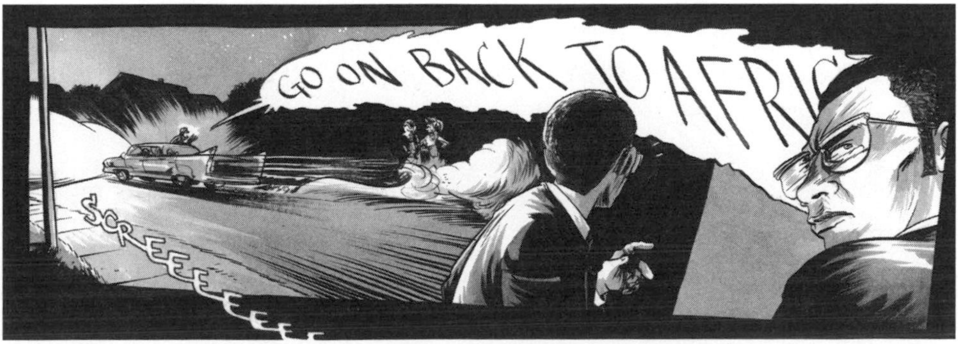
GO ON BACK TO AFRIC
SCREEEEEEE

After SNCC was banned on campus, TSU students began a boycott of classes, and on May 17 staged a sit-down protest on Wheeler over conditions at the nearby city garbage dump. The protest evolved into an infamous police riot that night. An undercover officer was shot and over 200 officers responded by pouring rifle and machine-gun fire indiscriminately into the men's dormitory. The police later stormed the dormitory and arrested 489 students after a policeman was shot and killed. All but five of the students were released the next day. They came to be called the "TSU Five" and were charged with the murder of the slain officer. Only one of the students stood trial—in Victoria, Texas, due to publicity in Houston. His trial ended with the dismissal of all charges against the five when it was discovered that the officer was shot accidentally by another officer.

Some details from these events—as well as names and details about my family and Larry's—have been changed for storytelling purposes in *The Silence of Our Friends*. Creating a book like this one requires finding a balance between factual accuracy and emotional authenticity. What we have striven to create is a story that offers access to a particular moment in time, both for those who lived it and those who are just discovering it.

Dr. King said, "One day the history of this great period of social change will be written in all of its completeness. On that bright day our nation will recognize its real heroes. They will be thousands of dedicated men and women with a noble sense of purpose that enables them to face fury and hostile mobs with the agonizing loneliness that characterizes the life of the pioneers." We've used King's words elsewhere in this book, and those of his nemesis—George Wallace—to illustrate how even this little-remembered event reverberated through "Dixie." And how it echoes there still.

—Mark Long

To Mom and Dad.
        —JIM DEMONAKOS

*I'm grateful for the help and support of Paula Cuneo, Joanna
Alexander, Caroline Alexander, Nick Sagan, Judith Hansen,
Calista Brill, Patricia Long, Michelle Bennack, Julia Long,
Jared Gerritzen, and Jason Dean Hall.*
                —MARK LONG

*Thanks to Mark and Jim for the trust, openness, and
collaborative spirit; everyone at First Second; the spectacular
Rachel Bormann for sharing our lives together; and Erin
Tobey for crucial artwork production assistance.*
                    —NATE POWELL